Third Edition

ORAL COMMUNICATION

Skills, Choices, and Consequences

Kathryn Sue Young
Professor and Chair, Mansfield University

Howard Paul Travis
Emeritus, Mansfield University

WAVELAND

PRESS, INC.

Long Grove, Illinois

For information about this book, contact:
   Waveland Press, Inc.
   4180 IL Route 83, Suite 101
   Long Grove, IL 60047-9580
   (847) 634-0081
   info@waveland.com
   www.waveland.com

10-digit ISBN 1-57766-745-X
13-digit ISBN 978-1-57766-745-2

Printed in the United States of America

7 6 5 4 3 2

About the Authors

KATHRYN SUE YOUNG has taught at the college level for over 25 years at The Pennsylvania State University, Clarion University, and the University of Central Arkansas. She is currently a full professor and department chair at Mansfield University. She wrote *Group Discussion: A Practical Guide to Participation and Leadership*, 4th edition, with Wood, Phillips, and Pedersen, which is also available in a Korean translation. She co-authored *Communicating Nonverbally: A Practical Guide to Presenting Yourself More Effectively*, and *Business and Professional Communication: A Practical Guide to Workplace Effectiveness* with Howard Paul Travis. She has published numerous articles, including an article in a joint American–Russian publication, and has presented numerous papers at national conferences. She is active in the community, sharing her expertise in parliamentary procedure.

HOWARD TRAVIS taught at the university level for 37 years. His former students work nationally and globally in media as on-air talent, writers, producers, directors, technicians, sales executives, lawyers, public relations/promotion practitioners, media managers, and media CEOs. He retired early from his teaching career in 2002. Mansfield University of Pennsylvania awarded him professor emeritus status, and he holds the rank of Honorary Professor of Communication, Volgograd State University, Volgograd, Russia.

Acknowledgments

Inspiration challenges the human spirit to achieve the impossible. My willingness to take risks and do new things reflects the enthusiasm of unique people who crossed my path on life's journey.

The idea for this book came from Dr. Kathryn Sue Young, a former colleague. An innocent phone call to discuss a book idea led to a joyful collaboration. Her enthusiasm, intelligence, and patience made the writing process tons of fun. Thank you, Sue!

The book also allowed me to reconnect with friends and Montclair State alumni who shared my enthusiasm for this project. Their professional experience and thoughts are used as sidebars throughout the text. It's comforting to know so many corporate executives are interested in sharing what they have learned with future generations. Their lives continue to inspire me and make me glad to be alive.

Finally, teachers who open the door to information, imagination, professional discipline and global culture are remarkable gifts. Edward Stasheff, Zelma Weisfeld, Ralph Herbert, and Frederic W. Ziv were inspirational gifts to me. Thank you. Each one enriched my life and my academic career.

—Howard Paul Travis

Together, we would like to express a debt of gratitude to Bia Bernum, Assistant Professor of Communication, Mansfield University of Pennsylvania, for creating, developing, and writing a professional and innovative online instructor's manual for our book. In addition, she provided a criteria example in the reflective thinking section, the reasonable goals list in persuasive speaking, and innovative terms and concepts such as a "key" for organization. When we moved on to the second edition, she continued to supply unique examples from her classroom experiences for us to use. She also provided the new information in the second edition about the feedback and self-disclosure continuums in the Johari Window and the addition of the categories of bullying, delaying, and withdrawing in the conflict-resolution model. She is a valued colleague and extremely creative teacher.

Holly Pieper, Assistant Professor of Communication, Mansfield University of Pennsylvania, also gave us thoughtful insights and suggested new sections, such as preparing for the interview, that greatly enhanced the second edition. We would like to thank the professors who wrote to Waveland Press with suggestions for changes as well. The thoughtful editing and insightful commentary about the first edition by Raymond R. Ozley provided us with excellent guidance.

For the third edition, we would like to express our deepest gratitude to Michael Southard, who worked diligently to find the newest and most up-to-date materials for us to include in the new edition. In addition, Tom Walton and Lori Norin at University of Arkansas Fort Smith provided feedback that helped us to reshape some of the concepts.

—Kathryn Sue Young and Howard Paul Travis

First and foremost, this book is dedicated to all of my students, who continue to inspire me. I thank you for being in the classroom, for engaging with the material, and for continuing to teach me about communication and the world. Without you, I couldn't do the job I love.

Second, this book is dedicated to the people who have guided me to this profession or believed in me and mentored me. To Gerald M. Phillips, who educated, encouraged, and challenged me; to Arlie Parks, who guided me to graduate school; to Julia Wood, Douglas Pedersen, and Nancy Phillips, who gave me my first opportunity to write a book; to Herman Cohen, who always treated me as though I had something important to say; to all of my professors at Penn State University who taught me how to think and instilled a love of this field; and to Carol Rowe and the editors at Waveland Press, who continue to teach me about writing effectively—I am eternally grateful.

Third, this book is dedicated to the people who give me strength in my life: my husband, daughters, my parents, my friends—you all know who you are.

Finally, I dedicate this book to my coauthor, Howard P. Travis. This project is a great journey, and the synergy we experience is tremendous.

—Kathryn Sue Young

Professional Contributors Acknowledgments

The authors gratefully acknowledge the professional men and women who enthusiastically supported the development of the book. They share their thoughts with you as encouragement to pursue your dream. Your dream lies in the future, and you must walk forward. Your present and past experiences are your history. Learn from them, but never take your eyes off your dream.

Mandy Aikens, Director of NCAA Compliance and Academic Accountability Program Director, Nyack College

Julie Allen, Senior Human Resources Specialist, The Summit Federal Credit Union

Vincent Andaloro, President and Founder, Latin-Pak Direct Marketing

T. W. Anderson, Adolescent Therapist

Anonymous (a member of the professional staff at a large museum)

Maureen C. Baker, President, Highland Ventures, Inc.

Jim Benson, President, Vision Quest Productions

Helene B., Lead Programmer Analyst

Bia Bernum, Assistant Professor, Mansfield University of Pennsylvania

Robert Buchanan, Producer, NBC News/*Dateline*

Lori L. Burrows, Commission Legal Advisor, Arkansas Public Service Commission. Former Peace Corps Volunteer (1999–2001), Pohnpei State, Federated States of Micronesia

Greg Chesterton, former undergraduate student, The Pennsylvania State University

Robert H. Christie, Senior Vice President, Corporate Communications, The New York Times Company

Carrie L. Clarke, stay-at-home parent

Kathleen Corrigan, Legal Clearances, Grey Global Group

Emilee Danielson, Assistant Dean of Students, Shippensburg University

Jana Polsky Deneroff, Writer/Producer, Creative Services, CBS/Westwood One Radio Networks

Dean De Peri, Director, Human Resources, CIGNA HealthCare

Christina DeVries, Senior Account Manager, Spotlight Payroll Inc.

Angela Dickson, Marketing Manager for the American Architectural Manufacturers Association (AAMA)

Edward Gallardo, Playwright

Allynn Gooen, International Performance Artist

Dr. Aparna G. Hebbani, Lecturer, School of Journalism and Communication, University of Queensland, Brisbane, Australia

Lisa Hanasono, Assistant Professor, Bowling Green State University

Hyun Mook Kim, former international student, Mansfield University

Sarah Loher, graduate, Mansfield University

Alysa Lucas, Assistant Professor, Mansfield University

Barry McCauliff, Account Executive, The Investment Center

Cami McCormick, Network Correspondent, CBS Network Radio News

Dr. Larry Miller, Professor Emeritus, Mansfield University of Pennsylvania

Roberta J. Miller, Casework Supervisor, Retired

Wes Moon, Interior Designer

John W. Nichols, Executive Director, The Art Museum Partnership

Raymond R. Ozley, Lecturer, University of Montevallo

Eric Schmidt, nontraditional student, graduate, Mansfield University

Michael Southard, graduate, Mansfield University

Gene R. Sower, Vice President, Production, West Glen Communications, Inc.

David P. Strus, Law Enforcement Officer, Nutley, New Jersey

Tracy Synowsky, stay-at-home parent

Lance Walden, Northwest Regional Radio Promotions, Universal Republic Records

Raymond Weaver, New Programs Educator, Cornell Cooperative Extension, former secondary English teacher, Ilsan, South Korea.

Robert C. Weigand, Senior Manager, Project Planning and Administration, ABC

Corey D. Welch, Operations Supervisor, Arkansas Student Loan Authority

Stacy Wolfe, Internal Sales/ Manufacturing, Seaboard International

Contents

four
Nonverbal Communication   57

five
Communicating Interpersonally   83

six
Relationship Stages and Conflict Resolution   115

seven
Initial Speech Preparation   137

Preface

Welcome to the study of communication. Our goals for this undergraduate communication textbook are to: (1) engage you to think about the skills, choices, and consequences of your communication; (2) create a book you will want to read; and (3) convince you that success can be yours if you make solid choices in your communication style. You may not realize how important a good communication style can be. The strength of this book is the inclusion of communication observations from the careers of corporate professionals. These professional sidebars give relevance to the academic concepts and encourage you to improve your communication skills for success. Since you are ultimately preparing for a career, we hope you find the insights valuable and enjoy reading the shared comments of our professional contributors.

This book is designed to help you recognize the importance of your words and actions in communication. We cover topic areas such as intrapersonal communication, language, nonverbal communication, interpersonal communication, presentational speaking, persuasion, interviewing, and team orientation. Each section of the book helps you to appreciate the value of appropriate communication in your personal and professional lives. We use a chatty style to make communication fun for you to learn.

Career opportunities are lost when you fail to recognize your role in the communication process or to use appropriate skills. The ability to talk seems so simple. But, it is not. Once you master the skills of interpersonal and presentational communication, speaking becomes as simple as it looks. The discussions in this book will prepare you to make effective communication choices throughout your life.

Professional Perspective

Some of the professional people contributing to this book work with the international community. They translated their remarks into the language they use with some clients. We included the translations to encourage you to study foreign language and to remind you of the importance of speaking more than one language.

As companies enter global markets, English-only speakers will find themselves at a competitive disadvantage. Technology makes direct contact with customers and suppliers in other countries much more likely even if you never leave your office. In addition, one in five people in the United States speaks a language other than English (Coombes, 2004). At Nicholas Senn High School in Chicago, two in five students were born outside the United States. The graduates from the school in 2007 spoke forty-six languages and came from sixty countries (Brotman, 2007). People seeking jobs will find that foreign language fluency is increasingly necessary as companies recognize the importance of understanding the cultures of other markets. "The important thing about speaking another language is it allows you to stand in the shoes of that other culture and see the world from their point of view," states Thomas Zweifel, chief executive of a cross-cultural coaching firm in New York (Coombes, 2004, p. 4).

Zweifel describes an example where lack of cultural understanding was very costly. Microsoft hired programmers from Taiwan to translate Windows software for sale to China. While knowledge of the language wasn't a problem in this example, the programmers failed to set aside their political preferences and inserted pop-ups such as "Take back the mainland" and "Communist bandits." The Chinese government chose Linux over Microsoft—jeopardizing potential sales to 1.3 billion people (Coombes, 2004, p. 4).

Your home is the best place to be introduced to a foreign language and another culture. This learning advantage is possible when one or both parents speak another language in addition to English. An Italian family who lived down the street from me in Detroit used this educational concept with their children. Italian was spoken within the home, but when the family members left their home only English was spoken. All of the children grew up fluent in English and Italian. They were also educated by their parents to respect American and Italian cultural similarities, differences, and traditions. Each child became quite successful as an adult.

In an increasingly competitive job market, knowledge of a foreign language will make you more attractive to potential employers. Expanding your language skills also enhances your communication skills, making you more competent interculturally and interpersonally.

—Howard Paul Travis

one

Communicating for Life

O B J E C T I V E S

After reading this chapter, you should be able to:
- Explain the importance of studying communication
- Identify and describe the parts of the communication process
- Identify four types of communication
- Identify four principles of communication
- Understand the ethical considerations of being a competent communicator
- Explain the importance of adaptability

Eric enters his residence hall room for the first time. There are two beds: one by the window; the other next to the wall in the middle of the room. There are two permanent closets. One is next to the door, and the other is next to the sink. Two portable desks and dressers are across from the beds. As Eric looks around the room, his mother asks him where he wants to put his stuff. He's not quite sure what he should do. Eric has never met or talked to his roommate. He has some decisions to make: he can choose to arrange the furniture the way he wants it, or he can wait and discuss the arrangement with his roommate.

Eric likes fresh air while he is sleeping, so his mother puts his boxes on the bed by the window. Not wanting to seem pushy or to make a bad first impression, he leaves the rest of the decision making for later. He and his roommate can decide together how the room will look. Imagine what Eric's roommate would think if he walked in to find his new room completely arranged and its spaces assigned already. Does Eric's decision not to rearrange the room communicate a message? Absolutely. Do you think Eric's decision to wait will help him develop a more positive relationship with his new roommate?

Only a moment earlier, Eric learned from the RA that his roommate's name is Juan Martinez. Eric looks up just as his roommate arrives. Juan

1

looks Latino, as his name suggested he might be. Before Eric gets a chance to impress his new roommate by greeting him with "Buenos días," Juan introduces himself. He sounds like a typical midwesterner. Eric is relieved to learn Juan speaks English and is glad he didn't embarrass himself by speaking in Spanish. Did Eric's face show signs of surprise? Could he have said anything that would alienate or offend Juan rather than welcome him into what could be a great friendship? Relationships evolve based on the choices we make when communicating: one bad or ineffective choice could impair the development of the relationship between these two roommates.

CHOICES AND CONSEQUENCES

Should you spend time with your new roommate, walking around campus and getting to know one another? Or should you spend time with a person you know and with whom you already feel comfortable? What kind of impression are you creating with the decision you make? What are the consequences of these choices?

_____

_____

_____

_____

_____

Communication Basics

Each communication experience (verbal/nonverbal) is an opportunity to demonstrate your willingness to work with others. Appropriate words and actions make you appealing to strangers and open social/professional doors that lead to friendships, employment, and personal growth. You should understand the three basics of communication.

- Communication is a two-way process.
- Communication can be intentional or unintentional.
- Communication occurs even when the interpretation does not match the original intent.

In the two-way ***communication process*** people share meaning, verbally and nonverbally. You are familiar with verbal messages, but keep in mind every gesture you make, the clothes you wear, or even the way you sit in class communicates a message about you. Communication can be *intentional* or *unintentional*. For example, most of you can remember making a remark you never intended for someone else to hear. When the person overheard the remark, you communicated a message about your true feelings.

Finally, it is important to understand that while the goal of communication is to share accurate meaning, communication *occurs whether it is interpreted correctly or incorrectly*. When the meaning is interpreted incorrectly, it is called miscommunication, but it is communication nevertheless.

Your use of language relays cultural, social, educational, and technical competence to others. It is increasingly important to choose words carefully when speaking as well as when sending messages electronically. Believe it or not, many professional people are unimpressed when they receive messages with spelling errors in them. You may call a written mistake a typo, but some people will perceive that you don't know how to spell. Therefore, your unintentional mistake can cost you employment or career advancement. In the professional world, you are assumed to be a competent communicator until your actions suggest otherwise.

To communicate effectively for life, you must first understand the:

- Importance of studying communication

- Communication process

- Types of communication

- Basic communication principles

CHOICES AND CONSEQUENCES

Describe a situation where you said something and then had to convince someone that you didn't really mean it. What were the consequences of your communication?

_____

_____

_____

_____

_____

_____

Why Is Communication Important?

We communicate to initiate or improve relationships, get things we want, negotiate the best price, conduct business, meet people, function in teams, and learn new things. The more effective we are, the better the outcome. Good, solid communication skills allow us to move through life with self-confidence and a feeling of accomplishment.

Critical Thinking

Why are you taking this class? _____

What is your career goal? _____

If your university mandates this class as a general education requirement, think about the academic reasoning for this choice. Why would a class in communication be so important that everyone in the university must take it in order to graduate?

_____

_____

_____

Communication Process

Communication is an ongoing process. In order to be successful, people must effectively share meaning, but this goal is not always possible. Sharing meaning implies a person must comprehend the intended meaning of the other person's use of language. In order to understand communication, we must look at the parts that make up an interaction. Each interaction consists of **communicators, messages,** a **channel, circumstances, feedback,** and, in some instances, **noise.** A good communicator analyzes each of these parts to make the best possible choices in each communication interaction.

If you have a bad communication experience, you can analyze what the cause might be: "Was it me?" "Was it the other person?" "Was it the channel?" "Was the message worded incorrectly?" "Was there noise?" The answers to these questions will help pinpoint a potential problem and enable possible corrections.

TRY IT!

Take a moment to list the many situations in which you need to have effective communication skills:

_____

_____

_____

You can also begin to think ahead to future interactions. Be proactive about this. Thinking about problems that occur in communication is the first step in becoming a better communicator.

Communicators

Communicators are the people involved in a verbal/nonverbal exchange. Each communicator simultaneously sends and receives messages. During a lecture, for example, a professor sends both nonverbal (smiles, hand gestures, eye contact) and verbal messages (the lecture material). At the same time, each student sends messages to the professor by maintaining eye contact, writing notes, or yawning. Everyone is communicating, whether they intend to or not. Effective communicators are aware that they intentionally and unintentionally send and receive messages; they constantly monitor and reflect on their verbal and nonverbal behavior as well as on the behavior of others around them as they fine-tune their skills.

Critical Thinking

Now is the time to think about your personal *brand* (see chapter 2). According to Brenda Bence (2008), a personal brand "exists in the minds of others in the way they perceive, think, and feel about you" (p. 23). Daniel Gall (2010) notes the evolution of branding: "In an age of social media, the idea has migrated from a strictly business connotation and is applied to individuals" (p. 630). We will discuss the concept of branding more fully in chapter 2. The quick summary here is that you can brand yourself the same way that a company brands a product. You send messages that are consistent with your brand. Focus on your appearance, language, and nonverbal communication as part of your brand. Your appearance should represent who you are at all times. Whenever you speak, adhere to consistent standards; be mindful of the messages you are sending nonverbally. Your brand communicates everything about you to other receivers. Invest in the communication behaviors that help others to see you as who you want to be.

Messages

Communicators deliver both **verbal** and **nonverbal messages.** The process begins with a thought in a person's head. The person encodes the thought into words or actions. **Encoding** means a communicator reviews all of the available symbols or actions that could represent the thought and selects the most appropriate ones. The person then selects a channel to send words or actions to other communicators. The other communicators receive the words or actions and decode them. **Decoding** means thinking about the received symbols or actions, applying meaning to them, and making them into a usable thought for an appropriate response.

The more effective we are at encoding our thoughts, the more likely other communicators will decode messages correctly. This results in a better chance for shared meaning. It is important for communicators to be fully aware that other communicators could decode the message with a meaning that wasn't intended by the sender. For example, a slight pause before delivering an important thought could be decoded as "the following statement is not true." However, a pause could also mean the communicator was searching for the right word to start the message. We should be aware that our decoding of meanings can be inaccurate.

Nonverbal messages are actions without words. Nonverbals include our gestures, the way we use our voice (loud, soft, high, low), the clothes we wear, and the car we drive. Delivery can enhance or hinder the effective decoding of a verbal message. Characteristics of delivery include the tone, the pitch, the rate, and the projection we use when we speak. All of these vocal characteristics of a verbal message help to emphasize or de-emphasize key thoughts. If messages are not delivered appropriately, then our meaning may be distorted and decoded incorrectly.

In our example at the beginning of the chapter, Eric realized that if he arranged the room without Juan's input, he might send a nonverbal message that would make him appear to be pushy. In addition his clothes, gestures, haircut, and personal possessions send nonverbal messages to his new roommate. Both verbal and nonverbal messages have the potential to be decoded incorrectly by others.

Channel

Messages must go through a medium to get from one communicator to another. The different mediums are called **channels.** Each channel targets a different sensory receptor and must be chosen appropriately to accomplish your goal. Channels include a cell phone, pager, handheld devices, computer, newspaper, radio, television, books, notes, sound systems, social media, and face-to-face interaction. Technology has increased the number, reach, and speed of channels exponentially.

When thinking about channels, remember every communication situation necessitates an appropriate channel choice. For example, Melinda wants to break up with Anthony. She logs onto her computer, finds him on instant messaging (IM), and types in, "I'm breaking up with you. This hasn't been fun for a long time." She hits send and immediately blocks any return messages. Is using e-mail or IM an appropriate channel for this situation? By choosing to use IM, what does Melinda communicate? What will Anthony think of her actions? What message does she send by blocking any further messages from Anthony?

Critical Thinking

Describe a recent event where you chose the wrong channel to communicate an important message to someone else.

_____

_____

_____

When have you used technical channels to communicate important issues because it is easier than saying something in person?

_____

_____

_____

As you choose a channel for certain communication events, think about the purpose of the communication and the consequences of that choice. There are certain situations that warrant direct and immediate involvement with the intended receiver of the message. However, many people choose a technology channel because it is easier—eliminating the uncomfortable encounter of facing someone.

TRY IT!

What would be the most appropriate channel for the following communication situations?

1. A boss needs to inform an employee that she did not receive a raise.

_____

2. A groom wants to call off his wedding two weeks prior to the date.

_____

3. A student needs to tell a faculty member there has been an emergency at home.

_____

4. Campus police need to tell a student there has been an emergency at home.

_____

5. You need to tell your professor that you have a strep infection and can't stay for class.

_____

Circumstances

Circumstances refer to the context of the situation and to the fundamental nature of the communicator. A communicator's background, attitudes, beliefs, and values contribute to his or her *fundamental nature*. As we analyze a communication event, we must remember that people are different. For example, because Jose's father was verbally and physically abusive, he may react to conflict differently than his significant other, Sally. When Jose gets into an argument with her, he may avoid her eyes and look downward. Because Sally was raised in an environment where family members always asserted themselves, she may not understand why he is so passive.

The context in which communication occurs also contributes to the meaning of a message. What you say in one situation could be completely inappropriate in another. For example, you and your friends feel comfortable using jokes and calling each other names. In the context of your friendships, you are all satisfied with this banter. However, you may feel uncomfortable or be offended if someone from outside your group makes the same type of comments to you. Analyzing your circumstances, including your own fundamental nature and the context of the situation, allows you to encode messages effectively. Reflection about past communication choices will help you think carefully about future interactions.

Feedback

Feedback is the response one communicator gives to another. Feedback can be verbal or nonverbal. Feedback is essential to the communication process; it acknowledges the presence of the other person, lets the communicator know the message was received, and demonstrates that the communication is valued.

Noise

Noise is anything that interrupts communicators from encoding, sending, receiving, and/or decoding a message properly. There are three types of noise: physical, personal, and semantic. ***Physical noise*** is anything external, from loud construction sounds outside a window to a bug flying around your head at an outdoor concert. At many schools, it is inevitable that the maintenance employees will mow the lawn on the day that students give their final speech or that the Spring Fling celebration will be blasting live band music during an exam. Physical noise distracts us and competes with our thought processes. Think about turning down the car radio while trying to find a friend's house for the first time; it's easier to concentrate when physical noise is minimized.

How many types of physical noise can you list? _____

_____

_____

_____

Personal noise refers to the ongoing thoughts in our minds. Three types of personal noise can distract us.

- *Prejudice.* Prejudice occurs when we "pre-judge," or have a preconceived, often negative, view of someone or something. If, for example, you have biases against small towns, you may have a negative impression of anyone from a town with a population of less than 3,000. So when you come to college and find your neighbor is from Small Town, U.S.A., you may immediately categorize her as unsophisticated. How will your ability to communicate with your neighbor be affected by your preconceived ideas? Will you be able to learn from her? It is our choice to be aware of our prejudices and to try to refrain from stereotyping. Just as Eric realized how ridiculous he was to have assumed Juan would speak Spanish, we must also be aware of prejudices and choose to work toward eliminating them. If we don't, we will ultimately pay the consequences generated by our ignorance.

- *Closed-mindedness.* Closed-mindedness occurs when we refuse to listen to another person's point of view. Think about your opinion on a topic like immigration. Chances are you feel very strongly about the issue. Could you learn something by hearing information from the opposing side? Of course. However, many people who believe they are right refuse to listen to any information that conflicts with their own beliefs. This position harms the communication process.

- *Self-centered noise.* Self-centered noise occurs when we focus more on ourselves than on the other person. Think about how often you zone out in class thinking about your friends, the exam you have in two hours, your weekend plans, the party you attended the night before, or even what you will have for dinner. You may have learned the art of smiling and nodding and looking attentive even though you are not paying the least bit of attention to the message.

  A new category of self-centered noise is technology. Many people are constantly checking their phones and computers for new texts, e-mails, updates, etc. Not only does that communicate a lack of interest in the people you are with (and distract them), but it distracts you and dilutes your focus.

The third type of noise is **semantic noise.** Semantic noise occurs when the person you are communicating with speaks a different language, uses technical jargon, and/or resorts to emotionally charged words. In the case of a different language, it is easy to understand the difficulties in the communication process. But technical jargon is almost as confusing. It is the specialized language of a profession. If one communicator knows the terminology and the other does not, sharing meaning is difficult.

Emotionally charged words also block the communication process. The listener may lock onto a word rather than pay attention to the complete message. Recently one of our friends, who is 78, shared an example of this. When he visits a particular business in our town, the doctor always greets him with, "Hello, young man!" Our friend finds this to be condescending and insulting since the doctor is 20 years younger. While the doctor may think it is funny or ingratiating, our friend finds it to be an example of ageism, and it hinders his ability to listen to this particular doctor.

As you can see, every part of the communication process is important. Select your message and channel carefully. As a communicator, you must be aware of the process and accept responsibility for the choices you make. Always consider the circumstances of the people around you. You should be aware of noise during the interaction and work to eliminate it whenever possible or to adapt to the circumstances to diminish the effects of the noise. And you should do your best to provide proper feedback. These choices will make interactions as smooth and effective as possible.

Professional Perspective

In ethnic direct marketing it is essential to be able to reach prospective Hispanic households in their respective language. Not only must we acknowledge formal languages, such as Spanish, Chinese, French, or Japanese, but also differences and nuances within each language group. For example, Spanish spoken in Spain is different from the Spanish spoken in Mexico or Puerto Rico or Venezuela. This relates to all languages and their dialects. Good marketers speak the language(s) of their customers.

En la venta directa dirigida a los grupos étnicos es muy importante poder llegar a los hogares de los posibles compradores hispanos en su mismo idioma. No sólo debemos reconocer los principales idiomas, tales como español, chino, francés, o japonés, sino también las diferencias y matices dentro de cada grupo idiomático. Por ejemplo, el español hablado en España es distinto al español hablado en México, Puerto Rico o Venezuela. Esto es también cierto con respecto a todos los idiomas y a sus dialectos. Los buenos vendedores hablan el idioma de sus clientes.

—Vincent Andaloro
President and Founder
Latin-Pak Direct Marketing

The communication process consists of many parts. To be an effective communicator, you must make appropriate choices as you become aware of how each part influences the others.

Types of Communication

There are four basic types of communication.

- Intrapersonal communication: Communicating within yourself
- Interpersonal communication: Communicating with another person
- Small group communication: Communicating with 3–20 people (with 5–8 as the ideal size) who have a common goal
- Public communication: Communicating with a large audience

When we mentally review or rehearse conversations or experiences, we are engaging in ***intrapersonal communication.*** Think how often you do this. Before you meet with your professor, do you think about what you are going to say? When your alarm goes off in the morning, do you ask yourself, "If I hit the snooze button, I can give up the shower, sleep for another 18 minutes, and wear a hat"? We communicate intrapersonally when we meditate, reflect, and strategize. Intrapersonal communication helps us to be in tune with ourselves, to practice important communication scenarios, to analyze everything around us (including our own actions), and to think critically about past and future events.

TRY IT!

How many interpersonal interactions have you already had today? List as many as you can.

_____

_____

_____

_____

In contrast to the internal dialogue of intrapersonal communication, ***interpersonal communication*** takes place when two people speak with one another. Can you remember the discussion you had with a classmate about the final exam in one of your classes? The complaints you shared with someone about your roommate? The person you smiled at in the cafeteria? You should be able to list at least 50 exchanges in the last 24 hours. We use interpersonal communication constantly to help create and maintain our relationships. However, face-to-face interaction is quickly being overtaken by *mass interpersonal communication* (social networking).

Interpersonal communication becomes **small group communication** when the number of people increases. Generally, groups are defined as having 3–20 members. Group members share a sense of belonging and have common beliefs, goals, or reasons for getting together. Group members work together to accomplish tasks and/or relationship goals.

Groups with task goals meet to solve a problem or to complete an assignment. This type of group can be found in the workplace or in the classroom and generally consists of 5–8 people. When your professor asks five of you to develop a marketing plan for a new product, you are in a task group. On the other end of the spectrum, the primary purpose of groups with relationship goals is to fulfill personal needs of conversation and belonging. These groups may consist of close friends who eat dinner together or colleagues who go dancing every Friday night. Sometimes groups have both task and relationship goals. These blended groups can include a social fraternity/sorority, book club, study groups, and/or a religious gathering. In addition to relationship functions, these groups also perform tasks such as fund-raising, social service projects, reading assignments, and so forth.

Teams are a type of small group. Teams work on tasks designed to accomplish a specific goal. The members of teams employ a procedure to accomplish their goal. Teams are prevalent in many workplace environments. In this text, we focus exclusively on communication within teams rather than on the broader concept of small group communication.

Public communication occurs when a communicator informs, persuades, and/or entertains a group of people. Speakers have an organized message and an official audience, and they prepare for the event. Typically public communication comes in the form of school assemblies, oral presentations, political speeches, a keynote address at a conference, high school announcements, sermons, corporate announcements via in-house television, and messages delivered through electronic media. You

---

TRY IT!

How many interpersonal interactions have you already had today? List as many as you can.

_____

_____

_____

_____

_____

may think you will never have to give a speech except in this class; however, chances are public communication is in your future. You should learn the skills for effective public speaking so that you will be prepared when opportunities arise in both your professional and personal life.

Basic Communication Principles

Improving your communication skills takes time and dedication. It involves thinking before acting, making the best choices, and dealing with the consequences of those choices. Below are four principles to keep in mind when thinking about communication.

We cannot not communicate. Everything we do is received and interpreted by someone, somewhere. Even if we isolate ourselves, thinking we won't have to communicate, the very act of not interacting communicates a message. We communicate with family members, friends, coworkers, peers, professors, service personnel, significant others, and many more. Our communication skills are put to the test every minute of every day.

Communication is irreversible—whether it is intentional or unintentional. If you say something or do something that upsets another person, you can't change it. Once the words are out of your mouth, the damage has been done. You can apologize and hope to lessen the impact, but the communication can't be changed. When you choose certain words or act a certain way, there are consequences, some positive and some negative. Effective communicators understand this principle and think carefully before they speak. They monitor and reflect on all of their communication.

Communication is a continuing process. The bits of information we collect become part of our circumstances and affect our future communication. By being more aware of our goals and surroundings, we can improve our communication style and learn other perspectives. We all experience the world a little differently, so in addition to understanding and improving our own style, we need to remember that other people have unique styles. No one is a perfect communicator; instead, we have varying degrees of success in certain situations. Effective communicators are flexible because they adapt their messages to the circumstances they encounter.

Improving your communication skills is a lifelong commitment. You already possess communication skills; by increasing your repertoire you'll be able to handle the diverse situations you will encounter. When doing so, you don't need to imitate others or to compromise your values and ethical standards. Increased skills allow you to communicate effectively and to adjust to unexpected circumstances.

Communication involves ethical considerations. As you think about the fact that communication is an ongoing, irreversible process, you'll also want to think about ethical considerations. According to Pamela Shockley-Zalabak (2006), ethics are "moral principles that guide judgments about good and bad, right and wrong, not just effectiveness or efficiency" (p. 118).

Many communication situations we face on a daily basis include ethical choices. For example, do we repeat gossip we heard about someone? Do we take the time to investigate the comment prior to passing it along? Do we refrain from sharing the information altogether? On another day, do we refrain from communicating that we have a crush on another friend? Do we hide our feelings by remaining silent? Each of these choices has considerable ethical consequences related to credibility and judgment.

We can also use communication to uphold personal ethics and moral standards. We do so, for instance, in a grocery store when we inform the clerk that the register undercharged us, or when we tell a server that the dessert we ordered is missing from the bill. Our reaction to these situations reveals our ethical standards to others.

The better you understand your intrapersonal communication, the more you consider others' viewpoints when communicating interpersonally, the more you practice working with others to achieve goals in a group, and the more you choose to communicate publically, the better equipped you will be to handle common situations effectively and ethically.

Adapting

While you may believe that your communication style is a reflection of who you are and you are free to communicate how you want and when you want, there are consequences to this philosophy. Certainly you have freedom of speech, but if you want to have relationships with people and to succeed professionally, you may need to learn to adapt to different situations.

Professional Perspective

Adaptability is important in facing the unexpected in terms of the twists and turns your personal career can take.

—Christina DeVries
Senior Account Manager
Spotlight Payroll Inc.

Adaptability is the ability to choose the appropriate communication style for the situation and the participants. This may mean that you alter your language in a more professional situation or on a serious occasion. Or you refrain from saying something that is on your mind if the situation is not appropriate for your comment. Being able to adapt helps you to appear competent in all situations.

Professional Perspective

The world is such a hurried place today. We rush here, we rush there, we rush, rush everywhere! We are, at the same time, inundated with communication. We get it by television at home or, now (WOW!), in the car, by phone, at the movies, on a plane, and even sides of trains; we get it via the Internet or magazines, in our mail and even the halls, and, of course, at the malls. At all times someone or something, somehow, somewhere is speaking in an attempt to convince us.

—Corey D. Welch
Operations Supervisor
Arkansas Student Loan Authority

Summary

Think back to Eric and Juan. They have a lot of work ahead of them, but with some thinking, acceptance, and patience they will get to know one another and may develop a lifelong friendship. Eric is already aware that nonverbal communication plays an important role in the perception of others. If he continues to monitor and reflect on his communication choices, he will have the opportunity to share meaning and to develop a satisfying friendship. The knowledge you gain from this book is beneficial to your personal development and is essential to your professional development.

KEY WORDS

adaptability
channel
circumstances
closed-mindedness
communication process
communicators
decoding
encoding
feedback
interpersonal communication
intrapersonal communication
messages

noise
nonverbal messages
personal noise
physical noise
prejudice
public communication
self-centered noise
semantic noise
small group communication
teams
verbal messages

DISCUSSION/ACTIVITIES

1. Name a person you feel is an excellent communicator. Describe the specific skills they use to hold your attention.

2. Analyze the communication style of one of your teachers during a class period. Do they think communication is a two-way process? Are they receiver-oriented?

3. Describe a communication situation in which the speaker adjusted their message during the speech due to an unforeseen event. Was the speech still successful? Why?

4. Describe the number of daily situations in which you use verbal, non-verbal, and written communication. Name specific moments where you feel the most effective and least effective during communication.

5. How do you think your communication skills will be used in your career field? Describe.

6. What is your strongest communication skill? Explain.

7. Describe a time when you communicated something that you instantly realized was irreversible but that you wished you could take back.

In my career I think my communication skills will be used effectively. My approach to people will effect the message. The channels I use will change the view of the reciever. I think my communication skills will constantly be used.

two

Perception

After reading this chapter, you should be able to:

- Define the perceptual process
- Explain how people can have varying perceptions of the same phenomena
- Recognize instances of stereotyping and explain its relationship to the perceptual process
- Explain the difference between fact and inference
- Recognize communication problems caused by attributing meaning
- Explain the perception-checking process and practice the skill
- Explain how perception relates to self-concept and self-esteem

---

Imagine three people witnessing a car accident. When interviewed by the police, they give three different eyewitness reports. How can that be? Although each person saw the same event, they did not *perceive* the event in the same way. Because we all have different experiences and expectations, we all perceive events and behaviors differently. Competent communicators understand that perception affects how we encode and decode messages and are savvy enough to assess potential communication errors due to perceptual differences.

The Perceptual Process

While walking down the street talking to a friend, you encounter numerous sensory stimuli. You hear the sounds of cars, the honking of horns, and your friend's voice. You see other people and perhaps notice some of their characteristics and personal belongings; you also see store window displays, buildings, and vehicles. You smell hot pretzels, perfume, bakery goods, and fumes from a passing bus. Your conversational stroll down the street is filled with distractions and sensory input. However, you attend to only a few of these things.

If we acknowledged all of the sensory stimuli around us, we'd be so overwhelmed we would have trouble concentrating. Perception helps us sort through external stimuli for relevance. We compare newly received messages to past experiences we've had with similar situations. Past experiences help us to interpret what we sense in our daily lives. This **perceptual process** occurs in three stages: (1) selection; (2) organization; and (3) interpretation (McGaan, 2003).

In the first step of the perceptual process, your mind decides which of the numerous distractions are worth recognizing. As you walk with your friend, you pay strict attention to the conversation because you haven't seen each other in a long time. You are aware of people walking toward you in order to avoid bumping into them. You may notice a particularly nice car go by, or an outfit on a specific person in the crowd, or even a parent with a child. These choices capture your attention based on your personality, your background, what is unique in a particular object and sound, and what seems important to you at the time. At one point, you notice a pregnant woman with an armload of groceries moving through the crowd to a parked car. She reminds you of your pregnant sister who is in her eighth month. This woman stands out because you've watched your sister's physical condition change and have become more sensitive to the difficulties that pregnant women face. Your personal interest in pregnancy makes this woman noticeable to you, but not to the person with whom you are walking. This process of focusing on specific stimuli and ignoring others is called **selective attention.** While numerous other stimuli are there, you do not choose to pay attention to them.

In the second step of the perceptual process, your brain **organizes** the stimuli you receive by grouping them in meaningful ways. Recently we received the following anonymous e-mail:

> aoccdrnig to a rscheeahcr at an Elingsh uinervtisy, it deosn't mttaer in waht oredr the ltteers in a wrod are, the olny iprmoetnt tihng is that frist and lsat ltteer is at the rghit pclae. The rset can be a toatl mses and you can sitll raed it wouthit porbelm. Tihs is bcuseae we do not raed ervey lteter by itslef but the wrod as a wlohe.

This is a perfect example of how our minds group information. Most of us can read this paragraph with little or no trouble at all. Our minds fill in blanks when we group information. What do you see below?

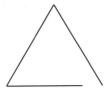

Most people would say this is a triangle. In fact, it is only three connected lines. However, our minds fill in the piece of missing information during the organizing process. We organize messages by comparing them with the information we have from past experiences. We think about similar situations, incidences, or behaviors from our past and use them to categorize the new information before assigning meaning. We expect future events to be similar to previous experiences. This helps us select and organize stimuli, but it also potentially limits our ability to perceive things properly. If we cannot view new perceptual input with an open mind, it is difficult to be an effective communicator. Our previous judgments can cloud our willingness to be open to new information. Have you ever seen this puzzle?

$$\bullet \quad \bullet \quad \bullet$$
$$\bullet \quad \bullet \quad \bullet$$
$$\bullet \quad \bullet \quad \bullet$$

The instructions are to connect all of the dots using four straight lines without lifting your pencil from the paper. Most people can't do it. Even after having previously seen this puzzle in various classes during their academic life, people often can't remember how to accomplish the task. The concept of staying inside the imaginary square is so ingrained that we conceptualize the problem by comparing it to past experiences, and we can't do the puzzle. (After trying the puzzle, see page 34 for the solution.)

How does this apply to communication? Well, when you see a 300-pound, macho football player, what kind of voice do you expect the person to have? Chances are that most large men you have met previously had deep, baritone voices. What is your reaction when this person starts to talk in a high-pitched, wispy voice? His voice violates your expectation of how he should sound and may make you uncomfortable.

Think about being in a business setting and management announces that a new administrative assistant starts today. Everyone is excited and immediately has expectations of what this person will look like. When the new assistant appears and is an obese man, would you be surprised? Upset? Bewildered? Would your nonverbal reactions convey a message to the new assistant? Are there possible consequences for these reactions? We need to be flexible and adapt to unexpected situations. If we rely *solely* on past experiences for organizing perceptual stimuli, we may experience difficulties communicating.

Once you have organized information by grouping it and comparing it to past experiences, you move into the third step of the perceptual

---

Critical Thinking

What does an administrative assistant look like? If we used a term from the past, such as secretary, would your description change?

_____

_____

How did you come up with this image?

_____

_____

---

process. Here you *interpret* what you sense; you assign meaning to it. Let's return to our street scene: Your friend's cell phone rings, and she decides to answer it. You pay attention to the call for a moment, but you become angry. The meaning you assign to your friend's nonverbal communication is that you are less important than the incoming call. Your attention shifts away from her toward other activities going on around you. Suddenly, you see a car coming toward you. It is weaving in and out of traffic. Without warning it veers to the right and runs up over the curb hitting a pedestrian who is waiting to cross the street. You hear screeching brakes. You smell burning rubber. You hear the scream as the person is hit. Your friend also witnesses the incident; each of you sees the accident but assigns meaning differently. The police question you separately. After providing a description of what you saw, you decide to go for coffee with your friend to calm down. You say, "I think the driver must have been drunk because he was losing control of the car before hitting the man." Your friend says, "What are you talking about? He obviously swerved to avoid hitting another car coming into his lane." Both you and your friend saw the car weave, but you assigned meaning to the event differently. Your selective attention also plays a role here. You focused on the accident, but your friend was involved in a phone conversation while the car was weaving back and forth. She only noticed the accident for a limited time.

Selective attention is natural for most people. However, someone who lost their hearing and then regained it (such as with a cochlear implant) has to relearn the selective-attention skill. Once the hearing is regained, an individual can suffer from an overwhelming amount of aural stimuli. He or she will hear every sound that others easily filter out. Imagine hearing every environmental hum, buzz, plink, or rustle. The process of relearning to filter out extraneous sound can take months to accomplish and cause great distress.

Perception Management

We mentioned the concept of personal *brand* in chapter 1. One of the smartest things that students can do early in their college career is to think about managing the perceptions that others have of them. While we can't control how others perceive us, we can do certain things that promote a personal **brand** for ourselves. How do you want others to perceive you? As smart? Kind? Ethical? Easygoing? Fun? Witty? Responsible? Outgoing? Shy? Private? Once you select the brand that you want, you can alter your communication style to enhance it.

Reality ✓

Lydia Ramsey (2011) advises: "When you meet someone face-to-face, 93% of how you are judged is based on nonverbal data—your appearance and your body language. . . . Whoever said that you can't judge a book by its cover failed to note that people do." What implications are there for your nonverbal behavior when you come to class on the first day dressed sloppily and schlump down in your chair with a disgusted look on your face?

_____

_____

_____

_____

We often find that students are not exhibiting qualities that they want others to perceive. For instance, one semester we had a student who wanted to be perceived as hardworking. Yet, every day, he arrived late to class. Often, he didn't have his homework completed, and the boxes in the chapter were not filled out. None of his behaviors led us to the perception of a "hardworking" peer.

Sadly in other semesters, entire classes of first-year students have been expressionless with no answer to the question, "How do you want to brand yourself?" "What do you want others to see?" While you cannot guarantee someone else's perceptual interpretation, now is definitely the time to start thinking about guiding others to the perception you'd like them to have.

Remember, though, that your personal brand must fit your personality. Brenda Bence (2008) says it is important not to try to manufacture a fake brand. You need to be true to yourself. Once you select the brand you want, you need to consistently choose communication behaviors that embody it. When you fluctuate in the impression you give others, you generate confusing messages that may damage your personal credibility.

TRY IT!

What do you do on the first day of class to help manage the perception the teacher has of you?

_____

_____

_____

Why do or why don't you think this is important?

_____

_____

_____

Varying Perceptions

People do not perceive the same sensory input in a similar way for a variety of reasons. For example, you receive the same sensory input from your instructor as the rest of your class. However, you may have different perceptions of the teacher. Some of you may think the instructor is funny—others may think he is a total bore and his jokes are cheesy.

So why do perceptions vary? How can two individuals assign meaning differently? Think back to the communication process and our discussion of circumstances. We talked about the fact that everyone has different backgrounds and experiences. Now, add that personal component to the perceptual process. In the organizing step, we are comparing current sensory stimuli to our past experiences. So if people have different experiences, it is reasonable to deduce that they can have different assignments of meaning for the same event when involved in interpersonal communication. Read the professional perspective below. The senior student had experiences that the first-year students did not

---

Professional Perspective

As retirement approached, I reviewed my evaluations by students over the years. One thing that stood out was the diversity of opinions that students expressed about my teaching. A comment that I particularly enjoyed was made by a CJA major who wrote, "I'm a senior, and I thought the course was very interesting. Some of the freshmen thought the course was boring. They haven't seen boring yet."

—Dr. Larry Miller
Professor Emeritus
Mansfield University of Pennsylvania

when evaluating the same class; therefore, the students' reactions to the course were different.

Think about your instructor again for a moment. Based on your limited exposure to this person, do you think the instructor owns a pet? If so, what kind of pet? Obviously you have no factual basis for answering this question, yet you probably have an opinion. How did you form this opinion? Chances are you looked for physical evidence (cat or dog hair) or based your opinion on something the instructor said. You may think about things the instructor has revealed in class that would indicate a lifestyle that is or isn't pet oriented. Or your instructor could remind you of someone who has a pet and that memory influences your perception. You may just look at the teacher and get an intuitive feeling about pet ownership. You may also look at the percentage of other professors you know who have pets and go with statistical probability.

In other words, there are a variety of personal experiences that shape your perception. You continue to relate new information to your past experiences as you try to interpret information. As each student in the class does this—and you all have different past experiences—you perceive the same phenomenon differently.

Critical Thinking

Think about three people viewing the Rocky Mountains for the first time. They are all witnessing the same physical object. What meaning do they assign to the object? How do they perceive it? Write a brief statement that would likely be the first comment of the individuals described below as they see the Rockies in person for the first time.

An experienced skier _____

A religious leader _____

A person with emphysema _____

Stereotyping

Stereotyping is the act of treating everyone with similar characteristics as though they were the same. We use the perceptual process when we stereotype. As stated earlier, we experience sensory stimuli and make sense of it by categorizing the information and comparing it to what we already believe is true. Stereotyping is an important part of the organizing step of the perceptual process. It develops from information we choose to hear and remember from our family, peers, religious establishments, teachers, community, and the entertainment media. Because stereotyping ignores the possibility of individual differences, it can be problematic. For example, thirty years ago men who wore earrings were stereotyped as homosexual. There was a transition period during which people interpreted earrings as a statement of sexual preference depending on whether the earring was worn in the left or the right ear. Today, many men wear earrings without being stereotyped.

ETHICAL CONSIDERATIONS

Is it ethical to live in a community that keeps certain people out? What about joining clubs that are prestigious, but restricted? Do you realize that both of these situations still exist?

_____

_____

_____

Stereotyping is something many of us do without thinking. Because we must organize stimuli in the perceptual process, stereotyping is a quick and easy way to group and analyze information. However, we have choices when it comes to assigning meaning based on those stereotypes. As Eric learned in chapter 1, his stereotype of people with Latino surnames was totally incorrect. While stereotypes allow us to organize information, they also limit our ability to look at people and situations objectively. This lack of objectivity could lead to communication misunderstandings. Once you become more aware of your stereotypical beliefs and maintain perceptual flexibility, you will be better equipped to communicate effectively with a diverse population.

Professional Perspective

Think about the stereotypes you hold. I was in a grocery store one day and ahead of me was a man with long hair, tattoos, and a worn leather jacket. Sitting in his cart was a boy who appeared to be about four years old. The boy was facing me, and the man was in front of their cart. As I stood there, the boy lifted his feet and pushed my cart. I was a little shocked at the child's behavior. As I looked at the child with disapproval, the man leaned down and whispered in the boy's ear. The child looked at me and said, "I'm very sorry I kicked your cart." Often we hold stereotypes about the competence of a parent/adult based on the manner in which they are dressed. Stereotyping this man based on his attire would have been a serious mistake; he was not a neglectful, uninvolved parent as some would think. By correcting the boy's behavior, he reinforced the expression, "don't judge a book by its cover."

—Belinda A. Bernum
Assistant Professor
Mansfield University

Critical Thinking

Do you claim you don't stereotype people? What do the following people look like?

Prostitute _____

Cop _____

Governor _____

Lawyer _____

Medical Examiner _____

Straight-A Student _____

How many people in these categories do you know? Where did you come up with your perceptions of what these people look like?

_____

_____

_____

Fact versus Inference

As you move into the third step of the perceptual process and try to assign meaning to perceived events, it is imperative to realize the difference between facts and inferences. **Facts** are observable phenomena. It is a fact there are clouds in the sky, the grass is green, and oceans contain water. We can observe the truth of these statements. **Inferences** are conclusions we draw about the facts we observe. For instance, if the green grass looks particularly inviting while we are on a trip, we may infer it would be a nice place to stop, spread out a blanket, and have a picnic. We have drawn a conclusion. When we start the picnic and are attacked by fire ants, we realize our inference was wrong. If we act as though a perception is fact when it is actually inference, we can run into numerous communication problems.

Reality ✓

You are driving down a busy highway and see a van on the side of the road with its door open. As you speed by, you see a man grabbing a small child.

What are the facts? _____

What are the inferences? _____

What is the truth? _____

Here is another example to think about from an interpersonal setting. It is a fact that Shakespeare wrote plays. It is a fact that Shakespeare's plays appear on your new significant other's bookshelf. Is it a fact that your significant other likes Shakespeare? No. You infer she likes Shakespeare based on the plays on the bookshelf. So, what happens when you give your significant other a ticket to a Shakespearean play for her birthday? The answer depends on whether you made a correct inference about the material you observed on the bookshelf.

Confusing fact with inference directly relates to the interpretation step of the perceptual process. Another concept to be aware of is how our emotional reactions to past and present experiences affect our inferences. We may infer meaning based on how we felt about something rather than on what we actually saw. This conclusion may often be incorrect. Let's say you are supposed to meet your significant other at 3:00 PM. You decide to show up a little early as a surprise only to find when you get close to his house, he is on the front porch hugging an attractive person goodbye. You immediately assign meaning to the sensory input based on your past experiences and state of mind. You feel your significant other must be cheating on you. Once the other person is gone, you confront your partner and yell accusations. When your significant other finally gets a chance to explain, you find out the other person is a sibling you haven't met. In this case, emotional reactions clouded the ability to infer accurately.

CHOICES AND CONSEQUENCES

Describe a situation where you have assigned meaning incorrectly. What happened?

_____

_____

What were the consequences?

_____

_____

What do you wish you had done differently?

_____

_____

Attributing Meaning

When we witness behaviors in others, we try to make sense of those behaviors and assign meaning to them. Creating meaning for behaviors is called ***attribution.*** It is very likely that from observation alone we can never know for sure what behaviors mean, but we often feel confident in our own interpretation. The process of attributing meaning can easily result in miscommunication.

Critical Thinking

Identify an instance of attribution theory in the description of the two friends walking down the street and witnessing the car accident.

_____

_____

Describe an instance where someone incorrectly attributed meaning to your behavior.

_____

_____

Imagine a scenario in which Tony sees Tina in the student center and waves hello. Tina looks at him and quickly looks away without responding. He feels hurt and angry. This is an emotional reaction that clouds his judgment. "Fine," he thinks. "Drop dead!" Tony has just created a meaning for Tina's action. He assumes she meant to ignore him. But is his assumption correct?

Tony has choices in this exchange. He can act as though his assumption is fact. Or, he can question his assumption immediately. He may also brainstorm for other reasons that would explain Tina's action. Or, he can be more direct and active by checking his perceptions (perception checking is discussed in the next section).

What do you think the consequences will be for Tony if he acts on his assumption that Tina has deliberately hurt him? What will he do next? Will he ignore her the next time he sees her? Confront her? How will this affect their future interactions? You can see that nothing good will occur if he acts on an incorrect assumption. Tony would benefit from recognizing other possibilities for Tina's actions or from doing a perception check immediately.

Critical Thinking

What are some other reasons for Tina's behavior? Can you list three? Six?

_____

_____

_____

_____

_____

_____

Perception Checking

Many of us choose to act on attributions, inferences, or perceptions without checking to see if they are correct. **Perception checking** is a skill that is used to double-check your understanding of what is going on with another person. Let's take a look at an example where perception checking would be valuable.

Judy is a 35-year-old who lives in a rural community where power outages are common. Judy decides to go on a brief trip five hours from her home. Judy has the type of relationship with her mother where she always e-mails her mom after she returns from a trip. The e-mail message lets her mother know she is home safely.

When Judy arrives home at 11:00 PM, she is exhausted from the trip. She pulls in the driveway and notices the power is out again. She could call her mom instead, but she knows her mom is often sound asleep by 9:00 PM. She assumes the power will probably be on within the hour, but she is so tired she falls asleep on the couch. Judy's mother, who is expecting an e-mail from Judy, doesn't find one when she wakes up. She calls Judy at 5:00 AM when she doesn't see the e-mail. Judy is groggy as she answers the phone and tries to process why her mother is yelling at her. Her mother says, "How can you be so irresponsible? All I ask for is a little e-mail message so I know you are okay. I haven't slept all night because I was worried about you. You are so inconsiderate of my feelings. It only takes a minute to send a message." In this case, Judy's mom would be a much more effective communicator if she used the skill of perception checking instead of making assumptions and acting on them as though they were fact. Imagine how awful she will feel when Judy says, "Mom, I tried to e-mail, but our power was out and it was too late to call. I was waiting for the electricity to come back on, but I fell asleep on the couch. I'm so sorry."

Perception checking consists of three parts. First, you give an *objective description* of what you sensed; second, you give an *interpretation* of what the situation meant to you; and, finally, you ask a *question*. In the previous example, Judy's mom could have said, "I noticed you didn't send an e-mail last night when you got home, so that I would know you were safe. I feel as though you are inconsiderate of my feelings. What is going on?" This would incorporate all three elements, but could alienate Judy. A simplified inquiry would be, "I was really worried when your e-mail didn't come in last night—did you send one?"

Here is another example. Your significant other comes home from school and seems to be in a bad mood. He hasn't even looked in your direction. Accusatory questions—"Hey, aren't you going to pay any attention to me?" or "What's YOUR problem?"—are normally ineffective. If you question the observed behavior by asking, "Are you mad?" the likely response is a defensive "no," or "Why would I be mad at you?" The "no" response stops communication and doesn't address your feelings of being ignored. You might say, "I'm getting the sense that you are mad at me" or "I feel you're mad at me when you don't talk to me. Are you?" Perception checking, in the majority of cases, is useful in creating a nonaccusatory, and therefore a nondefensive, communication environment.

Keep in mind, you should only use perception checking if there is a chance your attribution of meaning is incorrect. For example, it would be inappropriate to use perception checking in the following example:

Instructor: Michael, would you please close the door?
Michael: I'm getting the sense you would like to have the door closed. Would you?

Think of how annoying it would be to have someone constantly perception checking to see if you are mad at them. Sometimes people use perception checking when they really should take the time to stop and think for a minute about the situation. In our example above, if your significant other comes home and isn't talking, why is your first perception you have done something wrong? Why wouldn't you assume she/ he is tired or had a bad experience at work? Some people tend to think that everything is their fault when they should think through other reasons that might have triggered the behavior. You should use perception checking when you truly want to understand what is going on with the other person. If they are in a bad mood, and you are in a close relationship, sometimes you can choose to just let it go and stay out of their way. But if the situation continues to worry you, and you need to clarify whether you are the cause, then go ahead and check it out.

Finally, there are many people who feel awkward using the perception-checking skill. If you are reluctant to talk about feelings, then this skill will take a lot of practice before you can use it comfortably. Many people choose to simply ignore their own feelings and just accept their interpretation of the other communicator's actions. This is unfair to you as well as to the other person whose actions you may have misinterpreted. Another reason people are reluctant to use the perception-checking skill is because it is easier to assume what another person means than to ask questions. Although asking someone to clarify his or her behavior may be awkward initially, the value of accuracy in communication is immeasurable.

Critical Thinking

Describe a recent misunderstanding in your life that would have resolved itself more effectively if you had simply used perception checking.

_____

_____

_____

_____

Perception Related to Self-Concept

Self-concept refers to what we think about ourselves, including our physical attributes (short or tall, big or small), our aptitudes (good at math or at getting along with others), our physical coordination (good at sports or video games), and our skills (tying flies or gourmet cooking). Most of these attributes are factual assessments. We recognize whether we are tall or short, good at games, etc. We reach these conclusions as we assess and evaluate ourselves intrapersonally.

We also assess ourselves through comments others make about us. We take into consideration evaluations made by teachers, family members, significant others, friends, siblings, other relatives, coaches, and religious leaders. If, as a child, you hear that you are "pretty" or "smart" or "stupid" or "lazy," these labels shape your perception of yourself. Nicknames such as "chubby," "slim," "bubba," or "princess" also affect our self-concept. If we see ourselves through the labels given to us by others, we may develop a self-concept based on illusion rather than on reality.

A third area that influences our assessment of ourselves is when we compare ourselves to others. We watch someone else give a speech before we give our own, and we make a comparison. We look at some-

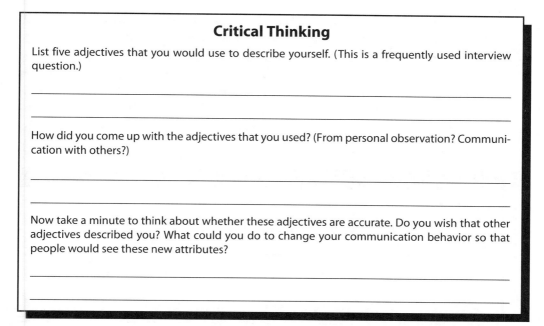

Critical Thinking

List five adjectives that you would use to describe yourself. (This is a frequently used interview question.)

_____

_____

How did you come up with the adjectives that you used? (From personal observation? Communication with others?)

_____

_____

Now take a minute to think about whether these adjectives are accurate. Do you wish that other adjectives described you? What could you do to change your communication behavior so that people would see these new attributes?

_____

_____

Professional Perspective

As a professional therapist it has been my experience that our self-concept is a result of the feedback we receive from others, especially those we love and trust. Their words are the chisels that form the person we become. If the feedback is constantly negative, we can change "chisel" to "weapon." _The Dead Poets Society_ gives the example of an adolescent who chooses suicide because he can't meet his father's expectations. I wish I could tell you this is fiction, but it is not. I write crisis intervention plans for my clients every day. And I shudder when I think of the millions of other therapists who must do the same. Feedback kills self-concept every day. Choose your words carefully and choose how other people's words will affect you. It is never all one person's fault. Choose only your level of responsibility. What your loved ones say is only their opinion; it is not fact. And focus on your positives. After all, your yesterday, today, and tomorrow is a matter of your choice. Choose wisely.

—T. W. Anderson
Adolescent Therapist

one else's outfit and compare it to our own. We notice how many friends someone has and note that we have more or less. This tells us something about our own abilities and traits.

Finally, we assess ourselves as we evaluate how well we hold up to our moral and ethical standards. For instance, if we believe cheating is wrong, and we never cheat, then we assess ourselves as an honest person. If we believe that cheating is wrong and then we find ourselves doing that, we may alter that assessment.

Once you have the whole picture of your self-concept, you need to realize that it influences your communication skills with the external world. Our presentational style, use of nonverbal communication, ability to interact on an interpersonal level, or our ability to function in a team environment grows out of our self-concept. If our self-concept is that we are shy, we are likely to have nonanimated nonverbals, a quiet disposition and presentational style, and we may be afraid to participate in teams. On the other hand, if our self-concept is that we are confident, we will stand tall, speak loudly, and actively participate in teams.

TRY IT!

If your instructor perceives he is shy, what kind of behaviors will he exhibit in the classroom?

_____

_____

If you hear you are stupid and unlikable all of your life, how will you interact with others at college?

_____

_____

Perception Related to Self-Esteem

Self-esteem refers to the value we place on self-concept observations. For example, Rachel, who is 5'3" tall, thinks she's short. Her self-esteem related to this concept depends on the value she places on height. In U.S. culture, research shows that tall people have an advantage in interviews, presidential elections, and promotions (Knapp & Hall, 2010, pp. 192–193). If Rachel thinks only tall people are attractive and desirable, her self-esteem will probably be low because there is nothing she can do to change her height. However, if she believes attractiveness does not depend on height, then being short will not affect her self-esteem.

Sometimes, we can be our own worst enemy. We can be either extremely critical or extremely supportive of ourselves. How you communicate intrapersonally affects your self-esteem. What do you say to yourself when you get an "F" on an exam? Do you say, "I can't believe how stupid I am! I can never do anything right." This negative internal communication can damage your self-esteem and affect future behavior. Or, do you say something positive to yourself, "Wow. I sure wasn't expecting an 'F.' I need to figure out what to do differently so I can improve my grades." It is important to remain positive in your self-criticism so you can solve your problem and improve performance.

Self-esteem and how we feel about ourselves influence our willingness and ability to communicate effectively. If you feel good about yourself, you may be more likely to approach and meet new people, to assert your ideas in a team situation, to stand confidently before an audience, and to try new communication strategies. If you don't trust yourself to discover new talents and instead rely only on past skills that make you feel comfortable, you constrict personal growth. If you feel your self-concept or self-esteem need to be stronger, there are numerous books and articles outlining the skills you can practice to strengthen your views of yourself. You may also want to seek professional assistance.

Summary

Understanding the perceptual process is critical to becoming an effective communicator. You must understand why you assign meaning the way you do to words, actions, situations, and people so you can improve your communication style and avoid miscommunication. Once you understand your own perceptions and how the perceptual process works, you'll be better able to analyze why other communicators perceive phenomena and assign meaning the way they do. You should be able to think more critically about concepts such as stereotyping and attribution.

There are fascinating challenges waiting for you as you acclimate to new situations, perhaps even new regions of the country with their unique cultures and people. As you work through the perceptual process of organizing and assigning meaning to unfamiliar behaviors and events, you must be aware of the potential for saying or doing the wrong thing. As you gain a more acute awareness about yourself and your ability to communicate effectively with other people, don't jump to conclusions.

Do your best to manage the perceptual process within yourself so others see you as a solid communicator and someone they would like to get to know. Take nothing for granted. The things that look easy are normally the hardest to conquer.

Professional Perspective

Once you master yourself then you can fully relate to the world and others around you.

—Lance Walden
Northwest Regional Radio Promotions
Universal Republic Records

[Nine-dot puzzle solution: Start (1) a diagonal line from *outside* the lower right-hand dot (at a distance similar to the spacing between the nine dots) up to the upper left-hand dot; (2) draw a horizontal line to the right through the upper dots extending, again, outside the area; (3) draw a diagonal line through the middle right-hand dot and the middle lower dot, extending the line to below the left-hand row of dots; (4) draw a vertical line up through the left-hand row of dots.]

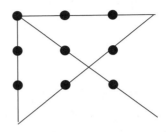

KEY WORDS

attribution   perception management
brand   selective attention
fact   self-concept
inference   self-esteem
perception checking   stereotyping
perceptual process

DISCUSSION/ACTIVITIES

1. What is the first thing you notice when you walk into the classroom? Why is your selective attention drawn to that item?

2. How would you describe the "brand" of your teacher? Explain.

3. What would your teacher say about your "brand" based on classroom observations? Is this description accurate? If not, how can you make a better impression?

4. Listen to a lecture on campus and identify the facts used in the presentation versus the inferences used in the presentation. Compare the results and evaluate the accuracy of the lecture.

5. What is your favorite color? How do gender and stereotypes play a role in how the color can be worn in clothing and jewelry?

6. Describe a time when you had an initial perception of a stranger that turned out to be wrong.

7. Thinking in terms of self-concept, what is your strongest academic skill? Why do you feel this way?

8. Is your self-esteem generally high or low? Why? What influence did your parents have on your feelings?

three

Language

OBJECTIVES

After reading this chapter, you should be able to:
- Explain the concept of symbols
- Define denotative and connotative meaning
- Understand content and relationship levels of meaning
- Describe how language influences our thoughts
- Explain the concept of rhetorical sensitivity
- Analyze your own use of rhetorical sensitivity

Lupita is attending your school for the first time. She speaks Spanish as her native language, and she is becoming quite fluent in conversational English. She has occasional difficulty, however, with some colloquial expressions used in the United States. Lupita attends a party in a room full of U.S. students. She notices her friend Maria preparing food at the refreshment table. She turns to Mark and says, "Oh, isn't that nice, Maria just cut the cheese for everyone." Mark spits his drink out on the floor and erupts in laughter. Four other friends who overheard her remark are also laughing hysterically. Lupita has no idea what is going on, but she is embarrassed by their reaction to her remark.

On another occasion, Lupita is shopping at the mall with Anita. They stop for a bite to eat in the food court. Anita notices an overweight man consuming three burgers, a large order of fries, a shake, onion rings, and dessert. Anita says, "Wow! Will you look at that couch potato?" Lupita is very confused because she can't see a sofa or a potato and wonders what Anita is trying to say to her. Anita proceeds to explain that this is a U.S. expression for people who don't move around much and are usually overweight from the consumption of too much junk food.

Language is the common tool everyone uses to communicate. In a basic communication course it is important for you to understand the fundamentals of the language process so you can make the appropriate choices in your remarks and avoid misunderstandings when speaking to others. Since communication is a daily process, solid language skills are essential for everyone.

Symbols

We cannot simply pour the information from our minds into other people's heads. We use **symbols** to communicate with others. All words are symbols. Symbols are arbitrary representations; we choose a word to represent an object or concept and then send the word across a channel to someone else. Because effective meaning relies on mutual understanding of symbols, we must be as clear as possible when we encode ideas into words. When someone says, "I saw an animal on my way to work this morning," what image do you see? Animal is a vague symbol—it could represent: deer, bear, squirrel, bird, cat, dog, and so on. Let's say the statement is narrowed to, "I saw a cat on my way to work." Do you have an accurate picture of the animal? How about, "I saw a black cat." Maybe we need to say, "I saw a big, black cat with a white spot on its chest." Now, we all have the same basic picture, but does your image of the cat have three legs? In other words, the clearer you are in selecting the proper symbols for a thought sequence, the greater chance you have of other people understanding your meaning.

Even when we carefully select symbols, we can run into problems conveying meaning because symbols are **arbitrary** and **ambiguous.** Symbols are arbitrary because there is no innate connection between an object or thought and the word we use to represent it. We say a patch of soil where plants, vegetables, or flowers are planted is a "garden." However, there is nothing about the site that necessitates it being called a garden. This is why other languages have different symbolic representations for the same word: in German, it is *der garten*; in Italian, it is *giardino*; in Spanish and French, it is *jardin*; in Japanese, it is *niva*; and in Russian, it is *caд*. Every language uses a different symbol, yet each word represents the same tangible concept—a piece of land where something grows.

Technically, we can use any symbol we want to represent an object or concept. If Lisa raises her young daughters to call a "desk" a "pickle," she could say, "Please sit down at the pickle and do your homework." They would understand their mother's meaning and use the word the same way. The only way the daughters would learn that their meaning for "pickle" is not a universally accepted definition would be when they interact with other children who have been taught to say "desk." While this is a highly unlikely scenario, it illustrates the arbitrariness of symbols,

Professional Perspective

Why should we learn foreign languages? "They should just speak English," I said! Then I became president of an international company working with Russian culture and sports. I found the language barrier had more to do with our use of slang than with their inability to speak English.

U.S. English is riddled with idioms. When speaking to people who do not speak U.S. English, leave out sports metaphors ("slam dunk"), Valley speak ("whatever"), and today's favorite buzzword (which, by the time you read this, will be yesterday's buzzword so you fill in the blank!).

English-as-a-second-language speakers are not deaf, so speaking loudly will not help them understand English better. Speak slowly, choose words wisely, and never be disrespectful.

When correcting foreigners, do so diplomatically! When the Russian culture minister said the Met was "so mickey mouse," he meant Mickey Mouse was a great American export, and he genuinely thought it was a good metaphor for one of the world's greatest museums.

Зачем нам изучать иностранные языки ? – «Они сами должны говорить по - английски », – думал я . Но вот я стал президентом международной компании , деятельность которой связана с Россией в сфере культуры и спорта . И я понял , что языковой барьер обусловлен не столько неспособностью людей говорить по - английски , а скорее тем , что мы сами используем сленг .

Американский вариант английского языка наполнен идиомами . При разговоре с людьми других национальностей американцам следует избегать спортивных метафор («slam dunk» – *термин , описывающий действия баскетбольного игрока* *), слов , заполняющих паузу («whatever» – *слово , имеющее различные оттенки значений , от «ладно » до «что бы то ни было »* *) и современных модных словечек (которые выйдут из моды к тому времени , когда Вы будете читать этот текст , так что решайте сами , какие слова можно было бы привести в качестве примера).

Если для кого -то английский язык не является родным , это еще не означает , что такой человек плохо слышит - соответственно , повышение громкости разговора не будет способствовать лучшему пониманию английской речи . Говорите медленно , правильно подбирайте слова и никогда не проявляйте неуважения .

Если Вы поправляете иностранцев , делайте это дипломатично ! Когда Министр культуры России сказал , что Нью -йоркский «Metropolitan Museum of Art» похож на Микки -Мауса, министр имел в виду , что Микки -Маус был прекрасным примером распространения американской культуры и искренне полагал , что нашел хорошую метафору для описания одного из самых известных музеев мира . В другой ситуации военнослужащий советской армии спросил меня , почему американцы всегда «pissed on» (*от слова «мочиться », «облить мочой »* *). Соответственно мне пришлось объяснить , что выражение «pissed off» («*быть рассерженным », «испытывать гнев или раздражение»* *) имеет совсем другое значение !

[* курсивом выделены примечания переводчика]

—Maureen C. Baker, President
Highland Ventures, Inc.

which we often mistakenly assume have universal meaning. We need to be aware that differences in symbols exist from region to region in the United States and from country to country. Can you think of a time when someone used a symbol that was unfamiliar to you?

Another problem in trying to create meaning for another person is that symbols are ambiguous. Because meanings are in people and not in words, this language vagueness blends with the concept of perception to make effective communication an exciting challenge. Each communicator decides what certain phrases mean.

Think about phrases such as "a lot" or words such as "expensive." Such words and phrases are all vague and ambiguous without a context. Compare your answers to the questions in the Try It! box below with those of other students in your classroom. Who has the highest number and who has the lowest number? Is the difference substantial? How can that happen?

Critical Thinking

What are some other creatively ambiguous lines that you have heard or used?

_____

_____

Professional Perspective

I once performed *The Three Little Pigs* in Japan, and the translator didn't show up. Not being able to translate "Little Pig, Little Pig, let me come in . . ." I just had the Wolf say, "Roar!" That worked until I told the pig to say "Oink, Oink!" That baffled a little Japanese boy . . . since only U.S. kids associate the sound "oink" with a pig.

—Allynn Gooen
International Performance Artist

Think about everyone's perceptions and backgrounds. If I say, "That sure is a tall building," you might think of a fifteen-story building. If you are from New York City, you might think of an 80-story building. That is a huge discrepancy. Speakers should be careful to choose the most concrete terms that are available when creating their message. For instance, "That 75-story building sure is tall" is a concrete way of explaining the picture that is in your mind to another person. The other person may not agree with your definition, but at least you have been clear. Clarity should be the driving force for any speaker when selecting symbols to express meaning.

TRY IT!

Take a minute to jot down a numerical answer to the following questions.

1. Roberto has a lot of money. How much money does he have?

_____

2. Alisha sends a lot of texts each day. How many does she send?

_____

3. The temperature outside during Mark's vacation was unbearable. What was the temperature?

_____

4. When I graduate and get a job, my five-year goal is to own an expensive car. How much will the car cost?

_____

There is an exception, however. There are times when speakers specifically choose ***creative ambiguity*** to mask a message that might be hurtful. If you notice that a friend is wearing a shirt you don't like and then asks your opinion, you might opt for a creatively ambiguous message: "Oh, it's really interesting." The creatively ambiguous message generally communicates a lack of excitement. If the receiver is perceptive, the message allows both parties to get out of the exchange gracefully and without any hurt feelings.

Critical Thinking

A hot sandwich can be called a hoagie, a grinder, a cosmo, or a sub. You might recognize only one of these symbols. List some symbols you have heard people use that were not familiar to you.

_____

_____

Can you identify the following from a region in Pennsylvania?

Gob _____

"Go red up your room." _____

Dippy eggs _____

What are some of the local symbols you have heard?

_____

_____

Some speakers choose creatively ambiguous terms to maintain their privacy or to mislead the receiver. Today we often hear an excuse from students that wasn't used 10 years ago: "I have a family emergency." What is a "family emergency"? Nine times out of 10, it means that the student wants to miss class but doesn't want to admit why. Typically if there is a true emergency, you provide details, such as "My very close uncle is in the hospital, and his condition is life threatening. I need to be there." But people know that others won't typically question them if they refer to a "family emergency."

However, there are times when people are trying to communicate real meaning, but their word choices are ambiguous. The discussion about word ambiguity becomes more challenging when a speaker uses abstract terms such as "love." What does the following exchange mean: "I love you." "I love you, too." Do these two people mean the same thing? Maybe yes, but probably not. If you have 100 people state their meaning for this exchange, you will probably find many variations. Some possibilities include:

- "I want to be with you until I find someone better."
- "I get goose bumps when I see you across a room."
- "I can't imagine living without you."
- "You are a part of my soul."
- "I will hold your head when you are miserably sick and throwing up into a toilet."

It can be very important to ask for clarification when talking about an important issue with another person. Asking questions prompts and provides more information. The question itself can help the other person identify possible areas of misinterpretation, and the answer sheds light on the specific meaning. Once both people fully understand each other, it is easier to continue the discussion and the relationship. As a speaker, you can use concrete terms to make your message more clear. By understanding the nature of symbols and the inherent problems of ambiguity and arbitrariness, you will be able to recognize potential miscommunications more easily.

Denotative and Connotative Meanings

Another important distinction when analyzing language usage is the difference between the denotative and connotative meanings of symbols. A ***denotative meaning*** is the dictionary definition of a word. The ***connotative meaning*** includes the feelings and emotions people attach to a word. If communicators don't share connotative meanings

Professional Perspective

Clear expression is important in business and is critical in the advertising/public relations industries. Most people don't realize it takes weeks—even months—to find the right words to successfully market a product. The problem facing advertising executives is how to "focus" on the one
selling point that is going to generate new sales for the client while staying within the confines of
the law and, at the same time, be "brilliant" for the consumer.

Clients love to win awards and relish praise from their peers for an innovative campaign. Conversely, clients do not like to spend time in court defending their claims. The simple expression of
an idea could lead to either outcome. Writers must be original yet critical of the ways they
express their ideas in order to satisfy agency management, the client, and industry watchdogs.
Remember the next time you fast forward through a commercial on a program you recorded that
what you perceive as simply 30 seconds of denture cleaner is the end result of a long, thought-
out, creative process. For the writers, the dentures aren't the only things that need to "shine."

*Chiarezza dell' espressione e' importante in affari, ed e' critica nell' industria delle pubbliche relazioni e
nella pubblicita'. La maggior parte del pubblico non realizza che si impiegano settimane, se non mesi,
per trovare le parole giuste per commercializzare con successo un prodotto sul mercato. Il problema
che si presenta agli operatori del settore e' su quale qualita' del prodotto focalizzare la campagna
pubblicitaria per convincere il consumatore restando nei parametri di legge e allo stesso tempo soddisfare i propri clienti con successivo incremento delle vendite. Lo scopo e' di ricevere premiazioni e rico-
noscimenti sia da colleghi che da concorrenti per una campagna innovativa, e non di dover passare
ore in tribunale per difendere i propri interessi. La semplice espressione di un'idea puo' portare ad uno
o all' altro risultato. Per i produttori e' importante essere originali, ma anche attenti nella maniera in
cui esprimono la loro idea, per cosi' soddisfare il cliente, l'amministrazione dell agenzia e i critici del
settore. La prossima volta che, usando il telecomando, magari vi soffermate su uno spot pubblicitario
per un prodotto di igiene delle dentiere, ricordate che se per voi e' solo un filmato di 30 secondi, per gli
addetti ai lavori e' il risultato finale di un lungo e creativo processo di produzione, dove non e' solo
l'oggetto publicizzato a dover brillare.*

—Kathleen Corrigan
Legal Clearances
Grey Global Group

for the symbols in the interaction, communication misunderstandings
will occur. Because there are so many connotative meanings for almost
every symbol, the possibility of misunderstanding is immense.

For example, think about the term "family." A denotative definition
for family is "a set of parents and children, or of relations, living
together or not." Family experiences are different for every individual
in our culture, including siblings raised by the same parents. For
Samantha, the connotative meaning for "family" is very cheerful and
happy. It is a place of support, encouragement, and love. In her experience, families eat dinner together, talk about their day, play games, and
go to sporting events together. For Tim, the connotative meaning for
family may be horrifying. His concept of family may be a place of physical and/or verbal abuse, sarcastic put-downs, or absolute emotional
neglect. His parents never gave him any attention; often, they would
come right out and tell him that he was stupid and would never amount

to anything. If Samantha and Tim are in a long-term relationship, imagine the difference in perception when Samantha says, "I can't wait to get married and start a family." Tim will probably have an immediate negative reaction to her statement. Samantha may interpret his reaction as an indication that he doesn't like her well enough to have a family with her. Instead, Tim is reacting to his connotative meaning of family, not to what she is saying.

This kind of misunderstanding happens all the time. For instance, Johnny and Ruth have been married for a year. Johnny says, "I can't wait until my birthday. It's the most special day of the year to me. I love birthday celebrations." Johnny grew up in a family where birthday parties were attended by lots of friends and included elaborate entertainment, decorations, favors, party hats, and fancy table settings. Ruth, on the other hand, grew up in a family where if she got a card on her birthday, she considered herself lucky. So on Johnny's birthday, Ruth hands him a very extravagant card, which she found after reading every card in the shop. She also went to a nearby specialty store and bought him a box of fancy chocolates. He appears confused and upset by her gifts. She has no idea why he seems so disappointed despite her generosity and effort. Ruth and Johnny have different meanings for the words birthday and celebration. You can see how different connotative meanings, coupled with the fact that language is ambiguous, can lead to communication difficulties in a relationship.

The meanings people attach to words (connotative meanings) are not necessarily in the words themselves. The best-intentioned communicator cannot guarantee how another communicator will receive and interpret spoken language. For example, Juliette visited her brother and his wife for a holiday. They had just purchased a French press coffeemaker, a new concept at that time. She was very impressed and said, "Wow, you guys are so trendy." Her brother was so angry he refused to speak to her for the rest of the day. While she had intended her comment to be a compliment, he interpreted the word "trendy" as a decidedly negative label. When they could finally talk about their misunderstanding, Juliette learned her brother felt the word trendy meant "following along with the crowd and not having a mind of his own." He was a person who strongly valued his individualism; therefore, "trendy" was a total insult. This misunderstanding would not have occurred, however, if her brother had simply used perception checking to discover her meaning for trendy. He might have said, "Are you saying that I follow the crowd?" This would have allowed them to discuss the issue immediately.

Critical Thinking

Describe a time in your life when differences in connotative meaning led to a communication misunderstanding in one of your interpersonal relationships.

_____

_____

_____

_____

Content and Relationship Levels of Meaning

Are you aware that there are at least two levels of meaning for every statement? The ***content level*** of meaning refers to the factual interpretation of the words. If you say to your significant other, "So I see you didn't do the dishes," the content level of meaning is that there are dirty dishes in the sink. However, you could also be trying to communicate something about your relationship. On the ***relationship level,*** the statement could mean, "You lazy person, what have you been doing all day?" Your tone of voice would distinguish that possible meaning from another, such as, "Oh my, is everything ok?" In the second case, your inflection would be different, and you would probably speak in a hesitant, questioning tone with lots of pauses.

The relationship level of meaning is particularly ambiguous and can lead to serious misunderstanding. Even when messages seem clear and direct, people may look for "hidden" meaning rather than accepting the content level of meaning. On the other hand, some people "hint" at their meaning by using the relationship level rather than just being honest and direct. Let's examine two scenarios.

Laura asks Scott if he is mad at her. Scott says, "No." Instead of accepting the content level of meaning, Laura begins an analysis in her head. "Well, he said that in a funny way, I wonder if he really is mad?" So she asks, "Are you sure you are not mad at me?" Scott, who just answered that question, is irritated to be asked again, and so he raises his voice a little, "No, I'm not mad." When Laura hears the raised inflection, she interprets the irritated tone as evidence her doubts were correct. She may even ask him a third time, which if you examine the situation from Scott's point of view is totally irritating. Laura would have done better to accept the content level of meaning in the message.

Another scenario involves people who insinuate meaning through the inflection and tone of the words. In this case, Kristen asks her partner Todd if he is upset about something. Todd says, "No" in a cynical tone. He is trying to get across that he really is mad without coming out and saying the words. This is a no-win situation for everyone involved. If Kristen reacts to the content level of meaning and says, "Oh good" and walks away, Todd will be angry. If Kristen recognizes his intent and plays along to find out what is bothering him, she is likely to be irritated because he didn't just come out and state the problem.

Think carefully about content and relationship levels of meaning. You should look for them and respond to each when appropriate. You should also try to say what you mean. Most people get annoyed quickly with people who play language games.

ETHICAL CONSIDERATIONS

How ethical is it to be indirect and hint at your meaning rather than directly saying what you mean?

_____

_____

How difficult is it to really say what you mean to others instead of hinting around?

_____

_____

The Influence of Language

The language we choose influences the way we think about things (Boroditsky, 2001). As we make symbol choices, it is imperative to think about how we view the world based on the words we use to describe it. For instance, think of a person on a diet who eats six chocolate chip cookies one day. There is a big difference in how the person will view the situation if he chooses the words "I cheated" versus "I made an unhealthy eating choice." Notice that "I cheated" has moral connotations. It makes the person seem unethical, weak, or appalling. On the other hand, the words "I made an unhealthy eating choice" focuses on the event itself rather than making a judgment. An individual can perceive the event as an unfortunate incident under his control or as evidence of a personality flaw. This choice of language will influence how the person thinks about himself.

Another problem occurs when we don't have a word to describe an event or a feeling. It is difficult for us to talk about something if we don't have any symbols to communicate our impressions. We avoid discussion and pretend the event or feeling isn't there. Julia Wood (2011, p. 121) points out that before there was a term for the horrendous behavior of date rape, victims didn't know what to call it or how to talk about it. Once the term developed, many people could begin to describe what had happened to them.

In 2007, the term "non-divorce" appeared in the media and described couples who are married but no longer in love. They are amicable, almost like roommates or brother/sisters. They have platonic relationships and no intent to divorce because of financial reasons, religious commitment, and/or issues with child-rearing/custody. Until now, there has never been a term to describe this situation among married people. Do you know a couple who fits this description? This word didn't really didn't catch on, but "staycation" became instantly recognizable during the economic downfall when people stayed at home to save money during their vacation time. Also the action of "defriending" someone has become commonplace among social network users.

In addition to the difficulties presented by the ambiguity of our language, we should also be aware of how **polarized** language is. We have words for opposing emotional positions, but no words for the "in-betweens." How do you describe someone who is 450 pounds? We might use the words "fat" or "obese." How do you describe someone who is 95 pounds? We might use the words "skinny" or "thin." How do you describe someone who is 165 pounds and 5′10″ tall? We don't have appropriately descriptive words for this condition. The person is "of average weight." But, the phrase "average weight" doesn't have the dramatic impact of obese or skinny to a listener. Sometimes phrases polarize our language to set up an either/or way of thinking. A group on our campus recently suggested using the following phrase to get people to vote: "It's a man's world unless women vote." While we agree that women should vote, we are not certain that we need to polarize men versus women in order to accomplish that goal. The fact that our language is polarized on numerous issues sometimes makes it difficult to find the appropriate symbols for proper communication.

When we create new symbols, we change how people think. Let's focus on a medical example. Some human characteristics have been reclassified as medical conditions so they can be treated.

> The medical community is giving names to "conditions" that used to be simply characteristics. So, what was previously a flat chest, for example, is called micromastia. . . . If doctors give something a name that implies illness, then they have something to treat. (Fellingham, 2003, p. 160)

The creation of a medical symbol for a natural characteristic of certain people spurs thinking about the characteristic as a disease. Will this change the way people think about themselves? Of course!

Language influences the way we think; this is why words are so important. However, meaning always resides in people. Some words are instantly offensive to some people while others have little or no reaction to the very same symbol. Rhetorical sensitivity is a concept that helps us navigate through fluctuating communication situations.

TRY IT!

Think about the influence of language and relate it to the previous chapter on perception and self-esteem. As we communicate intrapersonally, our word choices can make a difference on how we see ourselves. Keep track of how you talk to yourself for a day. Record the types of things you say and the word choices you use. Are the words positive or negative? Reflect on how those choices influence your self-esteem. Is it high or low?

_____

_____

_____

_____

_____

Rhetorical Sensitivity

Communicators must make thoughtful choices when using symbols, mindful of the difficulties created by language ambiguity and connotative meanings. Often you'll hear people talk about using "politically correct" (PC) language. Many people roll their eyes when PC is mentioned. What is the connotative meaning of being politically correct? Many people become outraged and state, "The First Amendment guarantees my right to say anything I want!" They are correct, of course. Others feel PC is "too much hassle." Roderick Hart and Don Burks (1972) introduced the term *rhetorical sensitivity* in an effort to help people cooperate. The term has come to mean reviewing all of the available symbols and using the one that is least likely to be offensive to the listener. That's not unreasonable, is it?

Think of the variety of messages you send on any given day. We may choose a *loaded word* without really thinking about it as we communicate with others. A loaded word is one that has a positive or negative connotative meaning in addition to its denotative meaning. For instance, the following words all have the same denotative definition. What are the loaded terms?

cheap	thrifty
tightwad	miserly
frugal	meager
penny-pinching	prudent
stingy	economical

Even though every one of these terms means that a person is careful with money, some have a virtuous connotation. Others have a pejorative connotation. Being rhetorically sensitive means that we choose the term that would convey the appropriate emotional meaning and be least likely to offend someone.

There are four main categories of potentially offensive language:

- Racist/Religious/Cultural Language

- Sexist/Heterosexist Language

- Noninclusive Language

- Profanity

If you are aware of these potential problem areas, you can avoid them in your own communication and can decode the communication of others with greater understanding.

Professional Perspective

Trying to be rhetorically sensitive has many challenges . . .

I have to tell you what happened at work today—a coworker and I put together a flyer announcing the company picnic, and I had to have it approved by our new Director of People Services (formerly human resources). She said it was ok but (and I quote), "On a personal note I prefer the words outing or team-building day or event over summer picnic. The historical origins of the word picnic are derogatory. They are from the term pickaninny, 'a black female child,' and evolved to the shortened version when southern whites would gather with their families and friends to hang a black person, and in a few cases Jews, in a lynching. Everyone gathered for the picnic."

Huh? says linguist Helene—isn't picnic derived from the French *pique-nique?* And who would ever connect picnic with pickaninny any more, even if it were true? And did she just throw in the reference to Jews because she knows I'm Jewish? I never heard a Jew object to the word picnic! But Ms. People Services is of course diversity sensitive, so we were ready to change it to "outing." Then I Googled "picnic word derivation" because I just didn't believe it, and the very first hit was snopes.com, the "urban legends" site, which states unequivocally that the story is FALSE. They also shared an instance where shifting to the term "outing" offended homosexual students at a particular university. (You can read the whole story at http://www.snopes.com/language/offense/picnic.htm)

In the end, we decided to call it a "summer event." It's silly, but better than calling the HR Director an idiot.

—Helene B.
Lead Programmer Analyst

Racist/Religious/Cultural Language

Racist language includes words that denigrate someone of a particular ethnic background. We are certain you know the obvious examples; however, there are many expressions buried in our language that you may not recognize as racist. A subtle remark such as, "Those people don't belong here" communicates volumes about a communicator's prejudices. During a school board meeting in a small town after an Asian-looking student offered her opinion on the topic under discussion, a community member said in a low voice, "Why don't you go back where you came from?" This student happened to have been born in that small town. The statement provided real insight into the prejudices of that community member. *Religious* expressions such as "I Jewed him down" are also prevalent and extremely inappropriate. *Cultural* expressions about "Oriental" people are also offensive. The term Oriental refers to objects such as rugs; people are Asian. Any term that is offensive to a group with different characteristics from the majority falls into this category as well. People who say, "Oh that is so retarded," may be perceived as denigrating people with intellectual disabilities. This is a perfect example of being rhetorically sensitive: it is just as easy to say "that is so stupid."

ETHICAL CONSIDERATIONS

Do you believe that you are unbiased? Do you use the phrases "Oh that is so retarded" or "That is so gay"? What kind of ethical compromise do you make when using those phrases? If you don't use these phrases, do you say anything when others use them? If not, what does your silence communicate about your ethical standards?

_____

_____

Sexist/Heterosexist Language

Sexist language denigrates someone based on their sex. For instance, the use of the term "girl" to refer to a grown woman is derogatory because it implies immaturity. Recently a term has been created to refer to the sandals that men wear: *mandals*. This is derogatory because we are denigrating men for wearing a particular type of footwear that should be available to everyone. *Heterosexist* language assumes everyone in society is heterosexual. It is much more rhetorically sensitive and inclusive to say "partner" or "significant other" when talking about people in a marriage or romantic relationship. Also watch out for terms or phrases that denigrate homosexuals or females, such as, "Oh that is so gay" or "You throw like a girl." Others may not appreciate your remarks about their behavior, even if you intended the remark to be humorous. Someone overhearing the conversation may perceive you to be insensitive, crude, or uneducated.

Reality ✔

You may think that we are overly sensitive by saying that you should think about refraining from the use of these phrases. However, at a high school in California, "when a few classmates razzed Rebekah Rice about her Mormon upbringing with questions such as, 'Do you have 10 moms?' she shot back: 'That's so gay'" (Associated Press, 2007). Rebekah was sent to the principal's office, warned about using hate speech, and a reprimand was placed in her file. Her parents filed a lawsuit charging that Rebekah's First Amendment rights were violated.

When do playground insults used every day all over America cross the line into hate speech that must be stamped out?

This incident raises some very interesting discussion points. The previous year two students were paid to beat up a gay student at the high school, which heightened the sensitivity to derogatory language. Yet the school took no action in this situation against the students who had teased Rebekah about being a Mormon. There are a number of religious and heterosexist issues here. As a group, discuss the following:

1. How often do you hear these types of remarks at your school? _____

2. Do you think Rebekah should have been reprimanded for her comment? _____

3. Do you think the religious comments should have been treated in the same way? _____

4. Knowing that a gay student was beaten up in the previous year at this school; do you think these comments should be classified as hate speech? _____

5. If you were the principal how would you have handled the situation? _____

_____

6. What course of action should the school have taken? _____

_____

Reality ✔

Before you read any further, fill in the rest of these sentences.

1. When an administrative assistant first arrives at the office, _____

2. After a nurse has completed training, _____

3. When a lawyer meets a client, _____

4. When a chef enters the kitchen, _____

5. If a flight attendant is late to work, _____

6. Before a judge can give a final ruling, _____

Noninclusive Language

Noninclusive language is changing. It was once considered appropriate to use the word "he" or "man" to mean both men and women; it is no longer considered acceptable. Some people do not understand why this gender issue is so important.

Wendy Martyna (1978) conducted a study using the phrases in the Reality Check box. Now—look at your answers. Did you:

- conform to traditional stereotypes (using "he" for lawyer and judge, "she" for parent and administrative assistant)?
- flip the pronouns so that "she" was used for the stereotypically male professions and "he" for the stereotypically female positions?
- avoid using "he/she" and substitute "they" or "one"?
- use "he/she" for each of the entries?
- use a random mixture of pronouns or the other choices above?
- use "he" in each case?

Martyna argued that if everyone truly understood the word "he" to be a generic pronoun meaning everyone, then everyone would use "he" in each of the above sentences. In 20 years of using this activity in class, we only encountered one student who used the generic "he." If you use specific pronouns, then you don't believe in the generic "he." Analyze your responses above carefully and decide whether you really believe noninclusive language means everyone.

When we modify our communication to eliminate noninclusive language, we are choosing inclusive language. The importance of inclusive language is reflected in research that suggests parents, teachers, and religious leaders who use male-oriented language in referring to professions limit young females' perceptions of potential career choices (Wood, 2011, p. 118). If you were aware of the effect of using male-oriented language, would you change your language so that you would not limit the choices for your daughter?

Religion often uses noninclusive language. References in religious teaching are frequently to men. Today, there is increased discussion about whether these historic references give the perception of excluding women. Some religious groups are trying to place women in positions of authority within the church hierarchy, while others are against this action. As another example of the changing noninclusive language in religion, notice during the holiday season that some boxes of cards now say, "Peace on Earth, Good Will toward All."

How can you change the following to be inclusive?

Fireman _____

Policeman _____

Mailman _____

Waitress _____

Stewardess _____

Profanity

Profanity is the utterance of irreverent, vulgar, or obscene language. Opinions about what is profane will vary depending on culture and socioeconomic factors. People normally use profanity for emphasis, shock value, or because it is a learned habit. A communicator takes a level of social risk when using profanity. There was a time when profanity was mainly an urban phenomenon, but this is no longer the case. Many people use profanity openly in communication. And yet, in regions such as the South, profanity is rarely used in public.

Think about your group of friends. Do you ever use profanity around them? If so, do you alter your language when you go home and talk to your parents or grandparents? If your language use does change when you go home, then you understand the importance of adapting your communication to your audience. Your use or nonuse of profanity should be an informed choice. Think carefully about the people who can hear you when you use profanity and the potential consequences of your language choices. There are people who will remember only that you use profane language. What if a potential employer calls them to ask about hiring you?

Frustrations

Many people find the discussion of rhetorical sensitivity extremely frustrating. They think it is too difficult to adapt to the ever-changing terminology in language. The cultural progression of language can be quite frustrating. But that does not mean you shouldn't think about it and decide if you should change your communication patterns.

In the past, we referred to people with a physical disability as crippled. Then, the term became handicapped. It morphed quickly into physically disabled. To sound more positive, it eventually became physically challenged. Finally, the word "persons" was added to the beginning of the phrase, "persons with physical challenges." The reasoning was that this places the emphasis on the person first.

Reality ✓

Since we wrote the first edition of this book, the terms have changed once again. If you look at the website for the Special Olympics, it is interesting to see the changes. In a previous section, we talked about the ethical consequences of using the phrase "that's so retarded." A perusal of the website shows that the organization has realized that people who use the phrase to mean "stupid" are slow to change. Therefore, the organization has changed their language. They now refer to their participants as "people with intellectual disabilities." Check out http://www.r-word.org/ for information on pledging to eliminate the R-word from everyday speech.

There is derogatory language for every race, religion, sexual orientation, and economic class in our culture. The obvious response in any discussion of derogatory language is to say, "Do not use words that offend other people"—easy to say and difficult to execute. How much should we monitor our own language? When should we speak up about the language we hear others use? You'll notice your reactions to the page 53 scenarios differ depending on the people with whom you spend your time. Your answers will also depend on your personal level of sensitivity to others and your geographical location.

A lot of our terms and phrases are linked to a specific period of time and to a specific generation. Try not to date yourself by using outdated language, and avoid offending people through your language choices. You should do your best to keep up with the current terminology. Your choice of a correct term should always be appropriate for any occasion, and it should consistently reflect your personal style. Consistency in style contributes to perceptions of credibility.

Some people say Americans are too sensitive. Others assert that they should be able to use profanity, and too bad if there are little kids, professors, or others around who might hear them. What is appropriate varies from region to region and situation to situation. As diversity increases, it becomes more likely that you'll run into a police officer, an employer, or a potential romantic partner who was raised elsewhere and is accustomed to the norms of another place.

Our choice of the appropriate language to use with a stranger may be incorrect, but the effort to make an informed choice is essential. You are free to choose whether to monitor your own language in the presence of others, but don't be surprised if you encounter consequences for using offensive language. Something else to consider is what to do if you are the offended person. What happens when people speak inappropriately in your presence? Should you blow up? Should you keep quiet? Probably the best answer is somewhere between those extremes.

CHOICES AND CONSEQUENCES

These are all real scenarios the authors have encountered. Which of the following situations offend you? Which do not?

1. Three 16-year-old boys appear at a playground and continuously use profanity very loudly in their conversation. You notice there are small children at the playground.

2. You and your friends are using profanity, and you notice there are small children around you.

3. You and your friends are on campus, and someone in your group makes a racist joke.

4. You are in the break room at work, and a colleague makes a joke about homosexuals.

5. Your 90-year-old grandmother makes a racist comment in a restaurant.

6. A stranger on the train makes conversation with you by telling you a racist joke.

7. You walk into an insurance business and you notice a sign hanging on the wall that says, "Unattended children will be sold as slaves."

8. You are at work when an anti-Semitic comment is made in the conference room. You aren't Jewish.

Each of the choices you identified has consequences for your reputation. Discuss with your peers what those consequences might be. What would you do in those offensive situations?

_____

_____

_____

_____

_____

_____

_____

_____

_____

_____

Think carefully about the consequences of derogatory remarks spoken within the corporate culture. These remarks could cost you your reputation, a raise, a promotion, and, in some cases, your job.

CHOICES AND CONSEQUENCES

You are standing with peers around the watercooler when one of them makes a joke about homosexuals. You are not homosexual, but you realize a joke like that can be offensive to homosexuals, to straight people who have relatives or friends who are gay, or to straight people who believe denigrating another group is morally wrong. List four ways you could handle this situation.

_____

_____

_____

_____

List the potential consequences for each of the four recommendations you made above.

_____

_____

_____

_____

Summary

Understanding the concept of symbolic representation of thought can help you avoid miscommunication. Recognizing the differences in denotative and connotative meanings allows you to use perception-checking skills to reach a shared understanding rather than allowing a situation to escalate into conflict.

Use of appropriate language symbols is a personal commitment to interpersonal and professional credibility. The decisions and adjustments you make right now can enable you to be successful in a diverse society or, conversely, can limit your personal and career potential. Because technology is bringing the cultures of the world closer together, you will need dynamic, globally sensitive language choices—both oral and written. The language battles of the twentieth century are now history. Whether you feel committed to rhetorical sensitivity or not, the concepts in this chapter illuminate the new challenges in communicating to the world. Look forward.

KEY WORDS

ambiguous

arbitrary

connotative meaning

content level

creative ambiguity

denotative meaning

language

loaded word

noninclusive language

polarized language

profanity

racist/religious/cultural language

relationship level

rhetorical sensitivity

sexist/heterosexist language

symbol

DISCUSSION/ACTIVITIES

1. List alternate symbols (synonyms) for the following ideas: happy, loud, exercise, full, and quiet. Describe other symbol choices for the same idea and why you feel your selection is the most effective.

2. Your roommate shows you a new exercise outfit and asks how you like it. You think it's ridiculous. Develop a denotative response to the question as well as a response using creative ambiguity. When is it appropriate to use each statement?

3. What polarized word or phrase bothers you the most when you hear it? Explain.

4. Describe a situation where one of your parents used a content level statement in conversation, but the other parent heard the comment at the relationship level. How did you react to the conversation as an observer?

5. Advertising uses the noninclusive language term "man cave" in its verbal and nonverbal imagery. Explain the meaning of this concept culturally.

6. Is the use of profanity in the home or community acceptable? Explain.

7. Is the language used in contemporary music changing public behavior? Explain.

8. Does the language of those around you help you to decide with whom to associate? Explain.

9. List the words or phrases you use to describe people from other cultures when talking with your friends. What do these words mean to you and should they be changed?

four

Nonverbal Communication

OBJECTIVES

After reading this chapter, you should be able to:

- Explain the concept of body movement
- Identify uses of emblems, illustrators, affect displays, regulators, and adaptors
- Explain the concept of time communication
- Explain the concept of smell communication
- Explain the concept of touch communication
- Define the term paralanguage
- Explain the concept of space communication and territoriality
- Describe the importance of artifacts

Nonverbal communication radiates from all of the senses but does not include the use of verbal symbols. We can communicate through sight, touch, smell, and sound. We send messages through our use of space, color, and time; our physical characteristics; movement; artifacts (furniture, clothing, and jewelry); and vocal sounds that are not words. Mark Knapp and Judith Hall (2010) remind us of the inseparable nature of verbal and nonverbal signals. It is important to make adjustments in personal style to make sure our nonverbal messages complement our verbal messages. A solid blend of nonverbal and verbal communication skills enhances your effectiveness with other people.

When we talk about nonverbal communication, it is important to remember one of the basic principles of communication from chapter 1: *we cannot not communicate.* Communicators assign meaning to all nonverbals. We can control some of these nonverbals, but not others. Although you have no control over some physical characteristics such as height, communicators will interpret nonverbal messages from physical characteristics. For instance, according to a University of Florida study, taller people earn more money; supervisors rated taller staff members as more effective (BBC News, 2003). It is imperative for you to be aware that nonverbals account for a large portion of our total communication package. You need to make careful choices about the nonverbals that you can control so that the overall impression is consistent with your message and your personal brand.

As we begin our exploration of the types of nonverbal communication, keep in mind that we send many nonverbal messages unintentionally. We may fold our arms in a cold room for warmth. However, a communicator observing our nonverbal position may perceive us as guarded and noninvitational. We have no intention of sending a message with our natural reaction to the temperature, but the receiver may perceive a meaning from our actions. It is important to be aware of the possible nonverbals we send unintentionally during any interpersonal encounter.

We may also perceive others' nonverbals incorrectly as well. Think back to chapter 2 on perception and all of the inaccuracies that can occur as we assign meaning to behavior. If we assign meaning to nonverbal behavior incorrectly without perception checking, our attributions may lead us to inaccurate conclusions. Think about the self-centered noise that we talked about in chapter 1. With the increasing use of technology and cell phones, many people are constantly checking their phones, which can send two distinct nonverbal messages depending on the receiver's interpretation: (1) that you are distracted and not paying any attention to them or (2) that you are an excellent multitasker who is paying attention to multiple important messages at once.

New technology creates another barrier to interpreting nonverbal communication correctly. If you are preoccupied with your technology, you are not reading the nonverbal communication of others around you. Think of how often you are wrapped up in your own handheld device, whether it is a phone, music app, etc. You are paying no attention to the people around you. Learning about the various areas of nonverbal communication can help you to change your behavior and to evaluate the messages you do receive from others more effectively.

Four Functions of Nonverbals

There are four basic functions of nonverbal communication

- They can substitute for a verbal message
- They can emphasize a verbal message
- They can contradict a verbal message
- They can regulate conversation

Nonverbals help us to communicate in a variety of ways. First, they can substitute for a verbal message. It is far easier to point to something than to explain where it is (see illustrators below). In this case, we choose a nonverbal message rather than on words. If you have seen the "talk to the hand" gesture, this is another very common substitution that is popular among young people.

Secondly, nonverbals can emphasize a verbal message. We can use a hand gesture to make a verbal statement more grandiose. Think of the times you've seen someone emphasize how big something was with a hand gesture for emphasis, "It was THIS BIG!"

Third, we have to be careful of contradicting our verbals with our nonverbal. Sometimes it is a nervous reaction to smile while telling very serious bad news. The conflicting messages are confusing and can undermine our credibility if the other party doesn't interpret the contradictory behavior to distress about delivering the unpleasant news. There are also serious interpretation issues when you send contradictory messages in romantic situations. We discuss this in the section on paralanguage below.

Finally, we use nonverbals to regulate conversation. We use eye contact to let someone know when it is their turn to talk, or we put up a hand to stop someone from interrupting us.

Types of Nonverbal Communication

There are a number of types of nonverbal communication. We will cover the following:

- Body Movement—Kinesics
- Time Communication—Chronemics
- Smell Communication—Olfactics
- Touch Communication—Haptics
- Paralanguage—Vocalics
- Space Communication—Proxemics
- Artifacts

Body Movement—Kinesics

Body movement (also known as **kinesics**) communicates volumes about who we are. We often don't think about what we are doing with our bodies, but even the smallest gesture or movement communicates information about us. Eye contact, gestures, facial expressions, and even head movements all contribute to the total package of communication and personal credibility.

Direct eye contact with other people is expected in U.S. culture as a sign of respect, but it is considered aggressive and disrespectful in other cultures. For most of us in the United States, a direct gaze makes a positive connection between people. If we turn our eyes away, we communicate that the words we are saying are difficult, or we are thinking about other things. How often has someone yelled at you for watching television while they were talking to you? Although you were listening, your behavior did not communicate attention. Some people feel they cannot communicate effectively unless there is direct eye contact. For this reason, sunglasses present a problem. When you wear sunglasses in a speaking situation, people feel disconnected from you because they can't see your eyes and read your reaction. In addition, eye contact makes a positive impression on others when using technology as well. Skype and Web conferencing sessions are perceived as more professional when there is eye contact with the lens of the camera throughout communication. The camera lens maintains the connection achieved through direct eye contact in face-to-face communication.

During group meetings, some people look away from a lecturer or write notes or use modern technology to send notes to others. This nonverbal behavior can communicate that they are not focused on the speaker's remarks. This is a risky move during a business meeting when the boss is speaking. Eye contact communicates caring and courtesy in U.S. culture.

Extraneous body movements can detract from your message. This is important to remember in public speaking situations, group meetings, and interpersonal encounters. Constant body motion should be controlled. Some people shake a foot or tap a pen during conversations. The person on the receiving end of the message may interpret this ran-

Reality ✓

The following example confirms the expectation of eye contact in U.S. culture and illustrates how quickly we can misperceive another person's nonverbal choices. In June of 2006, the president was holding a press conference when the following interaction occurred:

The President: Yes, Peter. Are you going to ask that question with shades on?

Q: I can take them off.

The President: I'm interested in the shade look, seriously.

Q: All right, I'll keep it, then.

The President: For the viewers, there's no sun. (Laughter.)

Q: I guess it depends on your perspective. (Laughter.) (Bush, 2006)

It was only after the press conference that the president was made aware that the man he was teasing was actually blind.

dom behavior as nervousness or an indication of impatience. Shifting body weight is another problem. A weight shift or two to relax is not problematic, but constant shifting is distracting. How do you watch a physically active speaker and still pay attention to her message? Place yourself carefully into a relaxed position and stay there.

Emblems

Emblems are nonverbal gestures that have a direct verbal translation. Their meaning is agreed upon within specific cultures or groups; emblems do not have a universal meaning across cultures. For example, there is no doubt what your friend means when he gives you a "thumbs-up" gesture after an exam. However, in other cultures, the thumbs-up gesture has a very different meaning. At the time the United States invaded Iraq, soldiers had a hard time deciphering the thumbs-up sign they were getting from the Iraqi soldiers. In Iraq, that gesture is the equivalent of our middle finger gesture. Soldiers didn't know if Iraqis were learning our meaning for the gesture and showing support for the troops or if they were displaying dissatisfaction with them for being there (Koerner, 2003).

In the United States the "V" sign stands for peace as well as victory, but in other cultures it is an extremely rude gesture. A former U.S. president visited Australia while a farmers' strike was in progress. As his motorcade drove past farmers gathered by the road to see him, he made the "V" gesture. Unfortunately, he was pressed against the inside door of the car and did not have room to turn his wrist to enable the gesture to be displayed palm forward. He displayed the gesture with the back of his hand visible to the farmers. The reversal of the emblem meant the same as the "middle finger" gesture means to Americans.

U.S. citizens traveling abroad need to understand how the emblems they use at home are interpreted in the culture they are visiting. Many emblems quite common in U.S. culture are considered to be extremely offensive in other cultures. You must understand emblem use prior to your journey and make the necessary nonverbal adjustments to avoid the consequences of an unintentional emblem display.

Illustrators

Illustrators are nonverbals used to enhance the understanding of a message. We can show how big something is with the use of our fingers or hands. We can point to direct the attention of our listeners. We often gesture automatically without thinking. Illustrators save us a lot of verbal banter. Think about being on a camping trip with your family. You are hiking over a mountain, and your father sees an amazing rainbow. Instead of saying "turn around and raise your head 45 degrees and look a little to your left and you'll see a beautiful rainbow," he will simply say, "Look at that!" and extend his arm in the direction of the rainbow. You react immediately to his illustrator and discover an incredible rainbow.

You can also misuse illustrators by emphasizing the obvious. For instance, when there are only two people on a stage and one person is introducing the other, an introducer may gesture to the other person as they say, "Today, I'd like to introduce Sally. . . ." There is no need for an illustrator in this scenario, because everyone in the audience immediately understands who is being introduced. Another cultural point to keep in mind is that in Asian cultures, pointing is considered to be rude. In many Asian cultures, people point with their thumb while their hand forms a fist, rather than pointing with an extended index finger. To Asians, pointing with their thumb on their fist prevents the rude gesture of pointing a finger directly at someone or something.

Be careful not to use too many hand gestures. In many cultures, gesturing for every comment is distracting. Gestures should always reinforce a specific content point in the presentation or assist with a thematic transition.

Affect Displays

Affect displays are facial muscle movements used to convey meaning. We communicate numerous emotions with our faces. Facial expressions reveal whether we are annoyed, happy, sad, angry, and so on. This is another reason why maintaining direct eye contact during a conversation is important. You won't miss facial cues that help you understand what the other person is saying, and he or she will receive feedback about the message. For instance, when talking to friends who tell us something surprising or startling, most of us raise our eyebrows slightly and widen our eyes. This conveys a message of surprise and allows our friends to know their messages were received properly. In a job interview, facial expressions can work for or against you. Imagine sending a message of surprise when you hear the salary range offered for the position. What might the interviewer think? Affect displays are sometimes hard to control because they are very spontaneous. However, many people are adept at masking a reaction to external stimuli of any kind—hence the term "poker face." Some people control their facial expressions so much that their communication partner may have no idea what they are thinking. When we can't read a person's nonverbals, communicating interpersonally is difficult.

Sometimes we emit facial expressions that are perceived incorrectly. For instance, in one of my (KSY) nonverbal classes, I noticed a young woman who had her arms crossed; she was leaning back and had a look of total disgust. I made a joke asking her whether she was tired or angry with the class we were having. This gave her the opportunity to laugh and to say that she was exhausted because her son had been up all night. Perception checking allowed me to get the true message and her to realize the unintentional message she was sending.

Regulators

Regulators are movements that direct the conversation. For instance, when the teacher asks a question and you don't want to be called on, you immediately look down at your desk. In contrast, the student who makes eye contact with the instructor signals a desire to answer. Eye contact is also used to let the conversation partner know whether to keep talking or when it is the listener's turn to speak. You can also communicate boredom by avoiding eye contact with the speaker.

Our choices with regulators can communicate attitudes about people as well. We often turn our eyes away from people who look different than we do. People who have had a stroke may have partial paralysis on one side of their face. Some people may have an unusual facial growth. We often avoid eye contact with these people because we are embarrassed or uncomfortable. We don't realize, however, that we are being disrespectful to them. Imagine feeling shut out of a conversation simply because you've had a stroke. This situation can also occur with people who have physical challenges. Think about how you would feel if you were in a wheelchair and people were always looking down at you. When communicating with a wheelchair user, you may want to sit in a chair next to the person, so your eye contact is at an equal level (however, do not squat down by the person as this nonverbal can be construed as condescending). This courtesy makes the person with physical challenges more comfortable, and the entire conversation is warmer. Try to see the situation from the other person's perspective and adjust your behavior to how you would like to be treated if you were the other person.

Head nodding is another potential problem. Women are often socialized to nod their head in agreement without even thinking about their message. Generally, men do not use this nonverbal technique. During a conversation, females tend to nod their heads so the other person knows to keep talking. However, some men may think a woman using this behavior isn't listening to what they are saying, especially if her head is moving through a portion of the discussion where nonverbal response is deemed inappropriate. This nonverbal movement could become an issue when a man and woman work together in corporate culture. He may interpret her head bobbing as trying to "suck-up" by always appearing to be in agreement. She may interpret his nonexpressiveness as disinterest or disagreement. Neither of these assessments may be accurate. So, it is important to be aware of our nonverbal actions as well as those of the people around us and make appropriate choices when analyzing a communication environment.

Adaptors

Adaptors are self-touching behaviors. Adaptors are often interpreted in a negative way by other communicators. A person who is always fussing with hair, glasses, or clothing is perceived to be nervous, self-involved, and/or not paying attention to what is being communicated. In interpersonal communication, it is important to understand that personal habits such as these should be controlled or eliminated. If your nose itches, you can usually scratch it, but in business situations, you may need to resist the temptation. What if your doctor covered her nose with her hand while she sneezed and then extended it to greet you before your examination? Would you shake hands? While the sneeze was involuntary, her choice of subsequent behavior could have been different.

Physical control is critical in corporate environments. In a small group meeting when everyone is listening to the discussion, imagine the reaction of other people if you begin to fuss with your hair, jewelry, a pen, or glasses. Their selective attention is drawn to your random

---

CHOICES AND CONSEQUENCES

You are speaking to a group of people, and your notecards suddenly fall from your hands to the floor. What are your choices and the consequences of those choices in this situation?

_____

_____

_____

You are part way through your presentation and the power goes off, disabling your electronically generated visual aids. What are your choices and their consequences?

_____

_____

_____

You are on a job interview and right before you are introduced to a potential colleague, you sneeze. What are your choices and consequences?

_____

_____

_____

movement. People may say nothing, but they notice your behavior and remember it. Sometimes if the wind is blowing you need to check the impulse to fix your hair and simply focus on the conversation; otherwise, you will be perceived to be more interested in your appearance than in the conversation. Pay attention to television reporters during a "live" broadcast as the wind grabs their hair. Do they try to straighten their hair? What impression do they make? If you interpret the nonverbals to symbolize vanity, make sure you don't repeat the same behavior when you are in a similar professional situation.

Time Communication—Chronemics

Kyle goes to a meeting with his graduate professor. The professor is in her office with the door open, but she keeps him waiting in the hall because she is examining a sheet of paper. He waits patiently. She finally invites Kyle in and asks him to sit down while continuing to examine the paper. He sees that the paper is a menu from a local restaurant. The professor's message is quite clear. She is using time to communicate her priorities.

Time communication (***chronemics***) is the study of the way that individuals and cultures use time. Our use of time sends messages about our character. Whether we intend these messages or not, people will perceive things about us and make assumptions about us based on our use of time. In the previous example, it is reasonable for Kyle to decide that the teacher is abusing her power as a faculty member and reminding him of his own insignificance in her schedule. Kyle had an established appointment, and she left her door open while reading a menu. As a graduate student, Kyle feels obligated to keep quiet and deal with her inappropriate behavior. He knows a different choice could compromise his ability to succeed in his graduate program. Two thoughts race through his mind: (1) write a letter to report this incident to the dean after he graduates (this may help his self-esteem by knowing he tried to do something); or (2) write a personal letter to the teacher, after graduation, to let her know how inappropriate her actions were.

Kyle also has a couple of intrapersonal choices. He can assume he is unworthy and allow his self-esteem to decline, or he can realize this is strictly a power play and the professor is the one who has issues. With the latter reasoning, his self-esteem remains strong.

Normally, we would encourage perception checking in this situation. However, because of the status differential between a professor and a student, Kyle needs to decide whether it is worth the risk to speak up. Depending on the professor, he may be able to ask, "Do you need to reschedule this meeting so you can finish your task?" That would call attention to the fact that the professor is making him wait. But Kyle knows from her past behavior during the term that she is using a power play, so he decides he is better off keeping his thoughts to himself.

If there is a valid reason why the professor must review the menu (the president of the university called and asked for an immediate decision on a luncheon choice), then the professor should offer that explanation to Kyle, "I'm so sorry to keep you waiting, but I've had an emergency phone call and must make an immediate decision. Do you have a few minutes or shall we reschedule?" This would have been appropriate communication. However, she was communicating for control and selected silence.

Think about your own time choices. How often do you walk into class late? We have noticed over the years there are certain students who constantly walk into class five or ten minutes late. If a student can be consistently late every class period, why can't he or she change the pattern to be consistently on time? Think about the assumptions the professor could make about the student. The professor might assume that walking in late demeans what the teacher is saying, distracts the attention of the other students in the class, and demonstrates a lack of respect for the students who arrived on time. The late student is psychologically manipulating the environment to demonstrate importance. Is this true? Probably not. But many professors could interpret the student's use of time to communicate precisely those messages. The reverse scenario is also true. Professors who are constantly late for class are communicating something about themselves as well.

Edward Hall (1966) described two contrasting ways to treat time. **_Monochronic cultures_** structure time into discrete units (minutes and hours) and treat it like an object. In these cultures, people "save time," "make time," and "have time." Activities are scheduled one at a time and in a linear sequence. Monochronic cultures compartmentalize time, and people are disoriented if they have to focus on too many activities simultaneously. In a business setting, formal appointments are the normal routine, and one "gets down to business" quickly.

Polychronic cultures plan many things at once, but time is unstructured and informal. The rhythms of nature (the weather, the tides, etc.) mark the flow of time. Relationships take precedence over activities. In fact in some cultures, if no relationship has been established, there will be no business activity.

The United States is a monochronic society. Time is extremely valuable, and we operate on a tight time schedule. Events occur at a specific time. What do we do at noon? Eat lunch. Does it matter if you are hungry? No. It's time to eat. Appointments start on time. Classes start on time. What do you do if a teacher begins a new concept three minutes before the scheduled end of class? Most students begin making nonverbal noises: packing up their books, rustling papers, talking to others, and putting on their coats even though the teacher is still talking. If you are a student in the classroom who wants to learn the new concept, do you say something to silence disruptive students? Do you expect the teacher to silence the students?

People in polychronic cultures don't feel pressured by time. If a person is two hours late, no one cares. Tasks are completed no matter how long they take. For instance, if a teacher continues to lecture beyond the posted class time, students sit and listen even though they will be late for another class or meeting. If a business lunch extends into the late afternoon, people would simply be late for any other activity they might have thought they could attend. Anyone waiting for them to appear would do so patiently. That's a difficult time concept for people in monochronic cultures to comprehend.

Think about how irritated we get when things don't go fast enough. Have you ever found yourself frustrated because your fast food was not in your hands in a minute or two? Think about how upset some of us get when we are standing at a sales counter or sitting at the drive-up window for more than two minutes. Our hearts beat faster, and we feel angry just because the high-calorie, artery-clogging food is not getting into our hands fast enough. Many Americans become annoyed at the slightest abuse of their time. And yet, these same individuals don't mind abusing the time of others. The use of time carries over into the business world as well. In corporate America, everything runs on a tight schedule. You will be judged by your respect for time.

Personal technical skills and attention to detail are a reflection of professionalism. The time you need to type a report, research information, accurately record a daily log, commute to work, etc. is known to you and you alone. Colleagues and employers are only interested in results, not the time it takes out of your day to complete your work. Therefore, it is useful to assess your own time requirements to perform tasks well as you assume more responsibilities in school and in the workforce. It is useful to leave additional time in planning every project, so you know you can complete your work on deadline and with the greatest degree of effort. The extra time you add to any assignment for its completion is contingency time. **Contingency time** minimizes personal stress as you solve problems while meeting the high standards you've set for yourself in daily life.

Critical Thinking

Describe a situation where your time was manipulated by another person.

_____

_____

Describe how you responded to it.

_____

_____

Would you handle the situation the same way now? Would another choice have been more appropriate?

_____

_____

Professional Perspective

"Half our life is spent trying to find something to do with the time we have rushed through life trying to save." Will Rogers [1879–1935]

This quotation illuminates the very American concept of time, its ability to control us, and its importance in our cultural marketplace. However, not all parts of the world are moderated by a clock or the need to make time equal money. In the Federated States of Micronesia, a country of tiny northern Pacific islands, time is simply not a driving force in the everyday course of things.

During a typical day in Micronesia, workers arrive two hours late and leave at least an hour early, funerals can last up to forty days, and women awake before dawn to begin the day's cooking and go to sleep well after every other family member has. While I constantly grappled with the efficiency of such a system, locals understood this "island time" so well they could set their clocks by it—if they had a clock.

Time is as much a part of Micronesian culture as it is American, but it plays a different role. In a place where the seasons do not change and the days are long, timelessness is a way of life and that way of life is simple. Now that I am back in the United States I remember to make time work with me rather than rule me. I believe that cultural sensitivity to different conceptions of time makes us all more efficient and more time effective in the long run.

—Lori L. Burrows, Commission Legal Advisor
Arkansas Public Service Commission
Former Peace Corps Volunteer (1999–2001)
Pohnpei State, Federated States of Micronesia

Smell Communication—Olfactics

Smells give us a lot of sensory input. Smells send strong nonverbal messages. While you may think this is humorous, scientific study about smell communication (also known as **_olfactics_**) is actually compelling.

We use smell to communicate messages about ourselves, our homes, our office environments, and our vehicles. Think about the large amount of money we spend on scents to alter our odor. We choose perfumes, colognes, deodorants, laundry detergents, aftershaves, shampoos, conditioners, and other products based on their smells. Aromatherapy is a field of study where people research how smells affect our moods and stress levels. The problem is people perceive smells differently. The scent you are wearing may not be appealing to a coworker, interviewer, or new acquaintance. If the fragrance is strong, people may immediately try to avoid you.

Now think about situations where there is no escape (sitting next to someone on an airplane or consulting with a coworker). Even worse, what if the receiver has allergies to the smoke lingering on your clothes, a perfume you've chosen, or the incense or eucalyptus in your office? At this point, the communication experience becomes intolerable for the receiver. The receiver may assume you are insensitive to people around you. This is not a good thing if the receiver is the interviewer, your boss, or potential romantic partner.

The smells in our homes (baking bread, cinnamon potpourri, or pet urine) all send messages to the people who enter. Does your home smell clean? Welcoming? The person visiting makes this decision, not you.

Our vehicles also carry smells. Why is this important? Well, you never know when you may be asked to give a ride to a professor, a client, a boss, or an interviewee. If your car carries the scent of smoke, and the passenger has an allergy, she may have to refuse the ride or suffer the consequences of being exposed to the allergens in the car. Neither of these impressions are ones you want someone to remember.

We become desensitized to the smells we enjoy, so we often increase the application. While we barely notice the fragrance of perfume or cologne we've worn for five years, the person we are meeting for the first time is getting an overdose. With the increase in allergy

TRY IT!

What do you think of people when you visit their home for the first time and it smells like . . .

Baking bread _____

Pet urine _____

The smells in our offices (incense, eucalyptus, floral sprays) also send messages. What is your impression of a business executive when you walk into her office and it smells like . . .

Incense _____

Floral spray _____

Linen Breeze _____

sensitivities, we need to be aware of the communication consequences as we choose appropriate scents for our bodies and our environment.

Touch Communication—Haptics

Touch communication (*haptics*) is one of the most powerful ways to send nonverbal messages. However, U.S. culture is particularly touch avoidant, and people rarely use touch in public. In fact, many businesses and schools have policies in place to describe inappropriate touching. In some elementary schools, teachers cannot even hug children who have done a good job or fallen on the playground. Teachers risk sexual harassment or abuse charges in these situations. The legal approach dictates no touching.

Women normally can get away with much more touching than men. Think of the times you've seen women dance together. No one thinks anything of it, but two men dancing together would raise eyebrows. Women also tend to hug each other when they meet much more frequently than do men in our culture. Men display touching behaviors in sports, and few observers react in a negative manner to what they do. However, if a male student were to slap another male student on the derrière to congratulate him on an "A," the reaction of observers might be quite negative. Context plays a major role in our determination of whether a touching behavior is appropriate.

CHOICES AND CONSEQUENCES

Think about yourself. Are you comfortable with touch or are you touch avoidant? In which situations? Can you handle meeting someone in the business world whose touch rules were different from yours? What are the consequences if you can't?

_____

_____

_____

_____

_____

How do we know when a touch is inappropriate? If it makes you uncomfortable, it is inappropriate. You need to find the words to tell the other person to stop the offending touch. The Human Rights and Equal Opportunity Commission defines **sexual harassment** as an unwelcome sexual advance, unwelcome request for sexual favors, or other unwelcome conduct of a sexual nature that makes a person feel offended, humiliated, or intimidated where a reasonable person would anticipate that reaction in the circumstances. Sexual harassment involves a patterned behavior. You must tell the person to stop the behavior. If you don't, your silence could be interpreted as consenting to the behavior. If the person continues with the behavior after you've asked or told him or her to stop, you may have grounds for a sexual harassment claim.

Some people attribute any form of unwelcome touching as sexual harassment. Someone who accidentally bumps into you in a public place is not guilty of sexual harassment. We get bumped many times during a day—on the subway, in a computer-training session, in the lunch line, on an elevator, or walking down a crowded street. These types of encounters, while they may be irritating, do not involve any attempt to create a hostile, offensive, intimidating, or abusive environment.

Our reaction to touching behaviors, such as having a hand placed on our shoulder or back, often depends on our family experience. If we grew up in families and cultures that were physical—where lots of hugging took place, where mom or dad put an arm around us as we walked down the street—we accept such touching behaviors as signs of affection or camaraderie. If we grew up in families where none of this touching took place, we could be extremely uncomfortable with touching and could even find the behaviors to be threatening. Be observant when involved in making communication choices about touching so that you can recognize and adapt to the comfort level of others.

Touching behavior varies with cultures as well. In general, Blacks and Latinos tend to use much more touching in their communication style with family and friends. Europeans are much more reserved. This difference in the use of touch can create barriers among ethnic groups. Please remember there is no one correct touching style. Try to be open-minded as you blend with other cultures.

A handshake is a touching behavior that varies from culture to culture as well. In U.S. culture, you must practice making your handshake firm (not bone crushing) and extending your arm out straight without bending your elbow. Ideally, your hand should not be sweaty (but avoid wiping it on your clothes first—this gesture sends a negative nonverbal message). If perspiration is a big problem, you can try an antiperspirant spray on your palms before a meeting.

You shake men's hands and women's hands in U.S. culture. In Europe, Asia, and Russia you should not shake a woman's hand. When you are traveling abroad, you might place a female business executive in an awkward position if you extend your arm to shake her hand. It is respectful to follow local customs.

Professional Perspective

Ancient cultural traditions are still followed in the Far East. When meeting a Japanese executive for the first time, you should extend your hand, but remember not to squeeze too hard. In Western culture, a firm handshake is considered important. However, in the Asian culture, a firm handshake is considered an aggressive and threatening act—not a good first introduction for your new Japanese boss.

—Robert H. Christie
Senior Vice President, Corporate Communications
The New York Times Company

In some cultures, you greet men and women by kissing them on the cheek. U.S. men, especially, need to be prepared for a different experience if they visit a foreign country. I (HPT) was at a university reception in Russia. My students had completed a study-abroad program, and I had completed a teaching assignment. A male faculty member kissed me on the lips during the reception. In Russia, this touching experience is reserved for men who have been lifelong friends. The moment was a gesture of acceptance and friendship, and I was honored. It made me feel like I had done a good job in an environment where I had been a total stranger. The kiss was unexpected, but I knew its meaning. Had I not understood the cultural meaning, I could have recoiled or been offended. This reaction would have embarrassed my Russian colleague. You need to study the customs of foreign cultures before you travel. It makes your communication much more effective.

Paralanguage

Paralanguage refers to the vocal techniques you use to emphasize and give meaning to words. We can say the same sentence and make it sound angry, happy, romantic, or indifferent just by altering our paralanguage (try it with "Glad to see you could make it"). The words remain the same, but the meaning changes. In addition, unintentional vocal noises can send messages. Have you ever heard anyone add a vocal element to a yawn? During a lecture, this action draws immediate attention and sends a different message from someone who yawns discreetly. Projection, pitch, rate, and pauses contribute to the meaning of the words you use to communicate.

Pitch, projection, and quality of voice play a large part in creating meaning for our message. Think about a petite, giggly young woman who says coyly, "Don't you talk to me like that," versus a large, deep-voiced man yelling it in a loud voice. Would both individuals be conveying the same meaning with the same words? Absolutely not.

Reality

Remember that the third function of nonverbal communication is that it can contradict a verbal message. Be very careful of using this in a dating situation. When your verbal message contradicts your nonverbal paralanguage, you are sending mixed messages that are not fair to your partner. For instance, Katie wants Rob to kiss her, but she feels that she can't really say yes because that would make her seem sexually available. So she playfully pushes him away saying "nooooo, don't kiss me" coyly with her paralanguage. If you read anything about gender communication, you'll find that Katie feels compelled to communicate that way because that is how she was socialized—to not be aggressive, not have an opinion, certainly not to have sexual desires.

However, the mixed message she is sending is dangerous. If we could convey one important change that everyone could make in their communication, it would be to clearly send messages when dealing with dating and sexuality. If you want to be kissed, say so. If you don't, say so. On the receiving end, ALWAYS operate on the content level of the message. If Katie says no in that coy little way that really means yes, get used to stopping immediately and saying "Ok, sorry." That will help her to adjust her behavior and keep you from overstepping a line that could get you into deep trouble.

And when you do say no, say it with as forceful paralanguage as you can muster. This is the time that you cannot have your nonverbals contradict your verbals.

Paralanguage definitely influences the way receivers interpret your message during interpersonal communication. When a parent said "Don't you use that tone with me!" they were pointing to your inappropriate use of paralanguage for the situation. Try to make sure you are mentally alert as you approach a communication situation so you can be flexible and accurate with your use of paralanguage. Words contain emotional meaning when paralanguage is used effectively. As you listen to different speakers in person and on television, analyze their vocal techniques (projection, pitch, emphasis, rate, and pauses) during their speech. Can you use some of their paralanguage skills to improve your own style? Practice conversational paralanguage so that you will be comfortable conveying your intended message to others.

TRY IT!

Pausing changes the meaning of a phrase. Note the difference in:

What's that up in the road ahead?

What's that up in the road, a head?

TRY IT!

Write the meaning of the sentence for each example.

Andre didn't say you were obnoxious.

Meaning _____

Andre **didn't** say you were obnoxious.

Meaning _____

Andre didn't **say** you were obnoxious.

Meaning _____

Andre didn't say **you** were obnoxious.

Meaning _____

Andre didn't say you were **obnoxious.**

Meaning _____

Think about the psychological meaning if you whispered the same message?

_____

_____

What if you screamed it?

_____

_____

Space Communication—Proxemics

The use of space communicates numerous messages nonverbally. People in positions of power can use their offices to communicate importance and to command attention. The president of the United States delivers speeches from the Oval Office to increase the impact of the message. In this section we will focus on the use of distance and space between people (***proxemics***) as they communicate.

Think about a couple sitting across from one another at a restaurant. The message they convey is different than if they chose to sit next to one another. Often people don't think much about the messages they send with their use of space, but the use of space influences perceptions—observers draw meaning from actions. Space and distance preferences depend on the particular environment and vary dramatically from culture to culture.

Most communication textbooks talk about research done in the 1960s by Edward T. Hall (1968) about personal distances.

- Intimate distance (0–18 inches)
- Personal distance (18 inches to 4 feet)
- Social distance (4–12 feet)
- Public distance (over 12 feet)

Hall's research used only white males, and his study is now over 40 years old. We will combine his historic findings with more current observations and guidelines.

Hall alerted us to the fact that we place an imaginary bubble around ourselves and only certain people may enter that space. The space is usually reserved for people who are close to us interpersonally—possibly our family members, a significant other, children, and close friends. However, there are also people who are not close to us whom we must accept into this intimate space, such as doctors, dentists, masseuses, and other professionals. There are additional situations where we allow total strangers into our intimate space as well. Think about being in a crowded elevator. We occasionally touch people we don't know. But what do we do to make the situation feel comfortable? We face forward, so there is no eye contact with strangers. We create the illusion of more space; we look at the floor or the ceiling. We also pull our arms closer to our bodies and try to shrink the amount of space we occupy. We stand shoulder to shoulder while remaining in our own world.

Notice the difference in two classmates standing shoulder to shoulder in front of the room versus the same individuals facing one another when the teacher asks them to turn toward each other. Immediately, the students shift eye contact to give themselves more psychological space.

Technology helps us to create the illusion of space as well. When we are crowded, pulling out a handheld device of some kind and keeping our attention focused on it helps us to feel that we are not so crowded. It also helps to keep people from bothering us.

Business conversations take place in vehicles, in offices, at dinners, or on escalators. Physical spaces vary, but you need to pick up on the cues that others are sending. You may need to adjust your comfort zone occasionally to work with business colleagues from other cultures as well as within your own culture. In many cultures, people stand much closer to each other when communicating than we do in U.S. culture. In some cultures, you are not close enough to another person unless they can smell your breath during a conversation. This intimate distance is much too close for most Americans, but be prepared for this experience as you travel.

Space may vary by gender. Women may be more comfortable being close to other women and more uncomfortable being close to men. Men in the United States often do not like to be close to one another publicly—yet in Spain, men feel perfectly comfortable hugging and walking arm in arm.

Too many people are afraid of hurting someone's feelings or making them upset by saying anything about space, so they sit in silence and deal with communication that is uncomfortable. What happens when someone invades your personal space? There is no need to be uncomfortable. A simple statement such as, "Would you mind giving me a little more space please?" stated in a friendly tone can be effective. Or, "I'm sorry, but I feel uncomfortable when we're standing so close to each other. Why don't you have a seat?" Never hesitate to speak up if you are uncomfortable. As you engage in this dialogue, don't forget the importance of paralanguage. Sounding sincere rather than sounding confrontational will help you to solve the problem with less chance for hurt feelings or misunderstanding.

Critical Thinking

Think about a time you felt your personal space was invaded. How did you handle the situation?

_____

_____

_____

_____

Territoriality

Territoriality refers to the imaginary ownership of a particular space. Most students walk into a classroom on the first day, choose a chair, and then feel ownership of that chair for the entire term. If you walk in and someone else is in "your" chair, you are annoyed because someone confiscated your seat. In apartment buildings or workplaces where there is a large parking lot, people often park in the same space. These people are annoyed if you park in "their space," even though the space does not belong to them. Territoriality is an imaginary social concept, but many individuals take the ownership of space seriously.

We also mark our territory by leaving a sweater or book bag on a seat. I (KSY) once went to a water park where every single seat was marked by a towel. There was not a vacant seat anywhere. I needed to find a seat for my father-in-law, since he was watching our sleeping baby who was in a stroller. Only 10 percent of the chairs were occupied, and yet the other 90 percent were not available either. It was amazing how strong the message of ownership was. We were not willing to move someone else's belongings. Think how angry you might be if you left your towel on a chair, and it wasn't there when you returned. Later in the day, management made an announcement over the loudspeaker that marking chairs did not reserve them for anyone. So in this scenario, the customers and management had to deal with an uncomfortable situation because of a territorial norm.

How territorial are you? Be honest about it. There are people who aren't annoyed when someone takes their space or moves their things occasionally. However, other people will go through the roof if their belongings are moved. Think about the communication difficulties that can occur when two roommates begin a semester together. Marcia sees her roommate's T-shirt on the floor, picks it up, and puts it in the hamper. The roommate comes home to see someone has touched her dirty laundry. She is extremely uncomfortable with this and a confrontation ensues. If Marcia isn't a territorial person herself, she will be shocked that this action upset her roommate.

The extent of our territoriality sends a nonverbal message about each of us. Others may think we are bizarre if our behavior varies from theirs. Some people may think we are unreasonable and odd; they may even think we are obsessed. It is important to remember that territoriality may be grounded in family experiences. In families where kids don't have any space of their own, they could become more or less territorial than the social norm when they are adults.

In addition to understanding your own use of space, it is important to respect the territoriality of others. Just as you want people to respect the way you use space, you need to return that respect to others and not question their position if they ask you to refrain from touching them or to give them some more space. This will help you avoid conflict and hard feelings with the other communicators in your life.

Critical Thinking

Do you feel your use of territoriality is reasonable or unreasonable? Describe three ways you use territoriality. Could you change?

_____

_____

_____

_____

_____

Artifacts

Artifacts are the objects we select to represent our identity. There are two categories. *Personal artifacts* include clothing, shoes, hairstyle, jewelry, eyeglasses, and other adornments. *Physical artifacts* include furniture, artwork, rugs, and other objects.

Artifacts are another area where miscommunication can occur. No matter how carefully we select items for ourselves or for our space, we cannot control how another communicator will interpret them. There are also many artifacts that we don't actually choose (Grandma sends you a piece of clothing). In our discussion, we focus on artifacts that are within your control.

Think about your personal artifact choices. What messages do you send with your clothing? How do you choose your clothing? Some people shop frequently so they always have the latest style; others take the first clean item off the laundry pile. Some of you may dress up, even when you could wear casual clothes; others wear only comfortable clothes even in formal situations. Many people select a specific color for most of their clothing. What do bright colors versus dark colors say about a person? Clothing that is tailored to fit sends a much different message than baggy clothing. People who wear colors that complement each other send a different message than people who wear colors that clash.

Clothing sends a strong social message, yet the meaning is not static—it changes with fashion trends. While jeans are a staple of today's wardrobe, they were not always viewed in a positive manner. In the aftermath of the Depression, jeans were considered a sign of poverty. Many people did not allow their children to wear them because they wanted to send a social message to others that they could provide for their children. In the late 1970s, jeans became a status symbol—and prices skyrocketed to match. Many people had to have "the right" designer's name embroidered on the back pockets to communicate that they knew the latest trends and were members of the fashion elite. Brands proliferated, and jeans became so common they went unnoticed.

Hairstyles send a message as well. Up-to-date hairstyles send a different message than hairstyles from the past. What do you think when you see someone who is still wearing a hairstyle from the 1980s, such as a rattail (a single, thin braid of hair longer than the rest of the cut) or a mullet (short in the front, long in the back)? What is the message sent by people who have multicolor or unnaturally colored hair? What do you think of shaved heads versus a full head of hair? One of our former students talked about the differences in the treatment she received from strangers during the two years she had her head shaved versus the subsequent years when she had a full head of hair. She was the same person, and yet when her head was shaved, the reactions of others were noticeably different. People will react to appearances that they perceive as unusual—even if the reaction is unfair or inaccurate.

Jewelry, eyeglasses, and other personal artifacts should be chosen to complement your build, your skin coloring, and your situation. We will talk about this in more detail in chapter 12 on interviewing. Some people like to reveal information about themselves through their use of jewelry, such as wearing a religious symbol. However, there are consequences to every choice. In a job interview, there could be a positive or a negative reaction to such jewelry, depending on the receiver.

Physical objects such as furniture, artwork, pictures, rugs, lighting, curtains, and other special adornments also communicate messages about you. Feng shui is the Chinese practice of configuring space to harmonize with the spiritual forces that inhabit it—the placement and arrangement of space to achieve harmony with the environment. Feng shui is now widely recognized as a guide for placing artifacts in your space to influence how they relate to your energy and production levels. Think about how you feel and what you think about a person who owns a space that is completely cluttered. How about a simply designed space without clutter, some beautifully placed artwork, and a wide-open feeling to it? Where do you feel more comfortable? Where could you accomplish more work? Where could you relax or concentrate? Removing clutter and minimizing the amount of furniture in a space are two of the first steps in generating a flow of positive energy (Ziegler & Lawler, 2003).

Quite often adults design work spaces to reflect their personal taste. We have assigned students to visit different offices on campus and to describe how they felt in each space. Student reports have varied from feeling welcome and calm to feeling distracted and claustrophobic. Think about artifacts as you move into the business world and create your own space. Your clients and colleagues will enter your space—send the appropriate message. Artifacts send such strong messages that many corporations have policies stating what employees can or cannot display in their office space. Some corporations will not even allow you to have a family photo in your office space. Other companies encourage people to decorate offices however they like.

These policies influence our perceptions of the companies who create them. When you go to a job interview, look closely at the offices. Do they resemble a place where you would feel comfortable working? Use of artifacts can tell you a great deal about the organizational culture around you. You may decide not to work for a company because you are uncomfortable with the absence of personal artifacts. Other people may decide they like a company that looks clean and neat with no hint of personal belongings in the environment.

ETHICAL CONSIDERATIONS

What are the ethical considerations when we judge someone based on their personal artifacts? How often does this happen?

_____

_____

_____

Professional Perspective

Upon entering an interior environment you are instantly affected by it on an emotional level. Color, and its application, is perhaps the strongest element sending signals in a space. The psychological effects of color are complex, as well as greatly underestimated. Further investigation into color psychology can teach you how colors signal aspects such as socioeconomic status and success, life experiences, and trustworthiness. On a subconscious level, color affects our perception of comfort, time, and quality. These perceptions flow beyond interior design and have a substantial effect on the people who inhabit the space.

The overall decoration of a space, in relation to design style, materials, and furnishings, creates an ambience that is a telltale narrative portraying the image of the inhabitants of that space, be it an office or home environment. As an example, when you walk into the lobby of an office, a few observations can quickly tell you if the inhabitants are modern or traditional, liberal or conservative, accomplished or flailing. This can be a useful tool to decide whether or not you wish to work for that organization or do business with them. Conversely, it has the same effect when people are judging you.

Good design is the key to conveying the image you wish to portray.

—Wes Moon
Interior Designer

Critical Thinking

Think about your current living space. If money were no object, what artifact changes would you make? What is the new message you would be sending to people who enter your room?

_____

_____

_____

_____

Summary

Your nonverbal choices have a huge impact on your ability to communicate effectively. Body language, time, smell, touch, paralanguage, artifacts, and space and territory all send messages. Understanding how these nonverbal communication symbols affect other people will help you make choices that will influence your career potential and the success of your interpersonal relationships. As the Professional Perspective below illustrates, unawareness of cultural norms for artifacts at a business dinner can create unintended consequences.

Professional Perspective

When I was in Japan, I became friends with a woman whose use of artifacts at a dinner party for a business associate of her husband unwittingly caused embarrassment. The woman stopped at a florist to bring a bouquet to the hosts. The host politely put them in a vase of water and placed them next to the table. After the dinner was over, she was told this was a funeral arrangement of flowers.

—Allynn Gooen
International Performance Artist

Image management assists the perception of others to see you as someone they want to have as a colleague or acquaintance. Consistent nonverbal behavior in appearance and use of space makes others comfortable while you are in their presence. It is useful to find an acceptable balance between your need to remain a unique human being and the need of others to see a colleague/acquaintance with whom they want to spend time. In most situations, a little polishing of your nonverbal image and behavior can accomplish this task and open the door to new friendships as well as employment.

KEY WORDS

adaptors	nonverbal communication
affect displays	olfactics
artifacts	paralanguage
chronemics	personal artifacts
contingency time	physical artifacts
emblems	polychronic cultures
haptics	proxemics
illustrators	regulators
kinesics	sexual harassment
monochronic cultures	territoriality

DISCUSSION/ACTIVITIES

1. Describe a gesture you commonly use to substitute for a word or phrase when speaking to others. Explain your behavior.

2. How do you indicate to others that you have something to say during a social conversation?

3. Describe an adaptor commonly used by a teacher, family member, or acquaintance that you find distracting or annoying.

4. Describe a smell that instantly allows you to recall a pleasant memory.

5. Examine two faculty offices on campus and describe the personalities of the occupants based on the artifacts contained in the spaces.

6. Sit in various locations within the classroom for two weeks. Do any of the locations make you feel more comfortable than others during the class? Explain.

7. How do you use physical contact to greet acquaintances, family members, and good friends? Where did you learn this behavior?

8. How do you let others know that you are uncomfortable with what they are saying without interrupting them verbally?

five

Communicating Interpersonally

OBJECTIVES

After reading this chapter, you should be able to:
- Recognize and use self-disclosure
- Discuss effective conversational style
- Explain the Johari Window
- Identify the 3 goals of listening
- Identify the six feedback styles and practice using them when appropriate
- Discuss the implications of technology on interpersonal communication

Interpersonal communication occurs between two or more people in a personal or professional relationship. From birth, everyone is involved in interpersonal communication, whether with family members, neighbors, educators, religious leaders, doctors, or peers. As we mature, we add friendships, romantic relationships, student-teacher relationships, employer-employee relationships, and professional colleagues to our social sphere. Each interpersonal relationship is unique.

The study of interpersonal communication is complex. Our discussion introduces you to the basic concepts of understanding others. The study of interpersonal communication will help you unravel why past relationships failed or were successful. Not every relationship fails because of another person. Many times, the failure is really yours. Good communication looks easy. You may think you are effective because you've communicated all of your life. Your skills, however, may not be as sophisticated as they need to be for all the encounters ahead of you. Skills improve once you understand the consequences of poor communication. As you recognize the importance of interpersonal communication, you can understand others better, get along with others, and be more effective in future interpersonal situations. Try to learn from past mistakes and acquire the necessary skills to prevent misunderstandings in the future.

Self-Disclosure

You enter your chemistry class and are assigned to a lab partner. How do you get to know one another? Most people begin with a brief conversation. **Self-disclosure** is the act of giving your personal information to another person. You need to disclose information about yourself in order for others to get to know you. Self-disclosure is a key building block in interpersonal relationships because, "When one individual takes a risk by disclosing to another individual, the receiver feels as though he or she is trusted. In return, the receiver is more likely to disclose information as well. Trust and security are developed when two people respond to one another positively over repeated interactions, which continually strengthens the relationship" (Bruss & Hill, 2010, p. 3). However, effective disclosure of personal information is done slowly and over a long period of time.

What are some of the common things we disclose when we first meet a peer? Our name, size of our family, hometown, high school activities, basic interests, and academic major are typical topics for self-disclosure on a college campus. Some initial self-disclosures are appropriate or inappropriate depending on the region of the country where people live. For example, when I (KSY) moved to Arkansas, I was in the car with a colleague and her 7-year-old daughter. The daughter looked at me and asked, "What church do you go to?" I waited for the mother to correct her daughter for asking an inappropriate question. From my perspective the question was too intimate for initial self-disclosure. Silence reigned. The mother was actually waiting for me to answer the question. In that region, "What church do you go to?" is usually the second question asked of strangers, immediately after asking, "What is your name?" The silence was extremely awkward because both of us were waiting for the other person to speak.

Self-disclosure will be different from culture to culture. Japanese students self-disclose less than American students in many different types of romantic and friendship relationships (Kito, 2005). In individualistic cultures like the United States, people celebrate uniqueness and are more likely to share what they believe distinguishes them from others. In collectivistic cultures like Japan, people prefer to blend in and are less likely to talk about themselves.

We have choices about how much we disclose and the amount of intimate self-disclosure we provide for others. There is no specific formula for what is appropriate and what is inappropriate. For example, very few students in a college classroom would volunteer information about a family member's personal problems, how much money their parents make, or their ultimate sexual fantasy. How do we know what information is appropriate to share with strangers?

Think through a couple of things as you decide to self-disclose. Is the information simply factual and innocuous? (i.e., I like the Yankees, Queen is my favorite band, my favorite color is purple). There is usually no problem with sharing those basic thoughts with people you don't know well. But if you share opinions about issues people feel strongly about (I believe/do not believe that abortion should be legal, I am homosexual, etc.), there may be unintended consequences. The situation plays a part as well. While sexuality may be disclosed in a close interpersonal relationship, it may not be appropriate in the workplace.

Also think about your motivation for disclosure. If you are disclosing to alleviate guilt (I stole from my company/I cheated on my significant other), you have now made yourself feel better, but you have compromised the other person. They now have to carry the burden of your disclosure. So ask yourself—will my disclosure become someone else's burden? If the answer is yes, then you should probably keep the information to yourself.

The more personal the information you choose to share, the greater the trust you must have in the other person. While intimate self-disclosure can make personal relationships closer, it also makes you vulnerable should the other person choose to violate your confidence. You should take only acceptable risks when you share intimate information with another person. The lesson of what is an acceptable risk is learned through life experience. You will get burned occasionally, but it's a risk you must take when you feel someone is worth knowing. All trust involves risk. If your trust is violated, you will at least know that you were willing to participate in open, honest communication. Although withholding information may be prudent in some circumstances, silence will not lead to close relationships.

Historically self-disclosure was only discussed in the context of face-to-face interpersonal communication. However, today we have millions of people who are willing to self-disclose via the Internet to a multitude of unknown receivers. Through Facebook, Twitter, discussion boards, and instant messaging (IM), people are posting all kinds of facts about themselves that were once reserved for sharing with close friends.

If there is someone we want to know about, we can quickly look them up and know their hopes, dreams, favorite movies, foods, songs, etc. Quite often, the person will list an IM address; their away messages often list when they are in class, in the cafeteria, and even in the shower.

Keep in mind that many people have access to these social networking (i.e., self-disclosure) sites. A recent graduate reported that she was told to pull up her MySpace site during a job interview. She was fortunate there was nothing compromising on her site. Most of our students aren't so prudent. Many post pictures of ethically questionable behavior, poses, and attire; use profanity; and list other information that potential employers could find objectionable.

Certainly, self-disclosing via technology can be used for good purposes. I (KSY) keep track of our alumni accomplishments and career moves easily through the use of Facebook. However, I also choose to post very limited information about myself.

Monitoring Self-Disclosure. One way to gauge the appropriateness of self-disclosure is by interpreting the nonverbal behavior of the conversation partner. People may demonstrate discomfort with self-disclosure through vocalizations, silence, or an instant change of subject. If this happens with your conversation partner, you need to be perceptive enough to stop the disclosure immediately. If you are in a position where someone is disclosing information and expecting you to disclose similar details, you may find it necessary to respond in a very calm manner with something like, "I'm not prepared to talk about that right now. Can we please change the subject?" This is a reasonable way to let the other person know she has overstepped the bounds of appropriate discussion without harming the relationship. Many people have different tolerances for what are appropriate topics for discussion. If you have not yet reached the same comfort level for disclosure, communicate how you feel, leaving the door open for the relationship to continue.

However, when we disclose on the Internet through Facebook and Twitter, we don't have access to nonverbal feedback. If we disclose things in bad taste or that make others uncomfortable, we aren't going to receive feedback immediately or possibly at all. The damage is done rapidly and with multiple people. In 2011, Gilbert Gottfried, the man who was the duck's voice on highly successful advertisements, was fired after posting jokes about the Japanese tsunami. He offended a large number of people with his self-disclosures, which he thought were funny. Had he first communicated those messages to a friend in face-to-face communication, he could have received feedback that his disclosures were wildly inappropriate in joking about a tragic situation. But by the time the feedback arrived, the damage was done, and he was unemployed.

Professional Perspective

It is amazing how a very common language term can be misinterpreted. . . .

Most college students are fully aware of the dangers of a Facebook or MySpace account, whether it be the "unbalanced" people that are out there or the companies and organizations that are using it to find out about potential employees. Regardless of the facts, many of us still choose to have an account.

My professor came into class one day with a surprise for us all. She had done some research on everyone in the class. She informed us that she had her own account on Facebook and MySpace! As she walked around the room, she informed us of something that was not appropriate about each one of our accounts. I was on the opposite side of the room thinking that I was in the clear because I had been very careful to keep my profile clean.

Come to find out, I was completely wrong! That day opened my eyes. Of course, as do most students these days, I have an Instant Messenger screen name that was advertised in my account. Are you familiar with a *crotch rocket*? Most people in my generation know this to be a sporty motorcycle. The professor, on the other hand, did not know it was a motorcycle. Until that day, I had not even thought about my screen name as indicating anything but a die-hard motorcycle fan! It totally took me by surprise. I was shocked and embarrassed by what the professor interpreted. So, before you post something, I encourage you to think carefully!

—Stacy Wolfe
College Student

Please remember that disclosures must happen for relationships to grow. Disclosure is fun and helps two people to learn about one another, support one another, and bond. There are some people who are unwilling to disclose anything personal. It is extremely difficult to build a relationship with people who never self-disclose. Keep in mind also that gender research supports the general conclusion that men tend to self-disclose much less than women do (Ivy & Backlund, 2008). This means two people in an intimate heterosexual relationship will probably disclose at different levels. The female in the relationship may feel the male isn't willing to get close to her emotionally, while the male may feel the female talks too much and too soon. There are certain things about yourself you should share openly with others and certain

Critical Thinking

What has someone disclosed to you that made you feel uncomfortable? How did you react? Do you still communicate with this person?

_____

_____

_____

_____

things you should not share immediately, if ever. This is a decision only you can make. Always be prepared for the consequences of your choices in every relationship.

Conversation

Conversation is an extemporaneous interpersonal exchange. Some communicators are better at participating in conversations than others. Think about the people you enjoy being with while discussing any topic. There is little that is more gratifying than an excellent conversation with someone you enjoy. Then, think about the people you may try to avoid when discussing certain subjects. What makes the difference?

As a relationship develops, a conversation needs to be a somewhat even exchange in self-disclosure. Each individual should share information about themselves so that both people learn more about each other. The information they are exchanging should be similar in both quality and quantity. A one-sided information exchange does not build a working relationship or an intimate relationship. And surely you've come across "*spewers*"—people who talk nonstop about everything they are doing but never have any interest in letting you into the conversation. This is not conversation; it is a monologue.

Effective communicators know there are three stages in the *conversational process:* the opening, the body, and the closing. The *opening* lets the other person know you would like to talk. You might use a smile coupled with eye contact, or you might use a direct verbal phrase, "Hi, my name is Rita."

Sometimes the opening includes *conversational setup*—the introductory remarks to the conversation that give the other person a sense of what is coming next. Setup is not always necessary, but if the information to be revealed in the conversation is important or surprising, then conversational setup should be present. People may say, "Have you heard what happened?" or, "I have some really bad news to share with you." In this way, the listener is not shocked by the information you share.

Keep in mind that if you use a lengthy conversational setup, you lose conversational effectiveness. Many people get annoyed with a person who starts a conversation with, "Oh hi, hey listen, I was meaning to ask you . . . now if you don't want to, please say no, there is no obligation, and I won't mind, so I really want to know what you think about. . . ." The listener may be annoyed by the rambling, disjointed opening and will be less likely to want to listen or respond.

The second stage, the *body,* is the longest section of a conversation. This is where you exchange information, share stories, tell jokes, or try to persuade. You may talk about superficial topics or topics of great intimacy. It depends on the relationship. Your self-disclosure rules apply here. Conversations end quickly if you launch into uncomfortable or insensitive information. If you want the conversation to keep going, you may need to listen intently and ask questions. (Be sure to incorporate the information about listening and feedback styles discussed later in the chapter.) However, certain questions and styles of feedback are notorious for closing conversations. So, pay attention to nonverbal or verbal cues that indicate you have plunged too quickly into sensitive topics.

Also be aware of your nonverbals during a conversation. While people can certainly listen without making eye contact, the communicator may legitimately feel there is a lack of interest or comprehension without it. Eye contact, in U.S. culture, makes most people feel connected to another person. It makes us feel as though we have the other person's attention. Eye contact and general attentiveness is essential in meaningful conversation. For example, Rowan and Seanan are business associates having dinner together in a restaurant. Rowan always looks Seanan in the eye while they are conversing. Any shift in Seanan's facial tension or eye motion gives Rowan the clues he needs to change or expand a topic. Rowan's eyes never move even though he is aware of everything around him.

Seanan has a harder time with this behavior. He finds himself distracted at times by peripheral phenomena. He looks at the servers walking by, people being seated, and couples in other booths. How do you think these business associates perceive each other's nonverbals? What attributions does Rowan create for Seanan's lack of eye contact? Disinterest? Short attention span? What does Seanan think about Rowan's constant gaze? Which of these associates is really listening to the conversation? Every aspect of nonverbal communication sends a message during conversation. Remember, a nonverbal message can support or detract from the message itself.

In addition to nonverbal habits, you also need to be careful regarding your selection of topics and the information you choose to share in a conversation. Many people just say what is on their mind rather than reflecting on how it will sound. Have you ever been standing in a checkout line at a grocery store and had someone self-disclose inappropriate information to you? Or have you done a double take when a friend has interrupted what you consider a serious revelation with a totally irrelevant point about his day? Or have you been talking to a friend about something important and personal when some friends interrupt your conversation and instantly begin talking enthusiastically about an upcoming event? After monopolizing your time without ever asking if they had interrupted something important, they leave as quickly as they came, leaving you wondering, "What was that all about?" These moments of inappropriate self-disclosure or introducing an irrelevant topic are constant reminders of why you need to monitor what you share with others. Don't repeat behavior you find to be annoying in others. Learn from the communication mistakes around you and apply that knowledge to your own choices.

ETHICAL CONSIDERATIONS

What do you do if you hear a message that was not intended for you? Let's say that you are in a bathroom stall when your boss comes in with another coworker. The boss says something about the job opening that your good friend is applying for. Do you tell your boss that you overheard the information? Do you tell your friend about the information that you really shouldn't know? Do you select another option?

_____

_____

_____

_____

_____

The third stage is the ***closing.*** In U.S. culture, we expect conversations to have an informal or formal ending. This brief statement allows the communicators to agree the conversation is coming to a close. A simple "goodbye," "see you later," or "nice chatting with you" is all it takes to alert each other that the conversation has ended. While the phrases may seem to be meaningless (obviously if I walk away from you, our conversation is over), it is a social norm to close a conversation effectively. Many communicators are aggravated by anyone who hangs up a phone without saying "goodbye" to close the conversation. We learn manners at a young age and apply our standards to other people. Years ago, I (KSY) was hanging up laundry when a 7-year-old neighbor was talking to me. I was somewhat distracted, but I did engage in the conversation. However, because of my distraction, when I was done hanging the laundry I picked up my basket and headed back to the house. The little boy called after me in a quiet, sad, and questioning voice, "Well . . . I'll see you later?" I was mortified at my insensitivity. Everyone expects—and deserves—some kind of closing to a conversation.

Remember, the most effective communicators can adapt to a situation and read nonverbal clues. If someone is giving you the nonverbal signs that she wants to end the conversation (such as glancing at the computer, reaching toward the doorknob, looking at her watch), then it is time to stop talking. We are constantly amazed at the number of people who have not learned this basic skill of observation.

Your mom calls while you are studying for a very important exam. She is still talking after 30 minutes. How do you end the conversation?

_____

_____

_____

You see a great-looking person at a party. How do you open the conversation?

_____

_____

_____

A friend of yours monopolizes the body of the conversation, never pausing long enough to allow you to participate. What do you do?

_____

_____

_____

Conversational Tips. There are some rules that apply to every conversation. Remember to be polite. Be concise. Do not waste another person's time. Keep the conversation focused. But also keep in mind that conversations vary from person to person and depend on the context of the situation. Specific conversational topics depend on whether you are talking to your friends, your teachers, employers, or parents. Preparation for the conversation is important if you must speak with someone for a specific purpose. If you are simply chatting with friends for enjoyment, no preparation is necessary. However, when you speak with a boss or an instructor, you must prepare for the body of the conversation. There have been times when students have come to our offices under the guise of a specific conversation topic, but they end up venting about something that is of no interest to us and is none of our business. You should converse appropriately with the appropriate people.

One of the best ways to ingratiate yourself with someone else is to care about the other person, to listen actively, and to engage in further conversation. So few people exhibit empathy that the person you are conversing with will recognize the interpersonal experience as a unique situation. People appreciate someone who lets them talk about themselves and who acts genuinely interested. By listening and engaging in conversation, you demonstrate to others that you value their thoughts—you make them feel important and validate their existence! Learning effective conversational skills is immensely valuable for every interpersonal relationship. These skills can help you tremendously in friendships, romantic relationships, family relationships, the workplace, and the job interview.

Critical Thinking

How satisfied are you with your conversational skills? What are you particularly skilled in OR what would you most like to change?

_____

_____

_____

The Johari Window

Psychologists Joseph Luft and Harry Ingham developed the Johari Window in the 1950s during research on group dynamics; the title of the model comes from the first names of Luft and Ingham. Once you understand the importance of self-disclosure and feedback in building relationships, the Johari Window is a tool you can use to analyze yourself and others. The **Johari Window** is a diagram of what we know about ourselves and what others know about us. The symbolic representation of that knowledge consists of four areas: information known to others, unknown to others, known to self, and unknown to self. Think of the areas as panes in a window that will vary in size depending on the individual. The Johari Window helps us understand how open or closed we are with others and how aware or unaware we are of information about ourselves.

Self-disclosure and feedback are the two continuums that determine the size of the areas. Your willingness or unwillingness to share personal information with others increases or decreases the size of the "known by others" area. The more you reveal, the more others know about you. People who self-disclose easily are more open; people who rarely self-disclose keep aspects of themselves hidden. If we process feedback from others by listening carefully to what they are saying about us, we can learn information about ourselves that we never knew, and our blind area will be smaller.

The **open area** refers to what we know about ourselves and what other people know about us: information you have disclosed and information you have learned about yourself from others. As you self-disclose and as you accept feedback, your open area will grow larger. It takes trust to open oneself up to feedback and self-disclosure, but it is necessary for healthy interpersonal relationships.

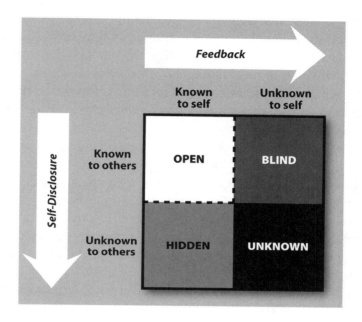

The ***blind area*** refers to qualities or characteristics about yourself that others are aware of but that you are not. These elements may include mannerisms, an unusual posture, a unique way of walking, or what your language choices say about you. The best way to discover the image you project (thereby decreasing the blind area) is to listen to and consciously evaluate the feedback others give to you. If you play with your hair when you give a speech and are unaware of your behavior, you will learn about yourself through feedback from classmates and/or your teacher.

People who have a large blind area typically overuse self-disclosure. They desire social relationships but are often unaware that they are talking too much to accept the feedback of others. They are unaware of listener feedback and keep talking because they are socially nervous, self-centered, or refuse to acknowledge the value of the ideas and thoughts of others.

A good way to reduce the size of your blind area is to elicit feedback from others through conversation. If you listen to others as they respond to your questions and process their information, your open area will become larger and your blind area smaller.

The ***hidden area*** refers to information you know about yourself but choose not to share with others. This is private information you never discuss with anyone. For most people, certain thoughts or actions remain hidden, such as an embarrassing incident or a mistake you made in the past. If you have a large hidden area, you are low in self-disclosure.

People who choose not to self-disclose certain information do so for a number of reasons: low self-esteem, trust issues based on a previous betrayal, embarrassment about past behavior, or a high need for privacy.

People with a large hidden area can listen to the feedback of others and actively participate in the communication process. They simply never share anything personal about themselves. Since self-disclosure is a key to building a relationship, the person with a large hidden area is very difficult to get to know on a personal level.

Finally, the **unknown area** refers to information neither you nor anyone else knows about you. For example, a parent who, with a sudden burst of adrenaline, is able to rescue her small child from a burning car may surprise herself and everyone else by performing an action she may not have thought she could do. Each person has unknown potential that is occasionally released when triggered by stress, an unexpected event, a burst of creativity, or through self-exploration. Communication can expand the open area and contract the blind area but it can't do much to change the unknown area. The synergy created in meaningful exchanges of self-disclosure and feedback could, however, set the stage for better understanding.

Reducing your unknown area is a journey of self-discovery. The more you self-disclose and the greater your willingness to listen to feedback from others, the smaller your unknown area will be.

Using the Johari Window. Now that you understand the four symbolic panes of the Johari Window a little better, think of them as a useful analytical tool for improving your interpersonal communication. The panes will not be the same size from one person to the next because people vary greatly in their ability to self-disclose information and listen to feedback from others.

If you analyze yourself and your relationships, you may be able to see whether you need to self-disclose more or less information and process more or less feedback to maintain a positive relationship. You may realize that you haven't been telling your significant other or close friend enough about yourself so she can get to know you. Relationships end when people don't share information about themselves. Maybe you are the socially inept person who can't seem to fit in with others, but you're not sure why. It's possible you might be revealing too much or inappropriate information about yourself. This information or behavior might make other people uncomfortable.

We also need to learn about ourselves from others. Are you listening to what others tell you about yourself? Are you listening at all? Or are you always talking? Do you brush off comments that others make about you? As you analyze feedback from others, there is a difference between harmful labels and constructive criticism. For example, if someone suggests that you cut others off when they are talking, you should reflect on that analysis and work on ways to improve your communication skills such as

What would your experience be if you are talking to this person?

_____

_____

How about this one?

_____

_____

turn taking. However, if someone has told you all your life that you are stupid, we would recommend that you don't internalize that message.

Personal awareness is the first step in the process of changing communication patterns. You can increase or decrease your self-disclosure as well as your ability to respond to feedback with a little practice. The Johari Window can become a tool for personal growth.

CHOICES AND CONSEQUENCES

Have you ever been around someone who was too open? What information did they disclose? How did you feel as a result of the self-disclosure? What were the consequences?

_____

_____

_____

_____

Listening

Most of us have the ability to hear from birth, but **listening** is an acquired skill. **Hearing** is a passive action. It is simply the process of sound hitting your eardrums and then being decoded for a possible response.

Professional Perspective

To become an articulate verbal communicator, I feel it is necessary to first become an attentive listener. I have always felt that I have been a good listener. But when I became the parent of a hearing-impaired child, my listening skills were immediately challenged. Hearing is an amazing gift, and I was just learning how amazing it really is. I had to listen carefully to my daughter's speech and then teach her how to listen and speak using Auditory Verbal Therapy.

Step one for everyone to become articulate verbal communicators: first listen, then verbalize. It seems very simple but, if you think about it, do you use this rule in your daily life? In every situation and phase of life, be it at school, your place of employment, or at home with family and friends, everyone wants and deserves to be heard. If you find yourself speaking and no one seems to be listening, chances are your auditory skills are lacking. If you interrupt, correct, and speak over people often, your listening skills will need some fine-tuning. Just being aware of having these habits is really the only step a person needs to correct them.

Remember, your auditory comprehension of others will not only determine what and how you verbalize your thoughts back to others, it will also determine how others perceive and respond to you. Listen—Think—Speak.

—Tracy Synowsky
Stay-at-Home Parent

Think back to chapter 2 on perception. We talked about the concept of selective attention. Remember how we are constantly bombarded by sounds? We hear everything, but we only pay attention to specific sounds based on personal need and preference. Listening is an active process where you selectively attend to and assign meaning to sounds. If we analyzed every sound within earshot, we'd be exhausted. Once we focus on which sounds interest us, we can process the information and respond appropriately.

TRY IT!

Take a minute and list eight sounds that you can hear right now:

_____   _____   _____   _____

_____   _____   _____   _____

Being an effective listener is a skill that takes practice. Some of us develop this skill to a much finer degree than others. Because every interpersonal relationship is unique, and because each communication situation has different listening requirements, we need to learn multiple listening styles in order to be a strong communicator. Many communicators learn only one feedback style and use it consistently, but this doesn't allow for the uniqueness of situations. As you progress from situation to situation, flexibility and the ability to adapt to new information are tools that will help you to become an effective listener.

TRY IT!

List all the reasons you can think of why it is hard to listen to others. Think of situations with friends, parents, and teachers.

_____

_____

_____

_____

_____

Reality ✓

There are some quick and easy ways to improve your listening skills. When you are in a classroom or business meeting, sit up straight, make eye contact with the speaker, and take lots of notes. Note taking keeps you focused on the message. Make sure that you are briefed on the material of the day (either by reading the textbook or reviewing material for the meeting). Knowing the information makes listening easier. Also make sure to take proper care of your body. If you have adequate rest and proper nutrition, focusing on the message is much easier than if you are concerned with staying awake or a rumbling stomach.

As a speaker, you can help listeners follow your main points by using signposts and transitions (see chapter 8). This will help the audience retain the information more easily as well.

Goals of Listening

There are three basic goals of listening that will relate to the feedback styles below. We perform ***informational listening*** when we need directions, new information, insight, etc. If I ask you where I need to go, how to sew a seam, what was the president's speech about last night or why the earth rotates, I am planning to listen to the answer to gain information.

Critical listening is analytical listening. In this instance I'm comparing what I hear to other things that I know to be true. When a student speaker says that "when you eat at a fast-food restaurant, you should choose the salads because they are lower calorie and healthier than a hamburger and fries" we instantly shift into critical listening because we know that many fast-food salads top 1,000 calories while a typical small burger and small fries clocks in at about 600. In this case, what began as informational listening about how to cut calories shifts rapidly as we analyze the information.

Critical listening is vitally important so that we don't just accept everything we hear as truth. We don't want to go overboard, however. If we are enrolled in a beginning sewing class and the instructor is demonstrating how to install a zipper, we should stay in the informational listening mode. We have not yet acquired the expertise to make judgments about the information.

Active listening occurs when we engage the speaker to find out more. I would be involved in active listening if I asked the speaker, "Where did you get your information on salads being the healthiest choice?" Maybe she knows something that I don't know. But if she doesn't have an answer, my critical-listening skill has served me well.

Feedback Styles

As you process and respond to information others give you, it is important to remember there are actually six different ***feedback***

Professional Perspective

As a mom to five kids, I am my children's first teacher and model of communication. Knowing that I am helping to shape their communication skills and habits makes me very aware of what I say and how I say it. However, I often find myself spending more time listening than speaking. Active listening is vital to effective parenting. My kids know that I'm not truly listening to them when I'm reading the newspaper and mumbling "uh huh." Taking the time to use eye contact and interested body language, to ask relevant questions, and to reflect or repeat the thoughts or emotions I'm hearing demonstrates to my kids that I am listening and that they and their ideas are important to me.

—Carrie L. Clarke
Stay-at-Home Parent

styles. Some of them are more useful than others, but each one serves a purpose. The six styles are judgmental, questioning, directive, empathetic, interpreting, and active. In each of the situations below Frank approaches his friends and says: "I can't believe I got a 62 on my chemistry exam. I needed an 80 to pass the course. I don't understand. I thought I did really well."

A *judgmental* style of feedback means a listener makes a judgment about both the content and the speaker. Judith, who is a judgmental listener, tells Frank: "Well, I told you that you needed to study more." This response makes Judith sound superior because she "knew it all along." It also implies that Frank failed to do what he needed to do to pass the course.

Questioning is another feedback style. The listener asks probing questions of the speaker that are not necessarily supportive questions. They sometimes have a hint of accusation in their tone. Frank's brother, Jeff, who is a questioning listener, asks, "Why didn't you study harder?" While he is inviting more conversation, he is also placing a confrontational edge on the communication. He is implying that Frank did something wrong. This leads Frank to reply defensively.

Both questioning and judgmental listening and feedback serve to put the other person down without giving any support. We consider these to be the least useful feedback styles since they typically result in hurt feelings and don't advance any goals. While Jeff's question might offer a useful approach for the next test, it also identifies Frank as failing to prepare. He might be so discouraged that he won't think he is capable of doing better next time. Try to keep these styles to a minimum. Most people do not want to hear, "I told you so."

Directive style means a listener tells the speaker what to do. Giovanni tells Frank: "Well, the first thing you need to do is go talk to the professor. Then you need to. . . ." As a directive listener, Giovanni tries to solve the problem by giving advice.

Empathetic style of feedback means a listener gives the speaker an emotional form of support. Sarah says, "Oh, Frank, I'm so sorry. You must feel awful. Is there anything I can do?" Sarah tries to comfort Frank by being empathetic.

Did you think Giovanni's and Sarah's responses were stereotypical? We intentionally chose to use a male for directive listening and a female for empathetic listening because, in general, women are more likely to be empathetic listeners while men are more likely to be directive listeners (Wood, 2011, pp. 132–133). Directive and empathetic listening can be useful depending on the needs of the speaker. If you want to be emotionally comforted, empathetic feedback is great while directive feedback makes you feel like the person isn't listening. If you want to solve the problem, directive feedback is terrific while empathetic feedback sounds condescending.

The *interpreting* style of feedback means a listener tries to offer another explanation of what happened. This style can be very useful in helping the speaker to think of other possible explanations for an event or a better analysis of the problem. Svetlana tells Frank, "Maybe the instructor made a mistake. Did you think about going in to go over the test and make sure the grade is accurate?" As an interpretive listener, Svetlana helps Frank explore other possibilities for his dilemma. This type of feedback can help you see things that you may have overlooked. This feedback style typically evokes a, "Oh! I never thought of that," response.

Active style of feedback means a listener offers supportive questions and makes it clear that he is willing to listen. The listener tries to encourage more communication, using paraphrasing to ensure understanding. There are two types of paraphrasing that can be useful. You may use a content-level paraphrase or a relationship-level paraphrase. A content paraphrase summarizes the message the other person states. The relationship paraphrase checks on the emotional state of the speaker.

> *Content paraphrase:* "Oh wow, I'm sorry, so are you saying you won't be able to graduate?"
>
> *Relationship (emotional) paraphrase:* "Oh my, you sound really upset, is there anything I can do?"

The active listener may use either or both of these styles if they are appropriate. In many situations, you may not need either. But if you do use them, you might continue with some other questions, such as, "Would you like to talk?" "Is there anything I can do?" Active listening helps the speaker emotionally process her reaction to a situation. It doesn't superimpose a plan. The active listener acts as a sounding board and allows the speaker to discover the best solution for the dilemma.

Critical Thinking

Think about the people in your life. Can you think of people who typically use the same feedback style? List them below with a brief description of your last encounter:

Judgmental: _____

Questioning: _____

Directing: _____

Empathetic: _____

Interpreting: _____

Active: _____

Looking at the six people you list above, whom do you most enjoy going to when you need to vent? Why? Whom are you likely to avoid? Why?

_____

_____

_____

How many listeners do you know who can adapt their styles and select an appropriate style effectively? Describe your last encounter.

_____

_____

_____

What type of listener are you? Are you satisfied with that style? Are you an effective listener for your friends? What could you do to make changes?

_____

_____

_____

Think of the last time a good friend came to you with a problem. Write a brief description about the situation.

_____

_____

What was the problem? _____

What listening style did you use? _____

Would another listening style have been more effective? _____

Describe a response to the problem in at least two of the listening styles.

_____

_____

_____

Implications of Styles

Communication misunderstandings occur when people don't get the feedback style they are expecting. Think about how defensive you might get if you weren't expecting the questioning or judgmental response. If you are looking for help, sympathy, or an active listener to help you out, a questioning or judgmental listener will make you feel worse or angry. At this point, communication stops or an argument begins.

If you're looking for a shoulder to cry on, and the person begins directing you instead, you may feel the person is not really listening. In this situation, you already feel emotionally down, and if the listener begins to give you directives, you may resent being told what to do. All you really wanted from a listener was some sympathy. But, some people find empathetic listeners to be extremely annoying. These communicators prefer a more directive listening approach to help them solve their problem. They want to be told what to do.

It is critical for you to begin an intrapersonal analysis of the listening style that works best for you. Begin to discover your reasons for communicating with other people and think about the responses you

Reality ✓

Felippe and Marci have been married for 10 years. When they first got married, they fell into stereotypical gender communication roles. Marci preferred an empathetic listener when she had a problem. Felippe preferred a directive listener who could help him solve his problem quickly. When listening to each other, they responded with the listening style each preferred. When Marci came home from work one night, she said, "Felippe, I can't believe how awful my day was. My supervisor assigned four more cases to my workload, my coworker Barbara took my lunch from the refrigerator, my computer crashed, and I'm so tired, I could just cry."

In his reply, Felippe used the directive listening style because he wanted to help. He said, "Well, tomorrow when you go into work, go to your boss and tell him you can only do two additional cases. Then you need to have a conversation with Barbara and let her know to keep her mitts off of your food unless she's going to pay for it. Then you need to call the IT department and have a chat about getting a new computer. And tonight, I'll do the dishes so you can get to bed at 8:00." Felippe was very proud of himself when he offered this useful advice. However, he was shocked when Marci screamed at him, "You never listen to me. I don't know why I even talk to you!!!"

Imagine the same scenario with roles reversed. If Felippe described a similar day to Marci, she would probably respond, "I'm so sorry, dear. Tomorrow will surely be a better day. Why don't you sit down, and I'll order some food." Felippe would also feel Marci is not listening to him; her comments don't do anything to solve his problem. So Felippe says, "I'm going out for a while," and he leaves the house.

Felippe and Marci solved their communication difficulties by recognizing they weren't meeting each other's communication needs. They realized they each needed something different in the listening response if their relationship was going to work. Marci explained she needed supportive statements. Felippe told her he needed directive statements. Neither Marci nor Felippe really understood why the other person was helped by a specific listening style, but because they were committed to one another, they worked on practicing the listening style their partner needed.

receive. Are you unhappy when you hear the comments and questions peers and colleagues offer you? Could you be looking for one of the listening styles just discussed rather than the one people are giving you? You should tell the people closest to you why a specific listening style works for you. If they can tailor their responses to the feedback style that best suits your needs, you will feel better about the decisions you make and you will be closer to each other in true friendship. Your family, significant other, and close friends can't support you properly if you are not clear about the responses you need during a conversation. We encourage you to think about which listening style will work for you in a given situation. Then, communicate your needs to those around you. It is important to consider feedback style when you are in a position to critique the work of other people. Critiquing classroom speeches is covered in chapter 9.

Reality ✓

Saying to your partner, "I just need to vent for a couple of minutes" gives him/her the heads up to keep their directive comments at a minimum. Also, "I need some help with a situation I'm stuck in" tells the listener to put on a directive hat. Simple comments (rather than expecting someone to read your mind) can help relationships to run more smoothly.

Communicating with Technology

To be effective in interpersonal communication, we must now be adept at ***technical communication.*** At one time, people who were not communicating face-to-face generally spoke to each other on the phone. Paralanguage gave subtle meaning to the words being used in the conversation. However, we increasingly use computers to communicate. We now have e-mail, texting, and IM as a significant channel for our interpersonal communication. Paralanguage does not exist in the written form (except through emoticons). When communicating via the computer, it is imperative to recognize the difference between communicating with your friends and communicating with business associates, professors, or other professionals.

IM is becoming a new language. People write very quickly and with numerous abbreviations. A simple "Hello Professor, how are you?" is written "how R U?" While this may be an appropriate way to communicate with friends, it is not appropriate with teachers or business associates. The specialized jargon used in IM has the potential to isolate people and also may reflect negatively on your communication skills and credibility. Using these abbreviations in the wrong situation can make you appear to be illiterate. You may think you are clever, but most business people would assume you are sloppy, too casual, and a poor speller. The tone sent with these informal messages is appropriate for friends, but not for working associates. Would you walk into a boss's office and start the conversation with "Hey, wuzzup baby?" We hope not. Just remember where you are and to whom you are speaking at all times.

When you are e-mailing family and friends, you may not bother to proofread for spelling and grammar. But with anyone who is not a member of your inner circle, you must proofread e-mail as carefully as you would a composition. When other people read your e-mail and words are misspelled, they will perceive you to be careless or, worse, incompetent. Don't forget, it is extremely easy to type your note in a word processing program that can check for spelling and grammar. You can then copy and paste it into the body of your e-mail. But don't rely on these programs exclusively. You must reread everything before you hit the send key. Although this may seem like a waste of time, you will find that written mistakes can affect a promotion opportunity or advancement in any company. And besides, you look rather silly when you respond, "I am defiantly coming to the social event" rather than "I am definitely coming to the social event."

Professional Perspective

A clear writing style and a good grasp of grammar are essential! In every day of my working career, I have found being able to express myself in a clear, concise manner to be invaluable. I would strongly suggest that anyone preparing for a career in business take the time to brush up on the elements of English grammar. There is nothing more embarrassing than writing your first memo to your brand new boss with a terrific idea you've had and getting it back with grammatical or spelling errors circled in red! Yes, this has happened, and to more than one acquaintance of mine; so I know my eccentric employer is not the only stickler out there. The reality is that people will be distracted from the content of your writing, whether it is e-mail, general correspondence, or a major report, if there are glaring errors. Whatever you write, take the time to proofread. Before you send out anything with your name attached, be sure to print it out and read it as though you were the recipient. If you know yourself to be a poor speller, invest in a good dictionary and remember that spell-check button!

—Christina DeVries
Senior Account Manager
Spotlight Payroll Inc.

Remember, nothing you write or post on the Internet for friends or business associates is private. What you write may be read by others. A private note you wrote to one person may be inadvertently forwarded to another. This happened to a friend of ours. Person A asked a question of Person B and included a negative comment about our friend.

The exchange went back and forth a couple times with the original messages still included. At some point it became necessary to ask our friend a question, and Person B forwarded the entire conversation. Our friend, in looking down through the history of the message, saw the negative remark. With forwarding, copying, and pasting electronically, this type of incident occurs frequently.

A number of people now are using blogs (Internet journals) to post their opinions. While the electronic posting has replaced a personal journal for some, it is important to remember that anyone can access the blog. If you decide to post personal comments and criticisms, a coworker, potential employer, or a boss will have access to your statements. Depending on what you have written, there could be serious repercussions. Choose wisely.

Businesses may monitor internal and external communication. Your office computer is corporately owned. It isn't your play toy. Numerous corporations have rules forbidding personal software to be loaded onto an office computer. Companies also have policies about personal e-mail while at work. Some companies electronically store all communication. When you send an e-mail to someone, it doesn't mean that person won't send your comment to others. All electronic communication can be altered. Think of the implications every typed message might have. We are not trying to paint a gloomy "Big Brother is watching over you" picture, but you should be aware of the realities of the Internet. Privacy doesn't exist. Carefully consider the content of your e-mails and to whom they are sent. Making an immature or uninformed choice can bring unexpected consequences.

Voice Mail

We are so accustomed to voice mail that we often don't think about the very different contexts in which it plays a role. If you remember two cautions, you can avoid potential problems. First, the recorded message you create for others to hear needs to be concise and articulate. You never know who will be contacting you, and the caller will judge you by the sound of your message. Second, when you are the caller leaving a message on voice mail, you need to be equally concise and provide the following information: name, time, reason for calling, phone number where you can be reached, and whether you expect to be called back. If you are hesitant, the answering machine will cut you off, and you will sound incompetent when your message is played.

Let's say you and your roommate are in your senior year of college. You are having fun and enjoying your last year of freedom before graduating. You've found a new rock group you really like. You decide to record a fun message on the answering machine with you yelling and the music blaring in the background. In addition, you recently sent resumes to potential employers. One day while you are in class, some-one from human resources (HR) in a Fortune 500 company calls the number you've listed on your resume. The person hears the message you've recorded. Before the message is even finished, the person from HR hangs up and shreds your resume.

Critical Thinking

An employer calls your phone number and hears your recorded message. What impression does your message create?

_____

_____

E-mail Addresses

E-mail addresses also communicate on an interpersonal level. Think about the e-mail names you have seen. Some people use profanity, sexual innuendo, cultural insensitivity, nationalistic overtones, or religious meanings that are easy to misinterpret and could be offensive to some receivers. Because your e-mail address is on your resume, it sends a strong nonverbal message. It is a good idea to have two e-mail addresses—one for business and another address for friends. The one you select for business should have your name in it. You may say, "Good grief, doesn't anyone have a sense of humor?" The answer is "no." One simple, inappropriate choice says volumes about your lack of sensitivity, judgment, respect, and credibility. The perception of the receiver could have consequences you never imagined when you made your choice.

CHOICES AND CONSEQUENCES

List your own personal e-mail address and those of 10 friends. What messages do they send? What are the consequences of using these addresses on a resume?

_____

_____

_____

_____

_____

The technology channels themselves are now used differently by different populations. According to Rosa Golijan (2011), e-mail usage is declining with teens and middle-aged persons in the U.S. Facebook, Twitter, and texting have replaced e-mail for those groups. For individuals over the age of 55, e-mail usage is increasing. One possible reason for mature generations using more e-mail is that former neighbors and friends have retired and moved away, and the Internet is a convenient way to keep in touch. It will be interesting to track changes in the usage of electronic channels in the future. Older adults may eventually find social networks are an attractive alternative to e-mail.

Social Networking, Blogs and Tweets

In chapter 1, we discussed intrapersonal and interpersonal communication as two of the four types of communication. Technology has blended the two into a type of communication we might call "me-ism." A person's thoughts that previously were the domain of diaries and journals are now freely shared with anyone who cares to click and read/view an individual's posting. Intimate thoughts, visuals, daily schedules, etc. are posted for total strangers (a.k.a. friends) who choose whether to comment. Comments can be ignored or responded to if the blogger/sender wishes a conversation to continue. Many individuals who use social networking as a communication vehicle are very adept at streaming words, phrases and one-liners to an unknown viewing audience. Social networking empowers many more people psychologically than would have been possible previously without the Internet. Media channels were once the province of the powerful and wealthy; the Internet has democratized access to potentially millions of followers. It will be interesting to observe how me-ism on social networking eventually influences interpersonal communication, analytical thought, and global cultures.

Critical Thinking

Social networking sites may not be as private as you think anymore. "U.S. lawyers are trying to mine the private zones of Facebook and other social-media sites for photos, comments, status updates and other tidbits that might contradict what their opponents are saying in court. And increasingly, judges in civil cases are granting access to online caches that has formerly been considered off-limits. . . . This shifting legal balance between privacy and evidence gathering reflects the broader debate that has been raging over what level of privacy, if any, citizens can expect as they put more and more personal information online. And privacy, at least on this front, seems to be losing" (Grow, 2011).

You can create blogs and Twitter accounts for organizations while you are in school. Numerous organizations need assistance developing an online identity to build a membership base, promote activities, maintain membership, and allow the public to know more about who they are. If you have the time and energy to be creative while developing today's technical business skills, there are organizations who can profit from your willingness to get involved and be an online voice for them: honorary societies, sports teams, academic departments, alumni relations, local businesses, churches, social fraternities, nonprofit groups, etc. The time you spend building an informative, visually appealing, updated blog gives you an excellent talking point during a job interview after graduation, since the majority of businesses use blogs and have a staff maintaining them 24/7. Your skills can help an organization become visible while you become more knowledgeable on how to build an appealing, successful blog. A Twitter account can be tied to the same organization for members only or remain open to non-members as well. The more time you spend building a blog and using Twitter, the more you enhance your technical skills. As technology continues to evolve and businesses rely on its possibilities, you could find yourself applying for employment as a social media manager.

Frustrations

Because technology allows channels for communication to be open constantly, there are increasing intrusions on interpersonal communication. How often have you been annoyed by a cell phone going off during a meeting or presentation, or by a person who is not paying attention because she is working on an iPhone, a BlackBerry, or checking a pager? Some people do need to be available at all times, but these people are rare. Others feel a need to be connected constantly, even at the expense of being annoying to others or tuning out the people with whom they are talking face to face.

Reality ✓

I am barely sitting down when I hear a voice from the other stall saying, "Hi! How are you?" I'm not the type to start a conversation or fraternize in men's rooms at a rest stop, but I don't know what got into me, so I answered rather sheepishly, "Not bad."

The other guy said, "So what's up with you?" What a question! At that point, I thought this was the most bizarre situation I've ever been in. I said, "I'm like you, just traveling south."

Then I heard the guy say nervously, "LISTEN!!! I'll have to call you back. There's an idiot in the next stall who keeps answering all my questions, bye!" (Adapted from an anonymous e-mail.)

Keep in mind you always communicate! Every choice with technology leads to a consequence.

Interpersonally, what message are you sending when you answer your cell phone in the middle of a conversation with another person at dinner? What message are you sending when you are more concerned with your BlackBerry than with paying attention to the people in the group around you? You need to make appropriate choices for your communication in public. Some cities have already imposed bans on cell phones and pagers in restaurants and theatres. We seem to think we are invisible when using technology in public, but we need to remember: every communication action sends a message to other people.

Reality ✓✓

Increasing use of technology cuts down on the interpersonal exchanges that can happen between two people. The ten-minute time period between classes used to be a time when teachers could chat casually with their students. Now, more and more students are plugged into iPods and other listening devices. They sit at their desks with their heads down listening to music or texting their friends rather than interacting with the teacher or other students. What might a student miss out on by making this choice?

Frustrations also occur when the sender and receiver disagree on using a particular technology to communicate an important message. For instance, in today's society, more people are using wedding websites to announce their engagements, to send invitations, to respond to invitations, to register for gifts, and to distribute photos of the event. This is an inexpensive and easy way for the happy couple to share their joy quickly. However, it breaks a long-standing social tradition of sending a printed invitation with a response card. Many people are offended by the impersonal nature of an electronic invitation. The perception is that the couple is trying to add as many people as possible to the guest list at very little cost. We have listened to just as many people voice extreme distaste over receiving an electronic invitation as we have listened to people happy to use them.

Another area where frustrations may occur is when information via technology is mass mailed rather than personally addressed. If you are changing your job or have a "life update," do you send individual e-mails to people or just one message to everyone in your address box? Sometimes the information that is mailed to one person is not in a format that seems personal to the next person. While society is accepting of the fact that people are busy, friends and colleagues may desire a more personal message from time to time to keep up the interpersonal nature of the relationship. If you rely only on mass mailings, you may find that your close friends decrease in number.

Pulling together the concepts in this chapter, try to come up with some answers for the scenarios in the Critical Thinking box. There is no right answer. It may be useful for you to share your thoughts with others in your classroom and to explore the most effective answers together.

Critical Thinking

You just started a job to make some extra money in a local store near your university. Lars, your coworker, seems to be interesting, and at first you enjoy talking to him. As the relationship builds, you notice Lars only talks about his interests and what he is doing. He never asks you for your opinion or what you think. Even when you offer an idea, he turns it into something about himself. In fact, there are times he only asks you questions so he can talk about himself. (Did you get a haircut? When the answer is no, he launches into the haircut experience he just had.) You end up being a dumping ground for him. He tells you everything, but the relationship seems more like a self-help situation than a friendship. You feel a little sorry for Lars and would like the relationship to develop differently. What can you say to Lars to let him know you would like to be included in the conversation?

_____

_____

_____

_____

_____

You start dating Kelly on a full-time basis. Gradually you begin to think about the kinds of places you are going and the activities you are attending. You begin to realize you are doing everything that Kelly wants to do and rarely doing what you want to do. You don't say anything. In fact, Kelly talks you into changing your mind any time you resist doing anything. You are the kind of person who buys into the arguments and accommodates so there is harmony in the relationship. Kelly, however, is never convinced to try the things you want to do. You go to Kelly's family events and out with Kelly's friends, but Kelly refuses to see yours. Kelly proposes to you. By this point, you feel you are in love with Kelly, but you dislike yourself for the fact you are giving up what is important to you. What should you do?

_____

_____

_____

_____

_____

Lucinda sits next to you in class. She seems to enjoy your company, and you like her as well. She begins to show up at places where you are. She meets you at the cafeteria or shows up in the library. She always has attentive nonverbal communication. She seems to like you so much she even imitates some of your mannerisms and reads the same books you do. However, every time you try to have a conversation with her, she only uses one-word answers. You realize you are sharing personal information, but she never self-discloses. She seems like a nice person, but you feel very uncomfortable with the one-sided self-disclosure. You have asked her to share more feelings and thoughts with you and she promises she will, but she never does. What should you do?

_____

_____

_____

_____

_____

Randy is an RA on your dorm floor. He never lets you finish a sentence. He always tells you exactly what you should do and how you should do it. He is a true problem solver. You don't even get a chance to explain a situation that is problematic. By the time you have just started to explain a problem, he is spouting off directions for how you should handle it. He never allows you to process information. In addition, he comes up to you the next day and asks whether you have done what he told you to do. He gets on your case immediately if you didn't. You perceive that he only cares about himself, and you don't feel he is acting as the resource person he should be as an RA. What should you say?

_____

_____

_____

_____

_____

Delia is a good friend of yours. After high school, you go in different directions. You go to college, and she gets a job in a local company. You keep in touch by e-mail for a while, but you find you have little in common as the years pass. Delia begins forwarding to you every e-mail she receives plus all of the jokes she thinks are funny. Her updates on her life are sent to a list of over 50 people. You are not interested in the little details she is including in these e-mails. Even though you still like her, you realize you've changed dramatically over the years. You are disappointed by the fact you don't get any personal e-mail from her. You are now receiving information you no longer desire at least two to three times a day. What should you say to Delia?

_____

_____

_____

_____

_____

Summary

Solid interpersonal skills are an essential ingredient for successful relationships in your personal and professional lives. It takes time to develop critical listening skills, acceptable verbal and nonverbal techniques, and to discover how to self-disclose personal thoughts with new acquaintances and to build trusting relationships. Self-disclosure at some level is the key ingredient in making every relationship work—whether with a casual acquaintance or a true friend.

As you become more comfortable with technology, it is also important to think about how technology removes warmth from the interpersonal process. How important is it to you to hear the voice of another person? See the person's face? Simply be in the presence of others to discuss important issues? Your answer to these questions helps you to focus on the definition and meaning of interpersonal communication. How you balance verbal and nonverbal communication through various channels tells other people how you feel about them.

Interpersonal skills can be improved with a little effort on your part. Each improvement in your ability to communicate with others makes you more confident as you integrate into a diverse society. In turn, your confidence and skills allow you to be perceived by others as competent.

KEY WORDS

blind area
body
closing
conversation
conversational process
conversational setup
feedback styles (judgmental, questioning, directive, empathetic, interpreting, active)
hearing

hidden area
interpersonal communication
Johari Window
listening (informational, critical, active)
open area
opening
self-disclosure
spewers
technical communication
unknown area

DISCUSSION/ACTIVITIES

1. Describe the personal information you feel is appropriate to share with someone the first time you meet them.

2. Describe the "blind area" of an acquaintance which you have never discussed with them but you are sure is true about them. Why do you believe your thoughts are correct? Why haven't you mentioned your reaction to them?

3. Describe the feedback styles you use when communicating with others. Explain.

4. Describe the "hidden areas" of people that you feel are appropriate to never discuss with anyone else.

5. Explain why some individuals are easier to engage in conversation than others.

6. Describe a situation in which you made a mistake because you were not listening critically to what another person was saying. What were the consequences of your listening error?

7. Is it easier to communicate via technology rather than with someone directly in front of you? Explain your reasoning.

8. Discuss the self-disclosure styles of two people you know. Do you prefer one acquaintance over the other because of what they share with you? Explain.

SIX

Relationship Stages and Conflict Resolution

OBJECTIVES

After reading this chapter, you should be able to:

- List the five stages in relationship development
- Identify appropriate behaviors for each stage
- Explain the concept of "I" messages and practice incorporating them into your communication
- Understand the nature of conflict
- Identify the five conflict-resolution styles and analyze their use

---

As you communicate interpersonally, you will begin to develop many relationships. There are differences between business relationships, family relationships, friendships, and significant other relationships. Information on the stages of relationships will help you to navigate your way. At the end of the chapter we also talk about conflict resolution. Being able to resolve conflict effectively is one of the best ways to preserve the relationships you are building.

Stages of Relationships

Interpersonal communication becomes more complex as relationships mature. Family, colleagues, close friends, and significant others depend on competent communication to sustain and/or increase the closeness of the relationship. Some people allow the daily routine of life to alter their connection to others. They may concentrate on their careers and assume that relationships can wait until they have more time. Or, they may move and spend more time making new friends than communicating with those left behind. Physical distance is not an excuse to end communication with people who matter to you. Emotional ties with your friends can continue, but there must be a personal willingness on your part to show others they mean something to you. Keep in touch with people who make a difference in your life.

Specific difficulties occur when you communicate via a technology channel rather than face-to-face meetings. These difficulties can be overcome, however, if you are truly committed to a friend. How many people have you let drift away who had been close friends at one time? How many people have allowed you to drift away? These decisions can trouble you in the years ahead, so start to think now about the complex nature of interpersonal communication. Try to make appropriate decisions about relationships that really matter to you. U.S. culture values loyalty and credibility. Whenever you make a decision to call someone a friend, you should be committed to the relationship. Use words wisely as you build relationships. If you don't want to be hurt or disappointed by another person, be sensitive to any behavior on your part that might hurt others.

All of you have been involved in friendships, and some of you have been in romantic relationships. The definition of friendship is rapidly changing. We used to reserve that term for people who were very close to us and who would support us. Now with the advent of social networking sites, we use the term friend to mean even the most casual of acquaintances. As we progress through the rest of this chapter, we are referring to people who are truly a part of your life, not just a casual acquaintance.

As you analyze the relationships that are strong and those that have failed in your own life, you may not be aware there are various behavioral stages throughout a relationship. This lack of awareness makes it difficult for you to realize what is going on in a relationship, how to progress, or how to effectively end one. There are many models for **relationship stages,** but we think Mark Knapp and Anita Vangelisti (2009) provide the most meaningful one for college students.

- Contact
- Involvement
- Intimacy
- Deterioration
- Repair or Dissolution

Contact

Stage one is the ***contact stage.*** This is where you meet someone for the first time. You usually decide right away whether a person meets your criteria for someone you would want to get to know better. Sometimes we miss good potential relationships because our initial perception of another person dissuades us from pursuing a conversation. If we are in a hurry, we might not take the time necessary to learn if we have correctly assessed whether someone would be likely to develop into a friend. Or we could be too judgmental about artifacts, deciding someone isn't wearing the right clothes or driving the right car.

A new bonus of social networking is that you can peruse contact with a new, potential friend before ever making contact. You may be able to see a lot of information about another person that leads you to a conclusion to pursue a relationship or run in another direction. Remember that sometimes we draw the wrong conclusion from limited information. If you get to know a person, you may be able to overlook their conflicting political or religious affiliation. But knowing that information up front may convince you to never approach the person.

Once you see the other person and decide you'd like to communicate, a conversation ensues. We make a lot of decisions based on an initial conversation. If you haven't learned the conversational skills detailed in the previous chapter, you may have a hard time building relationships.

CHOICES AND CONSEQUENCES

Describe someone you met, and you immediately decided the two of you weren't on the same wavelength. Why did you make this decision? Were there any consequences?

_____

_____

_____

Involvement

Stage two is called **_involvement._** In this stage, we continue to get to know another person. We may start to see or contact him or her on a regular basis. We start to do some initial self-disclosure about our likes and dislikes, our hobbies, and our backgrounds. Remember our discussion about appropriate self-disclosure during this phase. It is important to move at a reciprocal rate. We may also experiment a little in this stage to see how the other person reacts to certain behaviors. For instance, we may not call when we say we will, or we may show up late to an event or try a public display of affection to see how the other person reacts. We call this testing the relationship.

The concept of involvement is changing with the online world of social networking, blogs, and journals. Individuals are building personal relationships without being in the physical presence of others. They become attracted to numerous personalities based on their writing, posted pictures, and written responses to the communicator's personal problems and thoughts. Eventually, some communicators meet with one another. It is at this point that individuals begin to deal with the traditional issues of relationships and conflict. A computer gives an individual the opportunity to respond to someone's questions/thoughts with time to think of the proper words to use to keep an online relationship going. However, what's missing in the online relationship is paralanguage and nonverbal cues during the response. A face-to-face meeting with someone flushes out the missing pieces of social interaction.

Technology has made participating in the involvement stage much easier. We can text someone a quick note to let them know we are thinking about them. We can post a public announcement on social networking about our new friend—confirming to others that we are hanging out with our new gal/guy. We might write notes to them to share information about our likes and dislikes. As we become closer through the self-disclosure process, we begin to move forward to the next phase.

CHOICES AND CONSEQUENCES

Describe the type of "testing" you have done in interpersonal relationships. Why did you try out this behavior?

_____

_____

_____

Were there any consequences to this choice?

_____

_____

_____

Intimacy

Stage three is **intimacy.** This can be either romantic intimacy or friendship intimacy. People commit to each other in different ways depending on their circumstances. Many people model themselves on the family relationships with which they are familiar. Some people commit through verbal exchange, expressing thoughts about what the other person means to them. Others commit by doing things for the other person. This is another area where males and females often misunderstand one another. In gender theory, the research demonstrates that the majority of females generally feel closer when they talk about a relationship, whereas males demonstrate closeness by doing things for others (Wood, 2011, p. 219). For example, Tom and Patricia are friends. Tom checks Patricia's car on a regular basis to make sure her tires are safe and her oil level is fine to show he cares about her. Patricia doesn't really notice his actions. She wants to talk about their feelings for each other. Without understanding the communication rules the other person is using, they may totally misunderstand each other. Their friendship could easily fall apart rather than grow and develop.

In addition to the commitment you make privately to one another in this stage, you may also do it publicly. You might update your relationship status on social networking. You might wear rings to signify your devotion to one another. You might get married. You might introduce your partner as a dear friend or significant other. Once again, our background plays a major role in our communication style. Some people float easily into the intimacy stage. These individuals become intimate with a variety of people in a very short time. Other individuals will avoid intimacy at all costs and leave the relationship when the first talk of commitment is mentioned.

Critical Thinking

Describe a relationship where you had misunderstandings about the intimacy stage based on gender differences.

_____

_____

_____

_____

Would an online relationship with someone you consider a close confidant change if they became your roommate for a year? In what way?

_____

_____

_____

_____

Professional Perspective

The intimacy stage of interpersonal relationships varies greatly by culture. Growing up in a small town, I'm accustomed to the philosophy of helping out your "neighbor in need." My first week in Korea, I was overjoyed to find that one of my coworkers was eager to give me a ride to and from work every night. Not only did this save me money every week, but I had the opportunity to get to know one of my Korean coworkers better. However, after a few weeks, our mutual ride to and from work turned into the talk of the office. I had students leaving anonymous notes on my desk asking if I was "interested" in Seen Jyon Jee.

A couple of weeks later, I was approached by another Korean teacher, asking me if they could join us on a date. I was confused, thinking that our ride together to and from work was merely a mutual traffic pattern. Only later did I realize that I was beginning to commit to a serious relationship. I discovered that in Korea, men approach women, and then pursue them, if they feel that the woman has something to offer them.

Unknown to me, I was participating in a mating ritual, without my knowledge. Whereas I thought I was simply accepting a ride, I was actually committing to a long-term relationship!

—Raymond Weaver
New Programs Educator, Cornell Cooperative Extension, Cornell University
Former Secondary English Teacher in Ilsan, South Korea

Deterioration

Stage four is ***deterioration.*** It is important to understand that most people try not to enter this stage if they truly care about the other person. However, it takes two people to sustain a relationship, and if one gives up, it is next to impossible to save the relationship even if the other partner wants to save it. However, it is possible to repair a relationship and move back to the intimacy stage if partners are willing to make adjustments. All relationships will fluctuate through the stages at various times. There are two types of deterioration: intrapersonal dissatisfaction and interpersonal dissatisfaction.

Intrapersonal dissatisfaction occurs whenever we feel dissatisfied with a relationship. This can happen for a variety of reasons. For example, one of your friends tells you their significant other is planning a surprise trip for them. Suddenly, you feel your significant other should do the same thing for you even though surprises have never been a part of your relationship. You begin to feel some dissatisfaction with your partner. You must try to determine if your dissatisfaction is real or imaginary. Sometimes we fall into the "grass is greener" syndrome when we look at other people's relationships or fantasize about others with whom we might have been involved.

Interpersonal deterioration occurs when personal dissatisfactions affect both parties. Partners make decisions to isolate or distance themselves. Little habits or quirks that we previously overlooked sud-

---

Critical Thinking

Describe a time when you felt disappointed in a relationship of your own after hearing about someone else's relationship.

_____

_____

_____

_____

---

denly become annoying. Comparisons with other people, usually reflecting negatively on the partner, become more frequent. Conflict situations become more numerous. It is important to remember that even at this stage of deterioration, if there is commitment from both individuals to save the relationship, they can repair it.

Professional Perspective

Technology has greatly changed the way we experience our relationships. Social networking sites, like Facebook, and online dating sites have increased the opportunities to meet new people. In fact, before two people meet face-to-face, they can get to know each other by viewing prepared profiles, viewing photos, and having conversations via e-mail, text messages, instant messaging, and Skype. Once, I had a student who described being attracted to a classmate, but he was afraid to approach her face-to-face. Trying to avoid potential embarrassment and rejection, he added her as a friend on Facebook to learn more about her and he pursued her through Facebook posts, e-mail, and chat. At the time he told me this story, he and his Facebook friend had been dating for a year! Certainly, technology allowed my student the chance to meet and communicate with someone he liked in way that was more comfortable and less threatening.

Once in a relationship, a quick text, e-mail, or Facebook post of "i <3 u" may be used to share affection with a romantic partner who is close or at a great distance. Moreover, a click of one's Relationship Status on Facebook to "In a Relationship" can let the world know that two people are committed in a relationship. However, making a relationship "Facebook Official" (publicly and virtually known) may cause difficulties for the relationship. For example, I have had students who have tried to avoid defining a relationship, but run into problems when the person they are dating changes their relationship status without asking them. Facebook takes the relationship into a public arena and, if the relationship ends, it takes the relationship dissolution into the public arena as well. One's friends can instantly know if the relationship has ended and are provided the opportunity to "like" and comment on the breakup. A student told me once, "I learned from Facebook that I had been dumped," showing that signing into one's Facebook account may be more informational than one would expect.

Although technology can make it easier to experience the stages of relationships, we have to be prepared to take the relationship "public." The best advice: Before you make a relationship "Facebook Official" or before one changes their relationship status from "In a Relationship" to "Single," the two individuals should have a good, old-fashioned, face-to-face conversation about the relationship!

—Dr. Alysa Lucas
Assistant Professor
Mansfield University

Repair or Dissolution

Following stage four, there are two options: ***repair*** or ***dissolution***. If you choose to move to the repair stage, then you have intrapersonal or interpersonal repair options. For example, Deidre and Arkiem have been married for a year. When Deidre was growing up, part of her family life involved playing computer games every Friday night as a family competition. She always felt this activity provided a bond within the family, and she always assumed she would carry this tradition into her own marriage. Arkiem, however, dislikes games and did not enjoy playing them when he was young. Deidre began to feel dissatisfied, missing what she perceives as an opportunity for bonding. If she wanted to repair her own dissatisfaction, she could do it either intrapersonally or interpersonally. Intrapersonally, she could give up the activity completely. She could convince herself that playing games is not an important activity for their relationship. She could decide that her need for games was too trivial to risk possible damage to her relationship with Arkiem. In this case, the relationship would move back to the intimacy stage. You'll notice the parallel here to the accommodating or consensus style of conflict resolution discussed later in the chapter. The same rules apply. If you are going to do intrapersonal repair and adjust your own expectations, it is imperative that you truly feel that way. Otherwise, your decision may come back to haunt you.

Critical Thinking

Describe a relationship where you did intrapersonal repair. Was it effective? How do you now feel about the decision you made?

_____

_____

_____

_____

Another option would be for Deidre to try some interpersonal repair. She might explain to Arkiem how important game playing is to her. She could try to get him to understand it isn't just a game—it's an activity that makes her feel very close to the important people in her life. She might ask him if there was some way he could try to incorporate this activity into their relationship on a semi-regular basis. They might negotiate which games are acceptable and how often they would play them. In this case, both people are working to resolve the problem.

There might be another solution too (compromise). Maybe they could invite some friends over on the weekend who enjoyed game playing. Arkiem could then hang out with the group while others did the actual game playing. There are always creative solutions (choices).

If you don't choose to repair the relationship, you have two options: (1) remain in an unfulfilling, dysfunctional relationship or (2) dissolve it. This is the moment in a relationship where you move away from each other physically and emotionally. Dissolution should be a conscious choice. First, be honest with yourself; decide if you truly feel you no longer want to be in a relationship with someone. Then, you need to be honest with the other person so he or she knows there is no possibility of repair. Be sure to use the appropriate channel for this communication. Many people choose the option of becoming antagonistic, hoping the other person will do the dirty work of breaking off the relationship. As an effective communicator, you should always take responsibility for your feelings and act appropriately.

CHOICES AND CONSEQUENCES

Describe the choices you made to end an interpersonal relationship. What were the consequences?

_____

_____

_____

_____

What would you do differently now?

_____

_____

_____

_____

"I" Messages

As we communicate with other people through the stages of relationships, it is too easy to use accusatory statements. Because many people are not comfortable talking about their own needs, they sometimes resort to the use of comments that attack or put down other people. For example, after three years of marriage, Nina tells Perry, "You never tell me you love me." Perry is stunned because he knows he has said those words many times. He feels he needs to defend himself, and quickly says, "I just told you that yesterday!" Now an argument begins. Nina would have been more effective if she had phrased her initial comment to highlight her personal communication needs.

"I" messages are designed to enable communicators to embrace their responsibility in the exchange and to state their personal needs clearly in a nonaccusatory manner rather than to accuse someone else of wrongdoing. This reaction only escalates conflict and sends relationships into a death spiral. "I" messages can be valuable in any of the stages of relationships, and you can easily see how they could help de-escalate the types of conflict we talked about in the beginning of the chapter. Imagine that one of the students in your classroom comes to class late every day. The professor is obviously annoyed at this behavior. Instead of saying, "What is your problem?" or "You need to get to class on time" (both create negative feelings and can escalate the conflict), an "I" message indicates what the person wants to have happen by explaining why it is important to them. In this example, the teacher can say, "I need you to arrive on time, because when a student comes in late, it disrupts me and the class." The student should feel less defensive toward this statement. The teacher is simply articulating a need and an explanation for it, and the student can say, "Tough, I'm not doing it," or "Sure, no problem," or "I'm sorry, but the teacher in my last class constantly runs overtime. What can we do about this?"

In business it may be helpful to tell your colleagues what your needs are. If you need to have information 24 hours ahead of time to do a good job, then let people know your timetable. If you don't clearly describe your schedule, you could be tempted to yell at someone, "You always wait until the last minute!" Such a remark could immediately ignite a conflict. The statement is accusatory. The only thing you really want your colleagues to do is to give you enough lead time to allow you to do a good job. What would be the most effective means of stating that goal? Remember to include a reasonable explanation for what you need.

At home, maybe you feel overwhelmed with the housework, which always seems to fall to you. Rather than yell at family members, "You never help around the house!" try an "I" statement. "I really need someone else to do the dishes this week so that I can study for finals."

While "I" messages can definitely de-escalate conflicts, not everyone feels comfortable with them. For some people it is difficult or downright painful to phrase communication this way. However, if you work on eliminating accusatory language and developing this skill, you may find yourself in fewer argumentative situations.

As a word of caution, if you have so many needs that you are constantly bombarding others with them, you will soon find yourself iso-

Convert the following examples to "I" messages:

You always leave your clothes all over the room. (to a roommate) _____

_____

You always use my things without asking. (to a roommate) _____

_____

You graded this assignment unfairly. (to a professor) _____

_____

Note: Changing the first sentence to "I feel that you always leave your clothes laying around" is not an "I" message! It's still an accusation.

---

lated from the interpersonal relationships you were trying to build. No one wants to be around someone they think is too needy (unless of course they want to be needed). Think of the person who verbalizes, "I need you to tell me you love me at least 3 times a day, and I need you to spend all of your spare time with me, and I need you to make me feel like I'm the most special person in the world." How would anyone be able to do all of that? They can't. And if you have that many needs, you may need to do some serious self-assessment.

But if there is something simple that your partner could easily implement that would help strengthen the relationship, then an "I" statement is the way to go. "You don't make me feel special" is a far different statement from "I'd love it if we could make it a priority to have a date night once a week." If something is really bothering you in a long-term, committed relationship, it is probably useful to explore the issue with your partner using "I" messages.

Obviously, not everyone can meet all of your needs, even if you use "I" messages. You occasionally have to accept the way other people work and think. If you can't accept them, then you may want to reevaluate the relationship. The purpose of an "I" message is to avoid an escalated conflict as you explore communication options in the varying stages of interpersonal relationships.

Don't forget though, all relationships involve compromise and giving and taking. You cannot always be the one demanding change. We need to accept others for who they are and determine whether we can make a relationship work given those constraints. A famous television character once made a humorous statement about hating relationships. She said that they were all about compromise, and after a while the men she was dating expected her to do it too. It was a great laugh line implying that she was not the compromising type. But relationships need both parties to work on each stage in order to provide a fulfilling outcome for both people.

There are many ways to incorporate "I" messages into your speaking style. Keep in mind the key concept is to identify your feelings or needs without accusing the other person of doing something wrong. Go back to the example at the beginning of this section. What are some other ways that Nina might express her feelings as "I" messages? How might Perry respond with "I" messages?

_____

_____

_____

_____

_____

Conflict and Conflict-Resolution Styles

Interpersonal communication is comprised of the elements we discussed in the previous chapter. However, interpersonal communication doesn't always go smoothly even when you are skilled. When you are listening, making language choices, self-disclosing, or engaging in conversation, conflict can often surface unexpectedly. Understanding the nature of conflict and how it affects interpersonal relationships will help you to be successful in your personal and business life.

Conflict occurs any time there is a disagreement between two or more people. While many people think conflict is undesirable, it is actually essential to any growing relationship. What is important is how you resolve the conflict that occurs. Resolving conflict can be ineffective or effective. In interpersonal communication, ineffective conflict resolution involves yelling and screaming, manipulating, issuing ultimatums, silence, or refusal to discuss issues. These strategies leave people feeling angry, used, scared, and/or frustrated. Do you know a parent who resolves conflict in the home by yelling ultimatums? Have you experienced a person who claims to have no opinion about anything? Has a significant other ever refused to discuss an important issue?

Effective conflict resolution employs a variety of styles that we discussed above, including "I" messages. Spirited discussion, active inquiry, effective listening skills, critical thinking, and problem solving are all components in effective conflict resolution. If two people care about each other, they want to find a solution to the disagreement without creating animosity in the relationship. If you are afraid of conflict, chances are that the outcomes of disagreements you have already faced were negative and uncomfortable. People who have engaged in effective conflict resolution tend to enjoy working out differences and coming to an acceptable resolution. A healthy working relationship between two people must include an environment where both participants feel they can share opinions and participate in resolving disagreement. Both people need to feel that they will be heard and that both parties will share equally in the resolution, rather than one person winning and the other person feeling ignored.

The potential for conflict exists everywhere in daily communication, from small choices like how to clean your apartment or where to eat dinner to larger decisions like whether to spend thousands of dollars on a car or house. You will encounter conflict in daily life. So will you employ the skills to resolve conflict effectively? Or will you use ineffective strategies? All conflicts, once they are recognized, can escalate or de-escalate. When we use ineffective strategies, we cause escalation. For example, if you mouth off to a parent, superior, or sometimes a partner, you may escalate a conflict tenfold. What other choices do you have? Think carefully about how to respond to someone. If you choose the right words and tone, you can de-escalate a conflict immediately.

TRY IT!

Describe an instance where someone you know resolved conflict ineffectively. What was your reaction?

_____

_____

_____

_____

_____

_____

_____

_____

_____

In their classic work on ***conflict-resolution styles,*** Ralph Kilmann and Kenneth Thomas (1977) identify five different styles and suggest you should have all five styles in your repertoire so you can select the most appropriate resolution style for any given disagreement.

- Competing

- Avoiding

- Accommodating

- Compromising

- Collaborating

You should become familiar with each style and use the one that will be most effective in a given interaction. Most of us tend to use the style with which we are most comfortable rather than selecting the style that best enables us to handle specific disagreements. The most effective communicators are able to apply all of the five styles depending on the situation. Learn to assess the needs of all parties, so you can select the style most likely to result in everyone having a positive experience.

Critical Thinking

After reading the following sections, think about various couples or friends you know. What are their conflict-resolution styles?

1. Couple #1 _____

2. Couple #2 _____

3. Couple #3 _____

Competing Style

When it is important to "win" the conflict at all costs, the ***competing style*** is appropriate. This style is effective when you truly believe in something or in a crisis situation where the conflict must be resolved immediately. One aspect of this style is a refusal to listen to the arguments of others; the goal is to prevail, not to share decision making. For example, when a 5-year-old says he doesn't want a coat and the temperature is 12 degrees outside, some parents say, "You'll do it because I'm the parent, and I said so!" This style is, however, ineffective in most interpersonal relationships. Most people do not want to be dominated, and competitive responses close the door to further discussion. A competitor does not listen to others and is not concerned with their thoughts or needs. Even children absorb this message when parents always use the competing style.

What happens when you have a friend or partner who uses the competitive style all the time? Are you willing to be in a relationship with someone who always has to win or be right? Sometimes in interpersonal relationships, the competitive style can turn into the subcategory of bullying. ***Bullying*** occurs when a person must be right no matter what, and they railroad you into doing or believing as they do. You may go along with the bully or end the relationship.

If someone has told you to "choose your battles," they might be indicating that you are unreasonably aggressive. Monitor your behavior to assess whether you could be perceived as someone who has to win every argument. The competing style works depending on the situation (in the courtroom or in debates, for example) and the parties involved. If two people are naturally assertive, they can enjoy a spirited discussion of an issue and competing to win. They relish the verbal sparring and appreciate good arguments supported with evidence.

Professional Perspective

As a police officer, conflict resolution is a constant challenge. My communication skills, verbal and nonverbal, are very important tools in facing a variety of situations. Responding to a domestic violence call requires instant decision making to restore order and to get both parties listening and talking to each other again. Separation of the arguing parties is the first priority, and then problem-solving discussions begin. This scenario assumes the police arrived during the verbal argument stage.

The two most important skills to possess in resolving conflict are patience and an outsider's eye. Patience gives you the ability to understand what other people are saying and to respond to them in a calm, thoughtful manner. And, the outsider's eye gives you perspective to assess the needs and goals of people in conflict so you can present reasonable options for conflict resolution.

My job is to protect and serve the community. Conflict is part of the interpersonal process I am expected to resolve. I think with patience and an outsider's eye before I speak. Try to develop these critical skills.

—David P. Strus
Law Enforcement Officer
Nutley, New Jersey

Avoiding Style

When people walk away from conflict, they are using an ***avoiding style.*** When a heated argument begins, some people's reaction is to leave; they physically remove themselves from the situation. This style is useful whenever there is any threat of physical or verbal abuse—either to you or from you. Unless abuse is an issue, the avoidance style is one of the least useful styles because nothing is resolved. One person leaves, but the problem remains.

There are two subsets of avoidance. Someone might ***withdraw*** from a conflict for one of two reasons: (1) He or she has no opinion on the topic or no vital interest in the outcome; there is no reason to engage in the conflict. (2) The person is truly afraid of conflict. If he or she can't handle the negative emotions they feel when people start raising their voices and arguing, withdrawal is a means to avoid those uncomfortable feelings. The second subset of avoidance is **delaying.** Delaying happens when someone is too upset to continue with the conflict at that moment. Whenever you feel that you might say or do something that you'll regret later, it may be best to delay the conflict until you calm down and can express yourself appropriately. In this case, it is best to let your partner or friend know what is going on. Saying something like, "I need to talk about this tomorrow," or "I'll come back in an hour to discuss it," lets the other person know that you aren't simply walking out.

Accommodating Style

When people give in to someone else to promote harmony in the relationship, they are using an **accommodating style.** This occurs if people are afraid of conflict, afraid to voice an opinion, or are so easygoing that they do not have a strong opinion one way or the other. However, if you have an opinion, you should not use this style. People who repress their own opinions in relationships may become hostile or depressed. Sometimes they even play the martyr role, which can be annoying to others.

If Maureen asks Erik where he wants to go for dinner and he says he doesn't care, he should not then reply "Oh I hate that place" after she picks the diner in town. When you have an opinion, learn to articulate your position. For example, Erik could have said, "Let's go anywhere except the diner." If Erik has a list of places he dislikes, then he should not imply that he is willing to let Maureen choose. The accommodating style is useful only if someone does not have an opinion and is willing to do what the other person wants to do without question or comment.

Compromising Style

When both people give in slightly, they are using a **compromising style.** Let's say you and your friend want to go out to dinner together. Your friend craves Kentucky Fried Chicken, but you crave a Big Mac. Neither of you is willing to budge. As a compromise solution, you might go to a local diner where your friend could get a three-piece chicken dinner, and you could order a huge hamburger. In this case, neither of you is getting what you really want, but you are both getting a little of what you want. A compromise can work well in some situations where there is no other resolution, but in this example, both individuals would probably feel cheated.

Collaborating Style

When people work through the problem-solving process to come to the best solution for each of them, they are engaging in a ***collaborating style.*** The collaborating style mirrors a problem-solving model called the standard agenda (Young, Wood, Phillips, & Pedersen, 2007) that we cover in chapter 13. By slightly changing the terminology of that model and applying it to conflict resolution, we get a six-step collaboration process:

1. *Define the problem.* In this step each party needs to identify that there is indeed a problem requiring attention.

2. *Explore the facts.* Each party identifies their needs. Even more importantly, they must listen carefully to learn the needs of the other party. If you cannot get through this step, collaboration cannot take place. Both parties must self-disclose honestly and completely.

3. *Brainstorm for possible solutions.* In this phase, people generate a list of solutions off the top of their heads—as many as possible without stopping to analyze.

4. *Set criteria to determine the best solution.* Generating a list of what satisfies each person helps to determine the best solution. The first criterion should always be, "Any solution must be acceptable to both of us." (There is more in-depth discussion of this concept in chapter 13.)

5. *Evaluate and select a solution.* Here each solution is evaluated against the list of criteria to determine which solution might work best.

6. *Finally, test the solution to see whether it will work.* Put the solution into action and see if it is effective.

Collaboration is very effective when each person needs to feel involved in resolving an issue. It does, however, take more time and communication than the other conflict-resolution styles. See the Reality Check box on the following page for an example of collaboration.

Reality

We know many married couples end up fighting about the little things in daily life.

For example, Shawn and Brenda have been married for five years. One of their daily fights occurs over the cap on the toothpaste. Brenda works as an advertising executive and is on a tremendously busy schedule. She leaves the cap off. Shawn is a stay-at-home dad who takes care of the kids and the house. He prefers the cap on. They recognize the toothpaste is a constant source of discussion.

In a true collaboration, they would:

(1) **Define the Problem.** "Hey honey, we have a problem with this toothpaste cap, can we talk?" "Sure, I agree."

(2) **Explore the Facts.** What is the issue over which they are having conflict? As they talk about it, Shawn discovers Brenda feels extremely stressed every morning trying to leave the house on time. She feels that every five seconds saved helps her to relax. She hates screwing the cap back onto the tube. Brenda discovers that since Shawn is responsible for cleaning the sinks, he hates having dripping toothpaste stuck on the sink like cement. He is also concerned about the germs associated with having opened toothpaste so close to a flushing toilet. He's heard that germs can travel six feet when a toilet is flushed. He feels the opened toothpaste could be a health issue for the kids. Once they hear each other's concerns, they have a better understanding of why they can't simply accommodate each other on this issue. They don't have to agree with each other (Shawn still thinks it is stupid that Brenda thinks this is a time-consuming effort), but at least the communication helps them understand each other's perspective.

(3) **Brainstorm Possible Solutions.** Shawn and Brenda brainstorm: (a) They could get separate toothpastes; (b) They could coordinate their schedules so that Brenda brushes her teeth then hands off the toothpaste to Shawn who would replace the cap when he finished brushing his teeth; (c) They could get the pump toothpaste so that no cap existed; (d) They could get a flip-top cap; or (e) They could remodel the bathroom and have separate sinks.

(4) **Set Criteria to Determine the Best Solution.** Shawn and Brenda establish the following criteria in order of importance:

1. Any solution must be acceptable to both of us.
2. Any solution must minimize the mess and health hazards.
3. Any solution must accommodate Brenda's schedule.
4. Any solution must be affordable.

(5) **Evaluate and Select a Solution.** Shawn and Brenda evaluate each solution against their criteria. Getting separate toothpaste tubes is acceptable to both; however, it wouldn't minimize the mess and health hazards. This solution does meet criteria 3 and 4. Coordinating when they brush their teeth is such a hassle that it doesn't really meet criterion 1, and it might slow Brenda down in the morning if she has to wait until Shawn is available. But, it does meet criteria 2 and 4. Getting the pump toothpaste meets criteria 1, 2, and 3. They are on a tight budget, however, and the pump toothpaste is very expensive. The flip-top toothpaste doesn't cost a lot and will meet criteria 1 and 3. It still gets a little messy, but not as bad as the regular tube, which is left open. Remodeling the bathroom is so far beyond their budget that it cannot even be considered even though it would meet the other three criteria.

	Separate	Hand off	Pump	Flip top	Remodel
Acceptable	Yes	No	Yes	Yes	Yes
Mess/Hazard	No	Yes	Yes	Yes	Yes
Accommodate	Yes	No	Yes	Yes	Yes
Affordable	Yes	Yes	No	Yes	NO!!!!!!

They determine that the flip-top toothpaste is the best solution at this point. Even though it costs a little more, it meets the other three criteria better than any of their other solutions.

(6) **Test the Solution.** Finally, they try it to determine if it will work.

Interacting with People Who Use Different Conflict Styles

Think about the number of people who must try to resolve conflicts with one another. How will they get along? There is no simple answer. Sometimes, two competitors will hate each other because no one can "win" the argument. We know two competitors, however, who get along well because they love to argue. In fact, this couple has had four-hour discussions on the following topic: "If you had to give up cake or ice cream for the rest of your life, which would it be?" Integral to their discussion was whether ice-cream cake is defined as a cake or ice cream because that would influence their decision. To most of us, this kind of discussion is unimaginable. But this couple really enjoys these discussions.

Putting a competitor in a relationship with an avoider may sound promising as a way to solve problems, but in reality it isn't. Think about people you know who use the competitive conflict-resolution style. How do they react when someone walks away from them? Most of them probably demand as loudly as possible, "DON'T YOU WALK AWAY FROM ME!"

ETHICAL CONSIDERATIONS

You told something to your significant other in confidence, asking them to never tell another person. You find out later that they told someone. What conflict-resolution style will you use to resolve this?

_____

_____

_____

_____

_____

Two accommodators would get nowhere—"Where do you want to eat?" "I don't care. Where do you want to go?" "I don't care." These people will starve to death before they resolve their conflict. They are also comical to everyone who overhears their apathetic exchanges. Can you think of other examples?

Reasons for Styles

It is important for you to think about your own style. Are you happy with it? Do you feel confident in your own conflict-resolution skills or would you like to change? Anyone can learn these styles and use them, if they want to. And in fact, the best communicators are the ones who can use each of the styles in the correct situation. But if you currently rely on one style, you need to think a little about why you use that style. Most traditional-age college students have spent the last 20 years developing their styles through interactions with their families and friends. Those of you who are nontraditional students have spent even more time developing your style in many contexts—in business and with families and friends.

If your usual style is to accommodate others, ask yourself whether you are doing this because you honestly don't have an opinion, you are very easygoing, or you were conditioned to use that style because that was how your family approached conflict. Children who grow up with authoritarian, alcoholic, drug-addicted, or verbally abusive parents learn very quickly to be accommodators so they can stay out of harm's way. You can work to change your style or to incorporate elements from other styles once you understand the reasons for your behavior.

Chances are if you are a competitor, you grew up in a family where arguments and discussions were openly encouraged. You were allowed to speak your mind, and sometimes you were encouraged to do so. Think back to the discussion about the communication process—it is essential for you to understand the other person's circumstances in interpersonal communication as well as your own. Let's say Nicole and Tiffany are good friends at school. Nicole grew up in an abusive family. Tiffany did not. When Tiffany wants to talk through a disagreement, Nicole just gives in to her. Tiffany perceives Nicole as spineless with no opinion. With Tiffany's background, these characteristics are not desirable. Nicole, on the other hand, is reminded of her domineering mother whenever Tiffany raises her voice and gets excited during a good discussion.

Once these friends can talk about their circumstances (for example, their backgrounds), each of them should begin to alter their communication style to keep the relationship going. If they do not, the relationship may gradually fall apart. Even if Nicole and Tiffany don't change their styles, their discussions will illuminate their differences and allow a greater understanding of each other's behavior.

Effective use of the five styles of conflict resolution will help you to smooth over rifts in interpersonal relationships. Since no style is appropriate in all situations, building your skills is necessary. You should practice using styles in different situations. Having the knowledge and adaptability to use the appropriate style in each interpersonal situation helps you to become an effective communicator.

Even if you learn to use all of these styles effectively, it is important to remember there are some conflicts that can never be resolved completely. Two friends may decide that certain topics are "off-limits" and yet remain friends. Their taboo topics are never raised when they are together, and they get along fine. Or, the friends may decide the disagreements are too important to suppress, and they may end the relationship.

Professional Perspective

After learning about the five conflict-resolution styles in college, I thought my conflicts could always be resolved. I never imagined that I would run into a real-life problem that was simply not resolvable.

After graduating college, I finally met the man that I wanted to marry. Everything in our relationship was fine, however, some members of my family didn't think so. They didn't accept the fact that my future husband and I were different races. My dad especially had the idea that interracial marriages were wrong. I did my best to sit down and talk to my family about where I was coming from, but nothing was ever resolved. There were multiple times that I thought I had gotten my point across, just to find out that my dad had another point to strike against what I had said. My father refused to attend the wedding.

My husband and I waited over a year and a half hoping that my dad, and some other family members, would come around, but they never did. On my wedding day I walked myself down the aisle, had the most picture-perfect day of my life, and realized that not all conflicts are able to be resolved. My mother was there for my support and I danced with my grandfather at the reception when traditionally most women dance with their dad. Although I was missing a few members of my family, I didn't focus on that for one second that day. Sometimes you just have to make your decisions and understand that everybody will not always come to an agreement.

My father and I still talk; however, he is still holding to his claim that he doesn't "accept" our marriage. Maybe one day he will change his mind, but until then, we all live our lives through the decisions that we have made and adjust to respect what others believe is right.

—Mandy Aikens
NCAA Compliance Coordinator & Head Softball Coach
Nyack College

[As a heartening side note, years after Mandy wrote this and after the birth of her first child, her father decided to alter his thoughts, and they now have a relationship again.]

Summary

Relationships are an essential part of social existence. Developing relationships and maintaining them are personal challenges for every communicator. If you find people who are worth knowing, the effort of maintaining good communication can enrich your life in many ways. It is important to know that relationships normally fluctuate through stages. There are good times and bad times. But, effective communication keeps a relationship healthy and successful. Set your own limits on how much you are willing to adapt to the needs of others and make your relationship decisions based on that answer. Treat other people the way you want to be treated in a relationship. You face yourself in a mirror every morning; make sure you honestly like what you see.

KEY WORDS

accommodating style
avoiding style
bullying
collaborating style
competing style
compromising style
conflict
conflict resolution style
contact stage

delaying
deterioration stage
dissolution stage
"I" messages
intimacy stage
involvement stage
relationship stages
repair stage
withdrawing

DISCUSSION/ACTIVITIES

1. Discuss a time when you accommodated the actions or directions of another person. Why was the accommodation style appropriate? If the same situation presented itself now, would you still accommodate the other person?

2. In what situations do you feel comfortable competing with others? Explain.

3. Have you allowed important acquaintances to drift away from you as you moved to a new location? Have you ever regretted losing touch with that person?

4. Have you ever been involved in an organization or club you now regret joining? What did you learn from this experience?

5. Discuss people and situations you try to avoid. Why are you uncomfortable in these situations? Do you think you'll face similar situations in the future and not be able to walk away from them?

6. Give an example of an experience when you compromised with someone else or a group to make a project work. What were the highs and lows of the situation?

7. Describe a situation from the past where you should have used an "I" message for clarification rather than reacting in a negative manner to what was being said.

seven

Initial Speech Preparation

OBJECTIVES

After reading this chapter, you should be able to:

- Identify the first seven steps of the speech design process. (There are a total of 11 steps. Steps 8–11 appear in chapters 8 and 9.)
- Select an appropriate topic
- Narrow a topic to fit into a time limit
- Find an effective key for a presentation
- Write a specific goal statement
- Write an effective thesis statement
- Explain the concept of audience analysis

Students often dread making an oral presentation. One of the reasons for the nervousness they feel is that they do not know how to construct a presentation. If you aren't confident about how to do something, you become very apprehensive. This chapter will help you learn to prepare for your speech. While these new skills won't make all of your nervousness go away, solid preparation will soothe some of the butterflies.

The Speech Design Process

Initially, you need to get into the proper frame of mind. One of the authors once heard someone say, "It is important to say 'I have a speech to give,' not 'I have to give a speech.'" What is the difference between these two statements? The first statement is positive. It says you have a topic you think is interesting and important, and you want to share it with your audience. The second statement implies an obligation, a dreaded task. Which statement helps your attitude and the psychological frame of mind to do your best? The first one, of course!

The next preliminary step is to understand the purpose for giving a speech. If speakers think they are giving speeches just to talk, they are missing the entire point of the speaking opportunity. Think about speakers you've observed who simply talk *at* the audience. They are there for the sole purpose of showing off, spewing knowledge at the audience, or listening to their own voice. An audience soon grows bored with these presentations—and should! To be a good speaker, you must always remember you are there for the audience. The purpose of a speech should be to share your understanding of a topic with the audience. Therefore, it is extremely important to keep the listeners in mind at all times.

Once you are in the right frame of mind and understand you are creating something for your audience, you can begin the **speech design process.** While there are a number of ways to approach designing a speech, we find the following steps to be the most valuable.

Speech Design Process

1. Select a general purpose
2. Select a topic
3. Narrow the topic
4. Find the key organizing feature
5. Write the specific goal statement
6. Write the thesis statement
7. Analyze the audience

Planning Stage

---

8. Research
9. Organize
10. Outline
11. Select delivery style, visual aids, and practice

Creating Stage

Why do we call this a speech design process instead of writing a speech? An effective speech is one that is assembled one piece at a time. The speech design process takes you through 11 steps. These steps keep you focused on your final product.

Step 1: Select a General Purpose

A **general purpose** is the overall goal of your speech. There are three main purposes for public speaking: to **inform,** to **persuade,** and to ***entertain.*** There is some overlap in these purposes because informative and persuasive speeches can also be entertaining. With an entertainment speech however, the main purpose is to make people enjoy the subject and your performance.

What is the difference between informing and persuading? An informative speech is a factual speech. You might describe, explain, or give the details about a topic. For instance, you could inform an audience about three cultural sites in New Orleans. However, if you try to explain why New Orleans is a great place to visit, you have crossed the line into a persuasive speech. You have added opinion to your purpose. "Great" is an opinion word. Someone might argue it's a fact that New Orleans is a great place to visit. The use of "great," however, makes this sentence an opinion statement, and the speech becomes persuasive.

As another example, someone may try to inform you that Queen is the best band ever. The use of "best" makes the speech persuasive. It is important to stick to the facts in an informative speech. If you begin to evaluate or express a judgment, the speech becomes persuasive. Finally, think of the goal for your audience. With the informative speech, you want your audience to *understand* something. With the persuasive speech, you want your audience to *believe* or *do* something.

Step 2: Select a Topic

The next part of the design process is to ***select a topic.*** This is generally the hardest part of the public speaking endeavor. What should you talk about? The first thing to do is begin ***brainstorming:*** write down as many ideas as you can think of without evaluating them. For example, start with a simple topic—pets. Pets remind you of cats, cats remind you of litter boxes, litter boxes remind you of sand, sand reminds you of the beach, the beach reminds you of the sun, the sun reminds you of tanning, tanning reminds you of burning, and burning reminds you of cancer. You remember your aunt was just diagnosed with breast cancer, and you think that it would be important and interesting to give an informative speech on the three warning signs of breast cancer.

This may seem illogical, but that's how brainstorming works. If you had stopped brainstorming when you hit the word litter box, you would never have arrived at breast cancer. Brainstorming is a nonjudgmental, creative process where thoughts are not necessarily regulated by logic.

As you try to decide which topics would be acceptable for your audience, there are a number of criteria you should consider.

1. Choose a topic that accomplishes your general purpose (inform, persuade, or entertain). If you are doing an informative speech,

you should not pick a topic you feel very strongly about. For example, it is possible to give an informative speech about being CPR certified. However, if you are passionate about this topic and feel everyone must be certified, it will be extremely difficult for you to stay in an informative mode without persuasive comments/words entering your remarks. You may do better to save that topic for a persuasive speech.

2. Choose a topic that fits within the time limit. A speech about the history of Asia will not fit into five minutes. You must begin with a reasonably narrowed topic.

3. Choose a topic that is appropriate for the audience. It should not be too technical or too trivial. It needs to be something that will interest them. Audience analysis is discussed later in the process, but start now to place your focus on the receiver, not yourself.

4. Choose a topic the audience does not know much about (if the speech is to be informative) or a topic the audience does not agree with or needs to have reinforced (if the speech is to be persuasive).

5. Choose a topic that interests you. If you are not interested in the topic, there is virtually no way to make it engaging for an audience.

TRY IT!

Write as much as you can next to each question without evaluating it.

1. What topics do you like to read about? _____

_____

2. What current events interest you? _____

_____

3. Where have you traveled? _____

_____

4. What hobbies do you have? _____

_____

5. What activities do you do in your spare time? _____

_____

6. What is interesting to you about your major? _____

_____

7. What campus or world issues do you care strongly about? _____

_____

Now look back over your list and think about which of these items could be a potential speech topic.

> **ETHICAL CONSIDERATIONS**
>
> Is it ethical to select a topic that you know nothing about? What if you plan to research it?
>
> _____
>
> _____

Step 3: Narrow the Topic

The next step is to **narrow the topic.** Beginning speakers often make the mistake of using a topic that is much too broad, such as the symptoms, causes, and cures of depression. When speakers have this much material to cover, the only thing they can do is to provide a list of facts: here are the six symptoms, these are the eight causes, and here are the three cures for depression. What does the audience remember? Nothing. If you narrow this subject and discuss only three of the symptoms of depression, the audience will remember more information from your speech. You can explain what each symptom is and give examples. Focusing on fewer specifics and presenting them in depth enhances understanding. Here are a few examples of narrowing a topic:

Ineffective: The band Maroon 5

Effective: The drummer from Maroon 5 uses three unique types of instruments

Ineffective: Edwardian furniture styles in antique stores

Effective: Edwardian-style furniture has three distinct characteristics

TRY IT!

Take the topic of "music" and narrow it to an appropriate topic for a five-minute speech.

_____

_____

Your word choices are extremely important as you narrow your topic. By simply changing your wording slightly, you alter the message of your speech. To accomplish your speaking goal, spend time at this point in the design process to make sure your word choices are focused properly.

Let's return to the possibility of a speech on depression. Although the topic could be an interesting one to share with your audience, a speech on "depression" is too broad. What can you cover in an eight- to ten-minute speech that allows you to introduce a new understanding of depression to the audience? You could narrow the focus to three symptoms, three steps in a treatment program, *OR* three types of drugs used to treat depression. You may find yourself saying, "But I want to talk about so much more!" Alas, there is a time limit. A brief overview of symptoms, causes, and cures leaves the audience with nothing new. With a focus, the audience learns something new about depression, and you've done your job as an informative speaker.

You'll notice our examples all include "three" of something. Three is considered to be a magical number in public speaking. Remember the second step of the perceptual process? We all organize information before we assign meaning to it. Our minds organize information better when there are chunks of three and four items. This is why a phone number is not a seven-digit number. It is a chunk of three and a chunk of four numbers. Your social security number and other pieces of information in our society are broken up the same way.

Imagine a student who attempts to give a speech on 14 places to visit in Boston. By the time she is finished with this "list" speech, the audience does not remember a thing or is sound asleep. If she had broken the speech into chunks of three: three historical places, three universities, three major ethnic groups, three major waterfront attractions, three cultural activities, *OR* three major restaurants, the audience would walk away with a clear understanding and appreciation of something they didn't know previously. That is good communication. If you are still

CHOICES AND CONSEQUENCES

You really want to talk about the artist Matisse. You are enthralled by his work. You want to cover his life history and artistic theories, the medium he used, and his relationship with Picasso. What are the consequences of talking about all of this for your classroom speech?

_____

_____

_____

What logical choices could you make?

_____

_____

_____

having trouble narrowing your topic, you may find the next section on finding the key to be useful.

Step 4: Finding the Key

The next step in the speech design process is to find a key. The **key** is the organizing feature that describes the similarity among your main points. Examples of a key are: steps, aspects, characteristics, parts, areas, or reasons (Brickman & Fuller, 1986, p. 42). If you choose to cover three different types of medications, the key is "types." For a speech on depression the three main points could be Zoloft, Paxil, and Prozac. If you choose three reasons to treat depression, the key is "reasons." The main points might be "better intrapersonal communication, better interpersonal communication, and better social communication."

Speakers sometimes choose three unrelated points—or loosely related points—instead of selecting a key. This makes their speech difficult to remember. If a speaker decides to talk about Bon Jovi and says, "I want to cover the band members, the music, and how they became famous," there is no key in this speech other than "stuff" about Bon Jovi. The three points are unrelated and difficult for an audience to follow and remember. If this student narrowed the topic and selected an appropriate key, he could choose among the following speeches:

The three main band members.	(key: band members)
The three best-selling songs.	(key: songs)
The three events that led to their fame.	(key: events)
The three characteristics of their music.	(key: characteristics)
The three characteristics of their instruments.	(key: characteristics)

You'll notice how much tighter the speech is once the speaker chooses an appropriate key. You don't want to have an "everything-you-ever-wanted-to-know-about-X" speech.

If you are having trouble finding a key, you may want to try some diagramming. By brainstorming visually on paper, you can see which keys are strong and which are weak. Let's say Alice wants to talk about tomatoes. But she's not sure of a key. She knows she wants to talk about how to plant them, the types, and the uses. If she chooses those three main points, the only key is "stuff." If she continues to diagram, she comes up with the following.

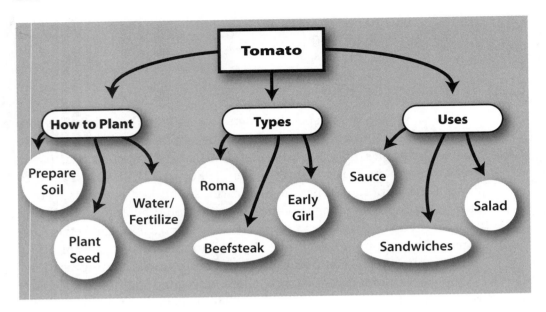

Looking at her diagram, she notices that "how to plant," "types," and "uses" all are strong keys. Each key yields three related main points. If she continued the diagram with "Roma" and listed "origin," "sauce," and "advantages," Roma would not be a strong key because the three main points are unrelated. This means she would have a "stuff" speech about Roma tomatoes. But if she continued the diagram with three advantages of Roma tomatoes, then she would have a strong key because the points all relate to one another. This type of brainstorming can be useful for finding a topic, narrowing a topic, or finding the key and main points. Additionally, if she goes with the three uses, she has an interesting catch phrase to help the audience remember her topic: The three "s's" of tomatoes!

TRY IT!

Use this diagram to brainstorm for three good keys for a speech about "music." Add more boxes where you need them or use a blank sheet of paper so you can put boxes wherever you like.

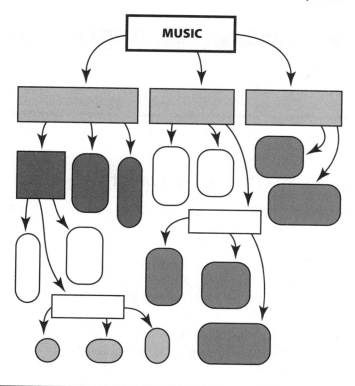

Step 5: Writing the Specific Goal Statement

Instructors will call this a purpose statement, a specific purpose statement, or a *specific goal statement.* The specific goal statement is for design purposes only. You write it so you know exactly what you want your audience to remember or learn. This statement places listeners in the central position; you want the audience to come away with an understanding of the topic.

A specific goal statement should be a full sentence. It should be limited to one idea. Generally, the statement will read:

After my speech, I want my audience to understand that:

- there are three different drugs that are used to combat depression.

- there are three steps in planting a tomato.

- there are three reasons why Bon Jovi became famous.

Notice that if you use the phrase "to tell the audience about..." in your statement, you are no longer receiver oriented. Focus on the receiver. If you write your goal statement correctly, it will reflect your key.

TRY IT!

Write a specific goal statement for your speech about music.

Step 6: Writing the Thesis Statement

The next step of the design process is to write the **thesis statement.** Some instructors call this the central idea. The thesis statement is integral for speech design purposes. You write it so you know what the main points of the speech will be. Keep in mind that the thesis/central idea in oral communication may be dissimilar from those you learn about in an English class. Oral and written forms of communication differ because the channel for information is different—spoken delivery versus written delivery.

The thesis statement is an extension of the specific goal statement. It clarifies what "three items" you are going to discuss. Thesis statements are written as follows:

Three different drugs used to fight depression are Prozac, Zoloft, and Paxil.

Three types of tomatoes are Beefsteak, Roma, and Early Girl.

Three of Bon Jovi's most popular songs are "Livin' on a Prayer," "Raise Your Hands," and "Keeping the Faith."

Once you've written your specific goal statement and thesis statement correctly, the rest of the speech falls into place nicely. As you begin to research your topic, collect only information that relates to the goal and thesis statements, and reject any unrelated material. The clear guidelines of the goal and thesis statements help you avoid the mistake of including information that isn't appropriate for the topic. All of the material in a speech must relate to your goal and thesis statement.

TRY IT!

Write a thesis statement for your speech about music.

Step 7: Audience Analysis

Since speaking is a receiver-oriented phenomenon, adapting your speech to the audience is essential. There are numerous choices to make as you design your speech: structure, language, the performance space, and time of day—just to name a few. When you think about your audience in each step of the design process, you create the most effective presentation. The two main considerations in **audience analysis** are the characteristics of the people and the characteristics of the situation.

Characteristics of People

Demographic analysis is an analytical look at the age, sex, socio-economic status, educational level, and professional experience of the audience. However, if you collect this information, what do you really know about the audience? In the 1950s, speech textbooks stated women preferred speeches on babies, art, and music. Men preferred speeches on business, science, and sports. Is this true today? Well, it may not have been true in the 1950s either. Here's a related example. If you are giving a speech to a group of women in their forties who have PhDs and all make over $50,000 a year, what do you know about them that would help you to adapt your topic for them? Nothing really. Let's say you want to give a speech on how to crochet a blanket. Is that appropriate for this audience? Many students automatically say no. However, this group may be in high-stress jobs. Crocheting is an excellent stress reducer. The topic could actually work. Or, it may not. Demographics won't provide the answer.

Certainly demographics are useful. We shouldn't talk about safe sex to a group of first graders, pro-choice to various religious groups, and retirement planning to high school students. But beyond those obvious conclusions, demographics alone just don't give us the information we need to shape our remarks. Should we give a speech about skydiving to a group of people age 60+? Well, it depends on the group. If we say they are too old, we are stereotyping. We know people who took their first jump from a plane after the age of 60. Should we exclude a speech on checking for breast cancer when we find out there are males in our audience? Perhaps not. Males should also check their chest tissue for cancer since 10 percent of breast cancer cases occur in men. And certainly speeches on breast or testicular cancer can be informative to the opposite sex because they may share the information with loved ones. When you make assumptions about the audience by looking only at demographics, it is easy to stereotype. An inaccurate assumption about the audience could ruin your speech.

So what do you need to know about your audience that would be useful in designing your speech? Some of the following questions could provide useful insight about *audience characteristics:*

1. How familiar is the audience with the topic?

2. How interested is the audience in the topic?

3. Why is the audience there?

4. How much experience does the audience have with the topic?

We need to know the extent of the audience's knowledge about the topic so we can present new information. If we open a speech with a statement that repeats information the audience already knows, we will bore them and lose their attention immediately. On the flip side, if a speaker is using terminology the audience doesn't understand, communication stops instantly. Think about a teacher who spoke in specialized language without defining terms. What was your impression of the teacher? It's likely you were lost, bored, frustrated, and did poorly on exams in this teacher's class. Make a conscious choice not to put your audience in that same situation.

It is often very difficult to recognize what the "general population" does or doesn't know about a topic. We have listened to students give speeches about their academic majors that were so far beyond the audience's knowledge of the subject that the speeches failed. For example, a student who wanted to give a speech on message encryption finally had to admit the audience did not have the background for the speech (or the interest), and the student changed to a much simpler computer-related topic. While this speaker was really interested in talking about message encryption, he realized that speaking is about the audience, not the communicator.

Is the audience interested in the topic? While the speaker should consider whether the topic will be engaging for the audience, it is also the job of the speaker to make the topic interesting. We always tell our students that we think oral communication is a fascinating topic. Do you think students agree with us? Is this the most riveting class you have at school? If we assumed you are as interested in this material as we are, we would be making a big mistake. We know we need to find ways to make the material interesting and applicable to you because speaking is critical for your future success.

In analyzing your audience, you also need to know why the audience is there. A captive audience is much different from one that comes to hear a speaker because they think the topic is interesting, or they've heard that the speaker is really good. But think how many times you've been disappointed when making assumptions about speakers prior to actually hearing them. As a speaker, you may have to work harder to interest a captive audience than an audience who chose to hear your presentation, but in both cases you must make an effort to maintain their interest.

How much experience does the audience have with the topic? This is another piece of information you can use to help design your presentation for the audience. Some speakers would only analyze the demographic of age. For example, in giving a speech to first graders on how to cook breakfast, the demographic of age would suggest you should cover simple items such as peanut butter toast with raisin smiley faces or pouring a bowl of cereal. However, experience is a better indicator of what is appropriate. In some preschool environments, little children learn the art of pouring milk, washing dishes, and doing creative baking, while in others, children may never have poured a cup of milk. The experience levels of these children could be quite different, and yet the children are all the same age.

Note that some topics are much easier for an audience to relate to than others. A speech about a popular band may not take much effort if your audience analysis reveals students are excited about that particular band. A speech delivered by a music major about the bassoon might be more difficult. In fact, in one class where a student did a speech about a bassoon one of the classmates had never heard of the instrument—she thought it was an animal!

TRY IT!

How would you make your topic of music relevant and interesting for your classroom audience?

Characteristics of the Physical Setting

Good speakers should always be familiar with the *physical setting* of the speaking situation. The arrangement of a room is important. You need to know where the audience is seated in relation to your speaking area. This allows you to develop a mental picture of how to make eye contact with each section of the audience when you practice giving your speech. If the space has a balcony, you need to look up in addition to scanning the main audience level. A speaker should be aware of the seating arrangement to be prepared for audience interaction. If an audience is seated in rows, members of the audience are less likely to interact with each other during a speech. If the audience is in a circle or in small seating groups, they may talk to each other more easily while you are delivering your speech. These more intimate settings can be challenging for a speaker.

You need to know what furniture is available for your use. Are you planning to use a lectern? What will you do if one isn't available? Many instructors ask you to deliver your speech without a lectern to give you practice standing in front of an audience. It is much easier to adapt to using a lectern than it is to stand in front of the audience. Do you need to have any special equipment? Do you need a microphone? Is a microphone necessary in a small space? An experienced speaker should know how to use a microphone and in what circumstances it is necessary. Always check your audio levels prior to speaking.

Is there a space to place your visuals? Work with your visual aids as you prepare your speech, so you are comfortable handling them. For instance, if you have a three-dimensional, round object, putting it on a flat surface won't work. It will undoubtedly roll off, distracting you and the audience. Some people arrive with a PowerPoint aid when there is no computer system available. Whatever visual you use, you must arrange in advance for all of the equipment you will need. We will return to this topic in chapter 9 on visuals.

Another aspect of the physical situation is the time of day. Time of day can affect the mood of your audience. The audience is in a captive situation. Audiences who have just had lunch will be sleepy; those who haven't will be hungry. Audiences who are there early in the day may be tired; those who are at the end of their day may be anxious and ready to leave. Anticipate the potential mood of the audience so you can adapt your speech accordingly.

You may also want to investigate whether there are fluorescent lights in the room that make a buzzing noise. If there is an alternative light source, you may choose to use it. Some audience members are so annoyed by buzzing lights they will be unable to listen to your message.

Electrical outlets are another item you need to check. If you are using any kind of electrical equipment, you need to know where the outlets are. Remember, electrical outlets may be there but the outlets may not work. Do you need an extension cord? We've watched many audiences lose interest quickly because the speaker couldn't figure out the technology. Be prepared. It's your speech, and you want to do well.

Regulating the temperature of a space is also important. A colleague reported that he used to be a member of a congregation that kept the building so warm that many in the audience were more likely to sleep than listen. The issue of temperature may seem to be trivial, but heat and cold can affect audience attitudes and behaviors. As a speaker you need to be sensitive to the physical comfort of the audience.

Finally, just seeing the layout of a room prior to a presentation can alleviate some of the nervous feelings associated with speaking in public. The more you know about the space, the more you can control the jitters as you prepare to speak.

> ### Professional Perspective
>
> Anyone over the age of four knows that words can be hurtful or offensive. That's a fact of life—both personally and professionally. Just as you're told to "think before you speak," it's equally important to "think before you write." I write commercials for a living. I help advertisers sell their products to millions of radio listeners. When you write copy for an audience, it's crucial to know who your audience is. You wouldn't market a drug for arthritis pain by using MTV-style slang because your target audience is people over the age of 50. There are still plenty of people out there who don't embrace new technology as easily as you do. There are ways to persuade people to try a product and to capture their attention without being "in your face." Be conversational. Don't insult your audience or "talk down" to them. And be honest. Don't promise what you can't deliver. In addition to creating possible legal complications for you and your employer, it will erase all levels of trust that a consumer might have for a particular brand.
>
> —Jana Polsky Deneroff
> Writer/Producer, Creative Services
> CBS/Westwood One Radio Networks

Summary

The speech design process is methodical and logical. Don't neglect any of the steps in your planning, because it will come back to haunt you on the day you deliver your presentation. Once you adjust to the fact you are going to deliver speeches most of your adult life, it becomes easier to remember this process and to follow the procedure without having to think about it.

Preparing to speak is like training for a sporting event. The process is repetitive. As your mind adjusts to the routine of learning, you plan your next speech more quickly and more effectively than the one before it. Speaking improves with practice just as your endurance improves with weight training and running. Your mind and your body need to remain healthy throughout your life. Work and patience now can lead to tremendous professional rewards in the years ahead of you.

KEY WORDS

audience analysis	narrow the topic
brainstorming	persuade
demographic analysis	physical setting
entertain	specific goal statement
general purpose	speech design process
inform	thesis statement
key	topic selection

DISCUSSION/ACTIVITIES

1. Discuss a recent class lecture that you feel was totally informative. Explain.

2. Describe a speaking situation in which the speaker's remarks were not targeted properly to their audience. Explain.

3. Discuss a speaker who lost their credibility because they had not checked the physical setting for the speech prior to walking into the room. Explain.

4. Define brainstorming and describe how it can assist in narrowing a speech topic.

5. Listen carefully to a class lecture during the next week of classes and identify the "key" for the lecture.

6. Listen to a lecture, religious sermon, or political speech. Identify its goal statement.

eight

Constructing the Speech

O B J E C T I V E S

After reading this chapter, you should be able to:

- Use various research outlets
- Explain the difference between facts, opinions, statistics, and examples
- Identify five organizational patterns
- Identify the parts of an introduction and conclusion
- Construct an effective outline

Chapter 7 introduced the planning stages of speech design and concluded with a discussion of the importance of knowing about the audience and the physical setting when you prepare your speech. Now we turn to the next steps in the speech design process, which will help you to construct your presentation: research, organization, and outlining. Each step helps you focus clearly on the presentation you are about to give. That is the real benefit of following this process. As you design a speech, each step becomes a piece of the greater puzzle—your presentation. You are the only person who will know how much hard work it took to organize the information. A good speech is a personal reward. Yes, the audience will enjoy it, but you are the one who has the greatest satisfaction in a job well done.

Steps 8, 9, and 10 are listed in order, but as we said above, the construction process is a puzzle. You may find that you do some initial research and then begin to organize and outline. Once you have an initial outline, you may need to go back to look for a particular piece of research—a statistic or an example that will strengthen your speech even more. After outlining, you may find that some of your points would make more sense in a different order. You should work back and forth among these last three steps to make your speech as strong as possible.

Step 8: Research

Once you determine the design elements of the speech, it is time to do your **research.** The first thing that you want to do is look at your key and your thesis. They provide you with your three main points and identify the place to begin gathering research.

Some students want to speak from personal experience. Other students believe themselves to be experts on numerous topics. Although you may be your own greatest resource, you still need research to bolster your credibility and to ensure the accuracy of your remarks. You'll notice we have citations in this book. We have over 60 years combined teaching experience. We consider ourselves to be experts in this field. However, we still use other resources and cite our sources. Even if you have been fly-fishing since you were 3 years old and your dad is the host of a popular fly-fishing television show, you can still reinforce your facts with a citation from *Field and Stream* magazine. Try to attribute all of your assertions to documented research. A simple citation makes a powerful impression on an audience.

Professional Perspective

[*Which of the elements of speech design is the most important? As this student humorously highlights with his main points constantly changing, they are all necessary and equally important.*]

So far in class you have covered some very interesting topics. I suppose the main point of your class has been **know your audience.** I mean, if you don't know your audience, then you could end up trying to tell your audience something they won't understand. I know I've had teachers who forget that you're an undergrad student and not some research scientist or something like that. And they were really boring, too. You have to use some energy when you speak. That's what I'm really trying to say here. **You have to use energy and emotion when you speak.**

Forget that stuff about knowing your audience—that was stupid. So, you've got to show energy and emotion. That way you'll be interesting to listen to. Some people get so caught up in their emotions during a speech that they even lose sight of their purpose when they are speaking. Never do that. Always keep your purpose in mind. That's it. Forget that baloney about using energy and emotion.

You have to **keep your purpose in mind.** I think that is my main point here. Because if you stick to your purpose, then everything will fall together. Sometimes I'll just go on and on and everything I say will be directed toward my purpose. I may jump around a little, but I usually manage to stick to my outline. I can't stand it when people go from one thing to the next without any organization. You have to be organized.

So let me start with that. **Be organized.** I mean, what if your audience is a little uninformed and here you are trying to talk about nuclear physics or something and you're jumping from one thing to the next? They won't understand. Which is why you have to know your audience. I guess that's basically it then—**know your audience.** That's what I'm trying to say here.

—Greg Chesterton
Former Undergraduate Student
The Pennsylvania State University

Places to Find Research

There are three places to begin research. You can look on the Internet, use library research, or conduct interviews. It is important to find the most up-to-date sources as you select information that will support your presentation.

The Internet

Most students go immediately to the Internet. If you know where to look and carefully analyze the quality of the source, the web is a tremendous resource for thousands of online journal articles. Many libraries have online subscriptions to journals, newspapers, and periodicals. Because online versions sometimes differ from hardcopy versions, be sure to specify in your citation which resource you used.

How do you know a credible Internet site from a noncredible one? First, analyze the address. An .edu extension indicates an educational site; a .gov extension is a government site; the .org extension is an organizational site; and .com can be any number of groups or organizations. Many of these sites contain facts, but they also contain opinions. You might assume the information is accurate, but you need to verify the information before you use it in a speech. It would be reasonable to expect the national site for Special Olympics to be accurate. While product sites may have some facts, the information is shaped to persuade you to believe in the product or the company. If we, the authors, created a university website, we would have .edu as our extension. What if we included medical advice from Dr. Young and Dr. Travis? No one would regulate this information. It would be up to you to determine that we are not medical doctors even though we use the title "Dr." You must evaluate the credibility of the site and the reliability of the information provided there. Be responsible and check the information against other sources.

There are some other factors to be aware of as well. If there is a tilde (~) in the website address, it means a subgroup of the original domain has published the site. The original site may not control the information. You should determine the credibility of the person who authored the information. Evaluate whether the information is fact or opinion. How current is the information? Look for a disclaimer on the web page and consider its significance.

Some students do not evaluate the credibility of site information. In an oral communication course taught by one of our colleagues, a speaker recently tried to convince her audience that hair dyes cause brain damage. When we examined her sources, we found there was indeed an article on the Internet about hair dyes causing brain damage. We read the article in disbelief. It used terms such as "dizzy blondes."

When we clicked on the "about this web page" icon, we found the entire news site was political satire. Not one statement on it was true! The student who used the information on this site in her speech was extremely careless. She presented information that was not accurate. If she had checked the information against other sources, she would not have made this mistake. Remember, it is your obligation as a speaker to make sure all information is correct and reliable. Furthermore, as an audience member you must listen critically. You should research any remark that sounds unbelievable or out of line.

There are thousands of websites. Many are inaccurate. Just because information is on the Internet doesn't mean it's true. What are the credentials of the people running a website? What if you discovered that a relationship advice website you were frequenting for personal help was run by a first-year student at your own school? How accurate do you think the advice you've been following is now? Would you be embarrassed? Angry? You may not think this is possible, but this is a true story.

Our best advice is to limit Internet sources. Use the most official website you can find and leave the rest behind. For instance, if you are giving a speech on the Special Olympics, their website is an excellent resource. Beyond that, look for some articles and interviews. And stay away from online encyclopedias. They may have been fine in the fifth grade, but you should be more advanced at this point.

TRY IT!

Name three of your favorite products. Now, find their websites and report briefly on the accuracy of the information provided there. How much material is informative and how much of it is persuasive? What other information could the site provide?

_____

_____

_____

_____

_____

_____

Library Research

Traditional research tools include hard copies of books, periodicals, magazines, journals, and newspapers. You should always supplement your Internet research with traditional research. By the time you enter college, you should be quite familiar with locating information in a library or finding library sources online through your school's search programs. If you cannot, it is time to take advantage of the resources your school offers and become familiar with these research tools. Most universities offer tours of their library facilities. Librarians are always glad to assist people who are looking for information. Ask for their help. A knowledgeable librarian is another great resource for finding information.

As you evaluate your library sources, think about currency. Depending on the topic, books may not be the best source for up-to-date information. When someone writes a book, the process takes months or years; the publishing process then consumes more time. By the time the book is printed, sources may well be outdated. If you are researching a historical event (a battle, the sinking of the *Titanic*, or the inception of the Girl Scouts), then a book can be a good resource. However, if you want AIDS statistics, any book you find will have seriously out-of-date material. You'll need to go to a periodical such as the *Journal of the American Medical Association* (JAMA), or you may need to go to a government website.

Don't neglect newspapers and magazines. Sometimes very current and interesting topics are covered well in large newspapers; you can access that information easily online. With all of the advances in technology, there is no excuse for not having a variety of up-to-date sources. If you find yourself saying, "But I can't find anything written on 3 types of dreams," then you need to go back to the drawing board of learning how to research.

ETHICAL CONSIDERATIONS

As you do your research, it is important to keep accurate records of what information comes from each source. Imagine that you have an important piece of information, but you can't remember where it came from. What would you do?

_____

_____

_____

_____

Professional Perspective

After you select your topic and begin to put some general ideas together, you will do some initial research on your topic; this will allow you to get an overview of the available information. You may, however, want to hold off on the in-depth research until you have a basic outline of your presentation.

If you immediately begin to thoroughly research your topic, your speech will be *research driven:* you will include only the information that you happen to find as you scour your sources. You may end up missing important support material that isn't directly associated with your topic. Instead, you want your speech to be *idea driven:* put a rough outline together, then ask yourself, "What information do I need?" and go look for that information.

I heard a speech several years ago about The Ration-D Bar, an energy bar that soldiers ate in WWII. One of the aspects of this energy bar was that it could withstand high temperatures. So in addition to telling us this information, the student researched average summer temperatures and told us how hot it got in Europe and the Pacific, where our soldiers would have been eating these. So in addition to including sources about The Ration-D Bar, she found other valuable but unrelated sources that helped her explain her point. The speaker went beyond the minimum sources required for the assignment and presented a thorough, interesting speech!

—Bia Bernum
Assistant Professor
Mansfield University

Interviews

You can also gather information by making a connection with members of your community. Interviews can yield useful information. Examples of local sources include teachers, police officers, politicians, doctors, counselors, clergy, lawyers, business owners/managers, or people involved with nonprofit organizations such as the Lion's Club. Don't forget to consult with the professional people on your campus. Every local contact adds credibility to your remarks. A local resource allows the audience to recognize the value of your discussion because a local connection makes the topic personal for them.

In preparing for an interview, it is important to:

- Schedule the interview well in advance.

- Know the background of the person you are interviewing to make sure he or she has the expertise you need.

- Know what part of the speech you want to reinforce with quotations from your source, so the interview is focused and you don't waste the interviewee's time.

- Plan your questions carefully in advance. This is not a brainstorming session; do not ask questions you have not prepared.

- Make sure to be on time.

- Check with the person the day before the appointment to make sure his or her schedule hasn't changed.

- Take notes while the person is speaking.

- Check in advance if the person will allow you to record his or her answers. Never ask this question once you are there. Always turn the recording device off if someone says, "This remark is 'off the record.'" Don't question this statement. The remark can never be mentioned to anyone. This is a test of your ability to respect the wishes of the interviewee.

- If the interviewee agrees, a phone interview is another potential source. Do not, however, record a phone conversation without permission.

CHOICES AND CONSEQUENCES

You read an article about a crime in the local paper. It interests you, and you decide to do a speech on the topic. You research national publications and the web for statistics and information. You do not interview any local community members. What are the consequences of this choice?

_____

_____

_____

Types of Supporting Material

Supporting material is the information you use to convey a point. Once you find your sources of information, you pull supporting material from them that will assist you in explaining your topic to the audience. As you draft your presentation, you may identify an area of your speech that needs additional support, and you'll do more research to find material to add to your presentation.

Supporting material can include expert opinion, facts, statistics, definitions, and examples that describe, illustrate, or explain. *Expert opinion* can come from a local source or quotations in national publications. Expert opinion helps boost your credibility.

Facts include information known to be true, such as dates, names, titles, and numbers. Facts are often defined as observable phenomena. The number of people who died in a local tragedy is a fact. *Statistics* are a descriptive use of numbers—and a good way to make numbers have meaning to a listener. For instance, on a campus of 3,000 people,

1,500 are male. Instead of reporting 1,500 males are on campus, it is more effective to say 50 percent of the population is male. A percentage is easier for the audience to remember. The speaker should, however, be prepared with the actual numbers in case an audience member asks a question. When using statistics, you must:

- cite the source;

- indicate the date the statistic was developed; and

- include the sample size if research was involved.

Present any facts and statistics in a way that connects with the audience. Sometimes using a smaller, more easily recognized number will make a greater impression on listeners. For instance, if someone falls 20 feet, you can say they fell two stories. Twenty feet may be more accurate, but it is also more abstract. The audience will connect better with the simpler form of the number.

TRY IT!

Be careful of stringing too many statistics together. While you mean to impress, often the audience just glazes over. Take this paragraph for example: "Statistics shows that a single person in one day can produce up to 4.39 pounds of trash. We create enough trash to fill 63,000 trucks per day. And during the holidays, we generate an additional 5 million tons of waste. 80% of this holiday waste is composed of shopping bags and wrapping paper, 2 items that could be recyclable" (*Ecoevaluator*, n.d.).

Now imagine this string of statistics delivered by a nervous speaker in rapid-fire delivery. What does it all mean? Does it have impact? Rewrite this supporting material to bring an in-depth understanding of this problem rather than a rapid-fire list of statistics.

_____

_____

_____

_____

_____

As a critical listener, it is essential for you to process the meaning of numbers carefully. Paul Krugman (2003) uses an example of Bill Gates walking into a bar. The minute Gates enters, the average person in the bar becomes a billionaire. You know the status of the people in the bar hasn't changed; however, statistically speaking, the average net worth of each person is over a billion dollars. This story illustrates how easy it is to manipulate numbers to support your conclusion. So, listen critically and analyze messages carefully when numbers are used.

As a speaker, you need to be ethical when using statistics to support your points. As another example, a news headline from 2004 announced "Child Antidepressant Use Skyrockets" (DeNoon, 2004). The story claimed that antidepressant use in children was up 100%. That sounds extremely alarming! However, the article goes on to state that "antidepressant use is up 100% to 0.16% of girls and up 62% to 0.23% of boys." Although the article included the actual statistics (each less than a quarter of a percent), it first summarized the increase as 100%—creating the impression that a shocking number of children were now using antidepressants.

Definitions are an explanation of a word, phrase, or concept. Definitions are important if the audience doesn't know the specialized vocabulary used in the speech. Be sure to think about your presentation as if you were an audience member. What may be perfectly common language to you may sound foreign to some audience members. In order to avoid sounding condescending, you may want to introduce a definition with a phrase such as, "As you may know. . . "

Analogies are comparisons. They show how one thing is similar to another thing. When we learn new information, we often try to compare that information to something that we already know. For example, in the South, a student was giving a speech about a ski slope and tried to explain the appearance of a newly groomed slope. Since the other students in the room had no idea, she used an analogy. Rather than saying the snow looks "bumpy" or "had long lines through it," she said, "A groomed ski slope looks like a Ruffles potato chip." Immediately the students could grasp exactly what she was talking about.

Examples are phrases or stories used to describe, illustrate, or explain a concept. They can be real or hypothetical. You should use an example any time you make a statement that may need clarification. If Laquan states, "Volunteering can be a rewarding activity," he needs to follow the statement with an example of a time when he volunteered and found it to be rewarding. The example he uses will help clarify the concept of volunteering for his audience.

To pull together relevant and up-to-date supporting material, make sure to listen to the news carefully for two weeks prior to your speech. Read the paper, listen to the radio, read magazines, and use the Internet (with caution). New information about your topic may appear in the news. Include it in your speech. This makes you sound totally up-to-date in your research and much more credible to the audience.

Another way to make your speech unique and memorable is to find information that the audience has never heard. Without new information, the audience doesn't need to listen to the speech. Most audience members are aware of basic information on a variety of topics. It is your job to pique their interest with new information, exciting examples, and interesting descriptions.

You should choose supporting material carefully. Think through how to explain your topic, and collect the supporting material that will best support your efforts. We now frequently hear speeches that sound like a string of sound bites. Students deliver one fact after an example after a statistic, etc. You need to figure out how these pieces of information relate to each other and to the audience and present the information accordingly.

Critical Thinking

Look at Olga's use of supporting material in the following speech.

"Low self-esteem is one cause of depression. [Adds definition and attributes source.] According to Young and Travis, authors of *Oral Communication: Skills, Choices, and Consequences*, self-esteem refers to how you feel about yourself. It is tied to self-concept, but it places a value on characteristics. [Add example to illustrate definition.] Young and Travis continue by saying that if a person is 5'1" tall and values height, then the person's self-esteem lowers. You can see how the person could get depressed if he were to dwell on an unchangeable characteristic. [Adds a more in-depth hypothetical illustration.]

"Let's look at Khineesha for example. She is an 18-year-old college student. When she was in high school, she got straight As with very little studying. When she came to college, however, she studied the same amount of time believing classes would be the same. She was horrified to receive a D on her first exam. [Explains how this relates to the topic.]

"What happens to Khineesha's self-esteem at this point? She has some choices. She can rationalize that the test was unfair, which would not lead to a change in self-esteem and/or depression. She can decide she did not prepare well enough for the exam. This probably wouldn't lead to a change in self-esteem either. However, if she decides she is not smart enough for college, then her self-esteem will drop [add statistic for effect]. If she continues to do poorly on exams, she may develop depression and join the 9.5 percent of U.S. adults age 18 and over who have a depressive disorder according to the National Institute of Mental Health."

Step 9: Organizing

One of the biggest mistakes public speakers make is to use a "slap-it-together" organizational structure. They simply place each point in random order. It is important for a speaker to choose an appropriate organizational pattern for her topic, audience, and speech. We will cover five **organizational patterns** for informative speeches; additional structures are included in chapter 11.

1. Time

2. Space

3. Topical/Classification

4. Comparison

5. Contrast

We will explore one topic and demonstrate how the focus changes within the structure. As you look at the structures, notice the integral relationship between the structure and the key. The key you choose will tell you which structure is most appropriate. Let's examine the topic: The City of Boston.

Time Structure

A **time structure** highlights steps in a process or a sequence of events. If you want to give a time-structure speech, you might present the following three steps in the process of making plans for a trip to Boston:

1. First step: decide how to get there,

2. Second step: make reservations, and

3. Third step: pack (key: steps).

Another time structure could highlight three events in the founding of Boston. You could include

1. First event: Thomas Dudley called the new settlement, Boston, after its English namesake,

2. Second event: a 1630 meeting between William Blackstone, John Winthrop, and Isaac Johnson decided the location of the new settlement, and

3. Third event: the first homes were erected in 1630 (key: events).

Space Structure

A **space structure** emphasizes parts and how they fit together to form a whole. You could give a speech on the four geographic areas in Boston. These would include

1. First area: North Boston/Cambridge,

2. Second area: South Boston,

3. Third area: West Boston/Chestnut Hill, and

4. Fourth area: East Boston/Waterfront (key: geographic areas).

Topical/Classification Structure

The **topical/classification structure** is used most frequently. This structure highlights keys such as the three types, aspects, characteristics, parts, or reasons. Here you could talk about three of the universities in Boston:

1. Harvard,

2. MIT, and

3. Boston University (key: universities).

You could also discuss three facts about Bunker Hill:

1. June 17, 1775 battle,

2. about 1,500 American militia fought against 5,000 British, and

3. 40 percent of British forces were killed (key: facts).

Comparison Structure

A *comparison structure* demonstrates the similarities between two things. If we compare programs at Harvard and Boston University, we could talk about the fact that both offer degrees in

1. English,

2. science, and

3. math (key: similarities).

As another example, we could compare Boston, Massachusetts, and Little Rock, Arkansas, stating they have

1. historical monuments,

2. interesting people, and

3. fine dining (key: similarities).

Contrast Structure

A *contrast structure* highlights the differences between two items. If we contrast three differences between Harvard and Boston University, we could talk about

1. type of school (private/public),

2. founding dates (1636/1839), and

3. location (Cambridge/Boston) (key: differences).

If we contrast the climate between Boston and Little Rock, we could discuss

1. temperatures,

2. precipitation, and

3. severe weather incidences (key: differences).

You can see how each of these structures gives you a different focus even with the same basic theme. If you choose a different structure, you get a completely different speech. For example, a classification speech about three types of transportation is different from a speech comparing air travel to bus travel. For each example we gave you, you could create many more. Each structure demonstrates how the focus of a speech changes. The diagram below gives you a visual example (Gormley, 1987). See how we visually represented organizing the topic of apples.

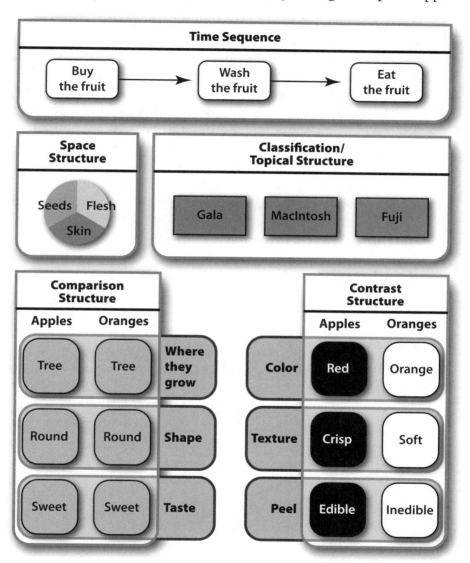

Interestingly, if you construct your key appropriately, you will automatically realize which organizational structure is appropriate for your speech. For example, if your key is "steps," then your organizational structure is time. If your key is "differences," then your organizational structure is contrast. If your key is "aspects," then your organizational structure is topical. Each of these structures gives you a different speech focus.

Step 10: Outlining

Many students grimace when their instructor requires an outline. Their attitude could change if they understood why outlines are useful. Think of an outline as a planning phase. When building a new condominium, the contractor doesn't just start building. First, she must decide on the structure. How many stories? What kind of building materials will go in the frame? How will the electrical and plumbing elements be roughed in so they coexist? These are all questions that she needs to answer before the building process begins. The contractor can look at the design and figure out if the pieces will work together. If there is a problem, there is time to reorganize before construction begins.

The same is true with your outline. When you organize your **main points** and subpoints in an outline format, you are building the structure of your speech. You want to reorganize or eliminate any information that isn't appropriate before you complete your project. While outline formats vary from instructor to instructor, the following includes the elements required for effective informative speaking.

Outline Format—Informative Speech
Title:

General Purpose:

Specific Goal Statement:

Thesis Statement:

Key:

Organizational Pattern: _____

> *This is a list of the design elements; you do not say these things in your speech.*

   I. Introduction

      A. Attention-Getting Device   *Your speech begins here with your AGD.*

         1.

         2.

      B. Connection

         1.

         2.

      C. Credibility

         1.

         2.

      D. Preview

         1.

         2.

         3.   *Transition from introduction to body*

    II.   Body

      A. (Main Point #1)

         1.

           a.

           b.

         2.

           a.

           b.

      B. (Main Point #2)

      C. (Main Point #3)

    III.   Conclusion

      A. Review

         1.

         2.

         3.

      B. Connection Restated

         1.

         2.

      C. Concluding Statement

         1.

         2.

Bibliography

Fill out the subpoints as necessary for your topic.

Transition between main points

Transition between main points

Transition from body to conclusion

The purpose of ***outlining*** is to make sure your thoughts are sequential and thoroughly developed. Never show up for a presentation and say, "Well, I thought I'd just answer whatever questions you have." The only message the audience receives from this statement is that you did not bother to prepare and that you're arrogant—and the audience is correct.

You use a ***title*** to capture attention since it is read by the emcee before you stand up to give your presentation. However, it should not give away your topic, nor should it be the topic. How does the title "A Vitamin a Day" grab you? Boring? You already know what the speech is about and who cares? Be creative with your title. Some good titles we have heard are:

Digging Up Your Dead Relatives (speech about genealogy)

I Melt for No One (speech about M&M's candy)

On the Rocks (mountain climbing)

How to Play with a Bear (trading stocks)

What a Relief (drawing techniques to reduce stress)

Could I Get Some Bacteria with That? (stop eating hotdogs because of Listeria)

Note that our sample outline includes the elements of the speech design process. These are not comments you will make during the speech, but they are part of the outline to keep the speech focused. Be sure to include your general purpose, your specific purpose, your thesis statement, your key, and your organizational pattern.

When you start to create an outline, you usually work on the body of the speech prior to writing the introduction. It is illogical to design an introduction for a presentation that is not yet created. Our discussion, however, will follow the order of delivery.

Professional Perspective

In the student loan business, communication is critical. It is of utmost importance that potential borrowers at the Arkansas Student Loan Authority first understand that the loan is an investment to better their future and they must repay it. Herein lies the importance of public speaking.

How do I convey such pertinent information? Capture the moment, of course!! The opening introduction can seal the deal or break the bank. Be knowledgeable, humbly secure in your purpose, and speak to the beat of the drummer you hear. Explain why that particular someone should be listening to you at that very real moment in time; reveal up front the need for your important communication. Feel it. Believe it. Conceive it. Communicate it. Achieve it. Simply plan your work then work your plan and above all else envision your success!

—Corey D. Welch
Operations Supervisor
Arkansas Student Loan Authority

Introduction

The ***introduction*** of any informative speech has four parts: gaining attention, making a connection, stating credibility, and stating the preview. Although the speaking time for an introduction is roughly 10 percent of your total speaking time, it is a key element of the presentation. Your audience should be ready to listen and engaged with the topic after listening to the introduction.

GAINING ATTENTION

The ***attention getter*** is the first statement you make. It should not be, "Hi, my name is . . ." or "My topic today is . . ." or "How are you today?" You need to prepare an effective opening that relates to the

Professional Perspective

A key principle for a student to remember is that your audience gets only *one* time to hear, understand, and comprehend what you are trying to tell them (unlike a newspaper or this book where a reader can go back and review something they don't understand).

—Robert Buchanan
Producer
NBC News/*Dateline*

topic to grab the audience's attention. There are a number of attention-gaining devices:

- *Painting a picture.* When you paint an image with words, you engage the audience. You might begin with, "It was a beautiful misty morning. From the window she could see dense clouds embracing the valley as though someone had poured milk from a stone pitcher. A fine mist fell on her upturned face." Speakers can use any description of a scene that encourages audience members to see a picture in their minds.

- *Quotations.* You can use literary quotations, historical quotations, or contemporary quotations. "Ben Franklin was quoted as saying, 'Many people die at 25 and aren't buried until they are 75'" (Voorhees, 2002). This quote could be a wonderful beginning to a speech about making the most out of every day.

- *Rhetorical questions.* This is a question where you are not expecting any response from the audience. We use rhetorical questions to set the tone of the speech. For instance, if you want to talk about a very serious topic like teenage suicide, you might ask the audience, "How many of you have been hurt, upset, and depressed to the point of thinking about taking your own life?" You aren't expecting audience members to raise their hands.

  While this may set the tone for a serious speech, it could also backfire. Imagine a smart aleck in your audience saying, "ME!" The audience giggles, and the mood evaporates. Sometimes people legitimately don't know whether you are using a rhetorical question. They may innocently raise a hand resulting in an awkward situation for you. You can set up a rhetorical question by saying, "Just think about this for a moment . . ." and then proceed with your question.

- *Actual questions.* You can also ask an actual question to get your audience's attention. You may need to set this up by saying, "Raise your hands if. . . ." But, make certain you know what the response will be. We have seen more than one speech introduction fail with the use of an actual question because the audience's response didn't match the speaker's expectations. It would be extremely rare for an audience member to have never eaten in a fast-food restaurant. So, you could use the question, "Is there anyone here who has never eaten in a fast-food restaurant?" It would be evident that everyone has done this because no hands would go up.

- *Startling or striking statements.* You must do this responsibly. Would it get your attention to hear the statement, "Americans are lazy and uncompetitive"? This might be a great attention getter for a speech that compares the work schedule of Americans and Europeans. Another example is to begin your speech in a foreign language. You could begin a speech on Madrid with a quote in Spanish. A student who wanted us to reduce our consumption of meat began by saying, "Did you know the average American eats over 20 animals a year?" Really? Yuck.

- *Personal references.* If you have a unique or strong connection with your topic, a personal reference can be useful as an attention getter, especially if your audience knows or likes you. One of the best personal references we have heard came from a student who had leukemia. She began, "Some people live without arms, and some live without legs, but I live without hair," and she pulled off her wig. No one in the class knew she wore a wig, and she had our immediate and full attention throughout her speech on leukemia. Note that this combines the personal reference with a startling statement.

- *An audio or visual aid.* Sometimes an audio or visual aid can be useful as an attention getter. One student who was going to give a speech on a Spanish festival played 10 seconds of festival music to gain the audience's attention. If you choose a topic of childhood obesity, you might begin with a visual of the number of obese children in 1980 vs. the number of obese children today. Typically if you use a startling statistic, having it visually available gives it even more impact.

- *Humor.* We urge caution with the use of humor. You should only use it if it is relevant to the topic. Sometimes, speakers tell a joke and then proceed with a presentation on a totally different topic. This is confusing to the audience. Humor must be appropriate for the topic and the audience. Any joke that is offensive whatsoever (and that really limits your choices) will lose the audience's attention instead of gaining it. Finally, the material must be genuinely funny. If a speaker delivers a joke and is the only one who laughs, that is an extremely awkward beginning. Given the diversity of audiences, we advise using humor with extreme caution.

Remember, an attention getter will not affect everyone the same way. Some of the examples above will appear more effective to you than others. Most importantly, the attention getter must be related to the topic in some way, must be appropriate for the speaker and the audience, and must actually attract the audience's attention.

TRY IT!

Write an attention-getting device for your speech on music.

_____

_____

CONNECTION STEP

Have you ever found yourself listening to a speaker and saying to yourself, "So what? What does this have to do with me?" That speaker forgot the second part of the introduction, which is the **connection step.** In this section of the speech, you must connect with the audience to let them know why the topic is relevant to them. Audiences are egocentric—they care about what relates directly to them.

You can make the connection with what the audience cares about in numerous ways. Looking at some of our attention-gaining examples, try to develop some connection steps. Why would an audience of college students need to know about Madrid or leukemia or childhood obesity? The need to know about these topics is a little less obvious than it is about some topics, such as time management, money management, or study skills, where you can immediately see the relationship to the college audience.

For example, you might state in the connection step for a speech on Madrid that learning about other cultures is valuable and that its architectural distinctions could be the subject of a future conversation, perhaps with a potential employer. You might address the connection step in a speech on leukemia by stating the percentage of children who get the disease, or the chance of having a child with it, or the likelihood of knowing someone who has it. You can then state what percentage of the audience is likely to come into contact with someone who has leukemia. Childhood obesity may not seem relevant to a college-age audience. Linking it with younger brothers, sisters, nieces, nephews, friends, or one's future children helps audiences see the problem as a national issue. If you don't make these connections, the audience will tune out because they cannot see how the information applies to them.

TRY IT!

Write a connection step for your speech on music.

_____

_____

_____

Professional Perspective

Lay members of our church are asked to speak during our services. While we have some wonderful speakers, others are less prepared and harder to follow. When I hear speakers at church, school, or in business, I find myself asking three questions:

- What is it you are trying to tell me?
- Why on earth should I care about what you're saying?
- Who the heck are _you_ to be telling me this?

If these questions aren't answered within the first couple minutes then I'm less likely to listen.

Speakers who make it easy for me to follow keep my attention. The best way to make it easy for me to follow is for you to tell me in the beginning what you're going to say and then stick to your points throughout the body of the speech. It is hard for me to know where a speaker is going when the points addressed are different from how they were listed in the introduction. If the points come out of order, or if the speaker adds points not mentioned in an introduction, I get lost easily. My mind wanders a lot without any help from anyone else! Speakers who wander in their presentation make it even worse and all I get out of it is what I was thinking—not what the message was about. Your audience can be distracted easily enough on their own. Why help them be distracted?

One way to help keep my attention and prevent unnecessary distractions is to answer the questions I mentioned earlier. Don't answer them just in the introduction; also look for ways to weave them throughout the entire speech. Doing this reinforces for your audience what you're saying, why they should care, and why they should listen to you.

Speakers who go the extra mile in their preparation and answer these questions gain and keep my attention and interest.

—Raymond R. Ozley
Lecturer
University of Montevallo

CREDIBILITY

Once you have the audience's attention, and you've convinced them the information is important to them, you begin to present information that allows the audience to assess your credibility. **Credibility** is the believability factor of a speaker. A critical consumer of communication should always ask, "Why should I listen to you?" Effective speakers present solid information in the introduction of the speech, encouraging the audience to believe they are credible. Speakers can mention their credentials (certifications, degrees), their research (articles, books), and their personal connection (experience with the topic).

Even though speakers present information concerning their credibility, the listener actually determines the credibility. A speaker cannot say, "I am credible because. . . ." For instance, as authors of this textbook, we cannot say we are credible. Instead, we might tell you we both have PhDs in speech, we've given numerous public presentations, and we have over 60 years combined college teaching experience in communication. This would state our qualifications and experience. Does that make us credible? Not necessarily. If you saw us in a public performance and we made a grammatically incorrect statement, spoke with vocalized pauses, or spoke with a local dialect (although using a local dialect would enhance your credibility with certain audiences), we could lose credibility instantly.

In the credibility statement, it is best to state your research and your experience with the topic. Then, the audience can assess your credibility initially and throughout the speech. Consider the following two examples. Robert is giving a speech on a software program for the home computer. He states he has done research in *Computer Journal* and has been writing software programs for three years. Bernhard is also giving a software speech, and he states he read an article in a weekly popular culture magazine. Who will have better credibility?

It is important to maintain credibility before, during, and after the speech. When Patrick goes to the front of the room, takes numerous deep breaths, and states how nervous he is, he loses credibility immediately. When Gwen does not attribute any of the statements she makes to reliable sources, she loses credibility. The person who stomps over to the trash to dispose of note cards immediately after presenting the speech, or, alternatively, makes a production of throwing a speech grade in the trash can, loses whatever credibility was established. Similarly, a person who gives a persuasive speech on picking up litter and later tosses a gum wrapper on the ground also loses credibility.

As speech professionals, either of us could create a dynamic speech to convince you to become a vegetarian. We know the right sources, the right persuasive techniques, and the right emotional appeals. However, we are not vegetarians; therefore, it would be unethical for us to try to persuade others to practice something we do not. The same rule applies

---

TRY IT!

Write a credibility statement for your speech on music.

_____

_____

to informative speaking. You must know your information and have valid facts and research. Misrepresenting yourself in any way is unethical.

PREVIEW

The final step of the introduction is the **preview.** This is the navigational tool for the speech. When you read something, if you become lost or confused, you can go back and reread the paragraph. But in presentational speaking, the audience has only one chance to follow you. By providing a preview that states your three main points, the audience can mentally join your journey through the topic. Audiences should know what you are going to discuss and the precise order in which you will discuss it.

The preview relates directly to the key you selected. Audiences have short attention spans, are egocentric, and may have difficulty seeing connections among main points. Reinforcing the commonality of your points helps your audience follow your speech. Be sure to use your key in the preview of your speech. However, try to be somewhat subtle in your preview. Speakers should not say, "My three main points are . . .", but they can say, "Today I'd like to cover the three historical aspects [key] of Faneuil Hall Market Place, which are its founding, the designer, and its original name."

TRY IT!

Write a preview statement for your speech on music.

_____

_____

TRANSITIONS

Transitions are bridging statements that tie the organizational elements of your speech together. You need transitions between the introduction and the body of the speech, between each main point, and between the body and the conclusion. A transition statement is another place where mentioning the key is imperative to helping the audience follow along.

In the speech on Faneuil Hall Market Place, our key was historical aspects. After previewing the topic and order as stated above, you might get from the introduction to the first main point by stating, "The first historical aspect is. . . ." You can get to the second point by a transition like, "Now that you know the founder, I'd like to tell you about the designer," or simply, "The second historical aspect is the designer." These are the standard types of transitions.

You may want to be even more creative with a transition, using something like: "The men and women who settled Massachusetts in 1630 needed to obtain goods and other commercial services for survival. A farmer's market where the community could gather socially and obtain food was developed by. . . ." This transition could be used after the preview and lead into the body of a speech about the founding of Faneuil Hall.

Body

In the **body** section of the outline, list your main points and all your supporting material. We recommend a **keyword outline**—a list of the words and phrases you need to remember to remain organized. For example, if you are going to give a speech to introduce yourself, you don't need to write out, "Hello, my name is Mark Henry. I am from Newark, New Jersey. . . ." Instead, you can just jot down the words "name," "hometown," etc., on a 3 × 5 card. You should use enough keywords and phrases in your outline so you don't forget what you want to talk about. But you should not have so much information that you are reading your speech. Keyword outlines allow you to practice extemporaneous speaking. Extemporaneous speaking simply means conversational speaking. (We will discuss extemporaneous speaking again in chapter 9.) The extemporaneous style is the best delivery style for a public speaker because you aren't reading to the audience—you are talking to them in a relaxed, conversational manner.

You should also include *source citations* in the main point section of the outline. In addition to your credibility statement, you build credibility throughout the speech by using proper citations. A citation includes the name of the research source. For a speech, you need to use either a title or author and the date for the source. "According to a March 2011 issue of *Time* magazine . . ." or "*Field and Stream* stated in an article published in February 2011 that. . . ." You do not need to include a full bibliography. The purpose of citations is to allow the audience to judge whether the information is current and from a legitimate source. You typically give the attribution prior to the quotation in public speaking. This helps the audience to understand that the words are not yours but those of an established source. Once you complete your main points, you are ready for the conclusion of your speech.

Conclusion

There are three parts to an effective **conclusion:** review, restatement of connection, and a concluding statement. The conclusion, like the introduction, is a short segment of your speech. You should not spend more than 5–10 percent of total speaking time on your conclusion.

The **review** is the same as the preview. This is your chance to remind the audience what your three main points were. It helps the audience to solidify the points in their minds, so be sure to mention your key one last time (So today I covered the three steps of . . .). It also lets the audience know you are wrapping up the speech. We recommend you do not say something like, "In conclusion. . . ." This phrase is not necessary for short speeches. It also shows the audience you lack creativity in your transitions. The audience will know you are concluding when you review your main points.

The second step of the conclusion is to **restate the connection.** Remind the audience why this information is important or relevant to them. It reemphasizes why the audience just spent their time listening to you.

A **concluding statement** is the last part of an effective conclusion. Unfortunately, many speakers do not plan their concluding statement, so they end up saying something like "that's it." This does not leave the audience with a favorable impression. A weak concluding statement destroys your credibility.

To maintain credibility, you need to find a unique way of restating the content of the speech to make a connection with the minds or hearts of the listeners. The concluding statement is the opportunity to strike a resonant chord with the audience. You want to leave them with a reaction of awe, joy, thoughtfulness, laughter, fear, sadness, or action. One student gave a speech on rock climbing. She ended it with, "The next time you hear 'on the rocks,' you'll think of another way to have some fun!"

When you finish your conclusion, check to make sure the thesis, preview, main points, and review contain identical information.

TRY IT!

Write a conclusion for your speech on music.

_____

_____

_____

_____

_____

Bibliography

At the end of your outline, you should always include a *bibliography.* We talked about keeping track of your sources in the section on research. There are different bibliographic styles, such as APA (American Psychological Association), MLA (Modern Language Association), and others. The order of elements, capitalization, use of quotation marks and italics are some of the differences in each style. Your instructor will tell you which style to use. We encourage you to consult published manuals or Internet sources that explain how to use each form of citation. The rules change with every edition of these manuals, so you need to check the most current edition.

CHOICES AND CONSEQUENCES

You procrastinate and end up working on your speech until the night before it is due. You don't have time to research and organize the material. What are the consequences of this choice?

_____

_____

_____

_____

Summary

Researching, organizing, and outlining information is a logical process. While it makes sense to follow these steps sequentially, you may find that you need to revisit a step that you have already completed. Once you have supported, organized, and outlined your information, you will be ready for the final step in the speech design process. The next chapter discusses choosing a delivery style and delivering the speech. Listen carefully to other speakers. Critique their speaking style by following the speech design process as an active listener. The more you analyze others, the easier it will be for you to improve your speaking style.

KEY WORDS

analogies	keyword outline
attention getter	main points
bibliography	organizational pattern
body	outlining
comparison structure	preview
concluding statement	research
conclusion	restate the connection
connection step	review
contrast structure	space structure
credibility	statistics
definitions	supporting material
examples	title
expert opinion	time structure
facts	topical/classification structure
introduction	transition

DISCUSSION/ACTIVITIES

1. Describe the various types of research that would assist the audience in paying attention to what you are saying.

2. How do you know that Internet sites are valid and reliable to use for a speech? Discuss.

3. Who is the most credible speaker you have ever heard? Explain.

4. What is the most memorable attention-getting opener you have heard for a speech? Analyze why it worked for you.

5. Jot down the factual statements used during a class lecture. Why do you think the statements you have written down are facts?

6. Attend a guest lecture on campus and write down the connection step used by the speaker to establish credibility on the topic. Do you feel the speaker is credible?

7. What speech organizational patterns do you associate with teachers in various disciplines? Explain.

8. How do interviews boost topic credibility? When were the interviews mentioned in a speech done?

9. Are local connections to a speech topic more intriguing to an audience? For example, if the topic relates to crime, did the speaker use local crime statistics as part of their supporting evidence? Does a local connection to the topic help you pay attention to the speaker?

Presenting the Speech

After reading this chapter, you should be able to:

- List the four styles of delivery
- Understand articulation, pronunciation, and grammar
- Explain the importance of visual aids
- Recognize effective uses of visual aids
- Explain the importance of practice
- Understand communication apprehension
- Understand how to critique a classmate

Your speech design planning and organization are about to pay off. The exciting final step of the design process is selecting the delivery style to highlight your detailed speech preparation. You have a mental picture of the entire speech as soon as you complete the outline. Now it is time to lift the words from the page and articulate them as sincere personal thoughts for the audience. This mental transition from thoughts to verbal communication is occasionally an obstacle for some speakers. Many people know how to compose an organized, logically written paper, but they don't have the vocal skills and confidence to translate their carefully prepared research into an oral presentation that will resonate with listeners. This final step may seem daunting, but it really isn't.

Step 11: Delivery Style, Visual Aids, and Practicing

We want to remind you that this discussion sets general guidelines for delivery, presentational style, and the use of visual aids. Each professional discipline presents its own variations of these guidelines.

Work closely with your academic mentors to find the presentational norms for your discipline. You must look and sound like a professional in your field when you speak to other professionals.

Delivery

There are four *delivery styles:*

1. *Impromptu:* speaking with no preparation at all

2. *Manuscript:* reading from a written paper

3. *Memorized:* written out and committed to memory

4. *Extemporaneous:* using key words and phrases to promote a conversational style

Everyone must do ***impromptu*** speaking at one time or another. If a teacher calls on you in class, you do impromptu speaking. You also do impromptu speaking in an employment interview when you answer an unexpected question. However, this style is not appropriate for a formal speaking situation. Very few people are talented enough to pull off an effective impromptu speech.

Some professionals use ***manuscript*** speaking. The president of the United States, for example, must speak from a manuscript during national addresses to ensure every word that has been planned is delivered correctly. The speech is read from a teleprompter to make the president look more natural to the television audience. The audience may think the president is talking directly to them during an address, but the president is actually reading from a manuscript.

There are very few speech occasions where a manuscript speech is appropriate. Audiences get annoyed when speakers read to them. How do you feel on the first day of class when an instructor reads the entire syllabus to you? Most students feel offended. Students can read the syllabus themselves—and in more comfortable places than a classroom seat. Manuscript delivery can remind you of your first-grade librarian who came into class and read a book. This is a condescending delivery style for an adult audience.

Memorized speeches also have problems. While memorized speeches sometimes sound very polished, they more frequently sound scripted, and the speaker usually lacks natural vocal variety. An actor works from memorized scripts because he or she is performing someone else's words, but a good speaker works from notes. Speakers need a relaxed conversational style. When we memorize, we concentrate on the fact that "this word" follows that "word," which goes after "this word." We do not think about the total concept and shape of the speech. Therefore, if we forget a word, it is much more difficult to recover mentally during the speech. We have seen numerous students who memorized speeches despite our warnings about potential problems. In almost all cases, either the speeches sounded unnatural, or the student forgot a word, panicked, and could not complete the assignment.

Extemporaneous speaking is conversational speaking. This is the preferred delivery style for most speaking situations. With extemporaneous speaking, speakers note key words and phrases on cards to help them remember the concepts they want to cover. They talk about those concepts, glancing at the written notes if they need to remind themselves about an example. If you want to call a company to lodge a complaint about a defective product, you might jot down some of the key points you want to remember. You don't write it out word for word or memorize it, but you refer to your list and make sure you cover all of the points on it. This delivery style helps listeners feel as though they are important because we are talking to them and not at them. The style also allows for adaptation on the part of the speaker. If you see that the audience doesn't understand a concept, you can add another example. If you see they are bored, you might add some humor or pick up the pace. One way to speak consistently in a conversational style is to imagine you are sitting at a kitchen table sipping a hot drink and communicating with a friend. An audience becomes your friend. This mental game keeps your voice warm and the delivery spontaneous.

Critical Thinking

Think about the last presentation you experienced. What style of delivery did the speaker use? How effective was it?

_____

_____

_____

_____

Articulation, Pronunciation, and Grammar

Articulation is the proper formation and release of the sounds that make up a spoken language. Using "proper" speech should be the goal of all speakers. Many local dialects don't use properly articulated English sounds, or they modify those sounds. For example, many people drop word endings. Going fishing becomes "goin' fishin'." In other regional dialects, people drop the "t," "k," and "p" sounds. So, gift becomes "gif."

A word like "fact" should actually be articulated as "fa-k-t," but some people drop the "t" sound and simply say "fak."

If you move to another location or into the business world, you may find that people will perceive you to be uneducated if you use the local dialect from the region in which you were raised. For instance, some people from the town of Scranton, Pennsylvania, drop the "t" and say they are from "Scran-in." While that pronunciation is usually acceptable in their area, people who travel elsewhere lose credibility when they announce where they are from. Most people would wonder why they can't pronounce the name of their own hometown correctly. It is your job as a speaker to monitor your sounds and compensate for any errors in your local dialect.

You may think a discussion of articulation is mundane; however, proper articulation is essential to make your message clear to a diverse audience. People who articulate well stand out. In fact, proper articulation is so coveted that in South Korea some parents choose tongue surgery for their young children to enable them to articulate English sounds more clearly ("A Short Cut," n.d.).

Proper articulation relates to proper **pronunciation** as well. Pronunciation is the accepted sound of a word according to the dictionary. A word like "get" is often pronounced "git." People say "you are taking me for granite" instead of "for granted." "Ask" in urban speech is pronounced "aks" or "axe." There is also an interesting pronunciation rule for the word "the." There is a difference between "the" pronounced

---

Professional Perspective

I was in the business 20 years before making it to the network level in New York. On day one, I was greeted by a coanchor who, after learning that I was from the South, replied, "Oh, diversity is good." But in fact I had gotten rid of my accent many years earlier.

When I started in commercial radio, I was 20 years old and going to college in Mississippi. My friends and family immediately noticed a difference in the way I spoke. Even though I was still surrounded by southern accents, my own accent hurt my ears when I would listen to daily "air checks." Eventually, I learned to correct the patterns that bothered me.

I also got some good advice in a college speaking class, including learning to pronounce the "e" in words like "get." I'd never noticed I pronounced it like an "i."

My editors still point out my accent on occasion. Especially the varying emphasis on words like umbrella, from "UM-brel-la" (southern) to "Um-BREL-la." I now say "in-SURE-ance," rather than "IN-sur-ance."

While I don't think a dialect necessarily hurts a person's radio career these days, I don't think one can work in radio worldwide without using universally recognized pronunciation. Throughout a long career, I've picked up dialects, vocabulary, and mannerisms from nearly every place I've traveled.

—Cami McCormick
Network Correspondent
CBS Network Radio News

"thuh" and "the" pronounced "thee." You should use "thuh" before all words that begin with a consonant such as, "thuh choir." But, you use "thee" before any words that begin with a vowel, such as "thee orchestra." This subtle difference can make you stand out to an audience.

Every time you read something out loud, focus on the rules of pronunciation and proper articulation. Remember your audience. The audience determines if you are credible as they listen to you. Your voice holds clues to your educational level and training. Do you want to be perceived as a professional? Then you'll need to practice pronouncing words correctly.

TRY IT!

Read the following out loud.

The girl and the iguana walked through the forest. They were going exploring. The girl and the iguana saw the orange and the apple hanging in the tree. The sight of the enormous apple whets their appetite.

Did you articulate the "t" and "ing" endings? Did you catch all the "thuhs" and "thees"?

Grammar is the set of rules that determine the correct use of a specific language. Usually people think about grammatical errors when they write, but grammar also applies to oral communication. Review your speech patterns for the following potential errors:

- One of the biggest errors in spoken speech is the adverbial form. People drop the "ly" ending from adverbs. For example, many people say, "Please drive safe" instead of "safely," or they use an adjective instead of an adverb, saying, "He draws good" instead of "He draws well."

- Some people also misuse pronouns. Someone might say, "It is a conversation between my brother and I." Because the pronoun in this case is the object of the preposition, the objective form is correct: "between my brother and me."

- Verb forms may also be skewed, particularly in broadcast sports speech. "That team was beat last night" rather than "beaten." Listen carefully to electronic media sports personalities and announcers at a local game. What do you hear? Do you mimic their mistakes?

Following are other delivery qualities that will affect your speech:

- *Rate* refers to the speed at which you deliver a sequence of words. You do not want to speak too quickly or too slowly, because either one makes it difficult for the audience to pay attention.

- **Projection** is important so that everyone in the room can hear you comfortably. Audiences lose interest immediately if they cannot hear you. But remember, a booming delivery style can also be uncomfortable for an audience who may feel as though a speaker is yelling at them. Moderation is the key.

- **Vocalized pauses** are a repeated audible habit used by some speakers. They occur when you fill a natural pause with an "um," "uh," "like," or "you know" rather than a preferable, thoughtful silence. While one "um" in a speech is not distracting, if you do this on a regular basis, your audience will focus more on your vocalized pauses than on the content of your message.

- **Inflection** is important in vocal delivery. Inflection refers to your vocal pitch going higher or lower. Most people can do this naturally to some extent. The key to natural inflection is a relaxed, conversational style. Inflection eliminates a monotone performance.

Try to work to improve your voice, but don't get frustrated. It takes time to retrain old habits. Work on introducing new motor skills into your speech or alter the way you've learned to say certain words a little at a time.

CHOICES AND CONSEQUENCES

You recognize you speak in a local dialect. What are your choices?

_____

_____

What are the consequences?

_____

_____

Visuals

Visuals are an important part of good presentational speaking. Use a **visual aid** whenever you wish to clarify a concept or enhance the understanding of audience members. Some people need a visual to back up the auditory message they hear—they need to see what you are talking about to understand. PowerPoints, DVDs, and streaming video are some of the many choices available to help engage listeners. When choosing a visual, think about which concepts in your speech may be hard for the audience to understand without seeing something. A good general rule is to make sure your visuals do not take any more than 5 percent of your total speaking time.

TRADITIONAL VISUALS

Poster boards, transparencies, or drawings on easels or chalkboards are now outdated and should not be used, perhaps because they appear far less professional than images prepared using computer technology. Only a few *traditional visuals* are still used today, such as objects and media clips.

Objects. Items such as sculptures, musical instruments, shop tools, running shoes, horse gear, a newspaper, a hundred-dollar bill, clothing, craft items, or sports equipment can attract attention. An object can bring a portion of your speech to life for an audience. But the object must fit the topic you are presenting and not be distracting.

Media Clips. If you use a media clip to reinforce a speaking point, keep it short. Generally, you need to limit media clips to about 10–20 seconds depending on the length of the speech. Make sure the segment you need is cued to the exact spot. If you aren't cued, communication stops, and so does your credibility.

TRY IT!

What traditional visual aid could you use for your speech on music?

_____

_____

VISUAL TECHNOLOGY

Visual technology refers to electronic equipment used to enhance a presentation, such as a PowerPoint presentation, laser pointers, a website, YouTube, and DVD players. However, many speakers forget the purpose of a visual aid when they begin to use technology. Speakers may have a great time with the technology, but they generally forget to focus on the audience rather than the technology.

Most of you have witnessed a presentation where the speaker dims the lights and puts a variety of words on a screen using PowerPoint software. PowerPoint is nothing more than an up-to-date filmstrip presentation if it is used as the entire focus of the speech. Some speakers use technology to entertain you. We have found that people who rely exclusively on PowerPoint usually are terrified of public speaking; they use PowerPoint to hide from the gaze of their audience. This is an abuse of technology, your time, and the speaking situation. When people use technology this way, they are eliminating the interactive and interpersonal dimensions of public speaking. Words on a screen are not a speech. Would you rather have someone hiding and showing you printed material on the screen that you could read at home, or do you want someone to talk directly to you in an exchange of information?

Of course, PowerPoint has its place in public speaking. When used correctly by selecting information that enhances the audience's understanding of a point, it can look professional and be extremely effective. But the use of PowerPoint must follow the same time guideline as any other visual aid in public speaking—five percent of total time.

To use PowerPoint effectively, make sure you check the color design combinations (yellow and some other light colors don't show up) and the font size (a 20–24-point font is necessary). You should have no more than five lines, no more than five words per line, and only one concept per slide (Weaver, 1999). The audience must be able to absorb the visual information easily without eyestrain. Some members of the audience may have color-deficient vision. The majority of these individuals see color images but with varying degrees of color intensity. You can be visually inclusive using color-designed aids such as PowerPoint if your presentation contains a great deal of color-intensity contrast (i.e., dark lettering on a light background or vice versa).

Rules for Visuals.   Simply having a visual to help the audience understand a concept does not ensure their understanding. The use of visual aids can enhance or detract from a presentation depending on how you use them. There are a number of things you can do to make sure that your use of a visual aid goes smoothly.

1. Make sure to practice with your visual. Visuals take time to set up and take down. You must also know how to run the equipment. You should never say, "Well, this worked before" or "How do you run the overhead?" The audience will assume you are incompetent and immediately lose any interest in hearing what you have to say.

2. Make sure the visuals are large enough to be seen and read by everyone. Most of you have heard a speaker say, "I know you can't see this, but. . . ." What is the point? The statement makes the speaker sound ridiculous. If an object can't be seen, then either figure out a way for the audience to see it or eliminate it. Sometimes a speaker can walk through the audience with a smaller object. Pictures can be scanned and the size increased so that the entire audience can view it.

3. Passing visuals through an audience is risky. It is distracting. Before the visual even gets past five people you will be on your next point. And, it never fails that the object will not make it through the entire audience before the end of your speech. If the purpose of the visual is to enhance understanding, then passing it is extremely ineffective. However, if you need your audience to refer to a paper during your presentation, you can explore the option of passing it out facedown ahead of time, so they have it to look at when you tell them to do so. Or if it is something that they should take with them after the presentation, you can mention that you have a handout for them to pick up before they leave.

4. Only show the visual while you are talking about it. A visual should be shown in a place where all audience members can see it. You should reveal it at the point where it will complement your information, and then you should remove it. When you are displaying it, make sure you continue talking to your audience and not to the visual aid. Never turn your back on the audience.

5. Explain the visual. Speakers have a tendency to show a Power-Point chart, graph or statistical information in such a hurry that it is on, then off, and you are left wondering what you just saw. Take a minute to explain to the audience what the visual means.

6. Do not bring anything illegal or harmful as a visual. Animals are generally not permitted in public buildings. Weapons of any kind (or even plastic guns, etc.) are inappropriate. Any kind of implement that could be used as a weapon is inappropriate as a visual (fishing knives, spears, etc.). Since alcohol is banned from college campuses, it should not be used as a visual.

7. Make sure to cite the visual source. If you got a visual from a website or a book, that citation should be at the bottom of your overhead or PowerPoint slide. If you borrowed the object from somewhere, you should be sure to credit your source.

8. Most importantly, have a backup plan. Projection bulbs blow out, volume controls aren't turned on, and equipment fails. You need

---

Critical Thinking

Describe a time when you saw a speaker use a visual ineffectively. What was your reaction?

_____

_____

_____

to be prepared for any of these situations. In some speaking situations, you may need to finish the speech without the planned visual aid. Don't panic. You have studied your topic thoroughly; use that knowledge to replace the visual information with a verbal description. Remain relaxed and in control.

Practice

It is essential that you *practice* out loud with a stopwatch. We do not recommend practicing in front of a mirror or with a tape recorder. The most important aspect of practice is to hear yourself say the words. One of our favorite student quotes is, "I didn't think I needed to practice. I sounded so eloquent in my mind." When you go through a speech in your mind, there are no vocalized pauses, no problems with transitions, no mispronounced words, no throat noises, and no delivery errors. But, there is no yellow brick road to a speaker's podium. You must practice out loud.

The first time you practice delivering your speech, it will probably sound pretty awful and will exceed the time limit. This is normal. The second time you say it out loud, it will get better and closer to the allotted time. By the fourth effort, you will start to sound like a polished speaker. You will change your wording during every practice session and even during the formal presentation using the extemporaneous style. Word changes are normal. Never panic. Concentrate. You will feel more comfortable with each practice session.

If your speech is consistently long on time, cut the material. Don't make the mistake of thinking you can shorten a 16-minute speech to fit a 6-minute time limit by speaking faster. If you are over the time limit, you need to cut the material to the essential points.

ETHICAL CONSIDERATIONS

Is it ethical to waste an audience's time if you have not properly practiced your speech?

GIVING THE PRESENTATION

You should plan carefully for the day of your presentation. Make a list of everything you need; gather and organize all the materials you need the night before a speech. Racing around before a speech or finding you have forgotten a crucial visual or required outline will only unnerve you. Try not to do this to yourself.

Know your own body chemistry. If you have an early presentation, but it takes you a couple of hours to wake up in the morning, you need to get up earlier the day of your speech to give yourself time to be mentally and vocally alert. Speakers should not take coffee with them to the platform. It's rude and distracting for an audience. Remember, your vocal chords take time to warm up. Your vocal chords are the key to good vocal technique. Articulation and pronunciation errors occur when your mind and vocal chords aren't working together.

If you are a little nervous before a speech, exercise can help you calm down. If that is not possible, you can try taking some deep breaths and exhaling slowly. The best way to make sure you are breathing correctly is to make sure your chest remains stationary, but your abdomen moves when you breathe. Abdominal breathing increases the support for your voice and helps you to relax. Search the Internet for hundreds of examples of relaxation exercises to prepare yourself mentally and physically for a presentation; try them and find one that works for you.

Potential Problems. Despite your best efforts to prepare, you might occasionally address an audience with members who present roadblocks to delivering your presentation. Lisa Hanasono created a typology and strategies for dealing with hostile, disruptive, disengaged, and overly engaged audience members based on her experiences teaching public speaking.

Professional Perspective

Tips for Dealing with Difficult Audience Members

1. **Disengaged Audience Member:** This person has mentally checked out during another student's speech. The person may be sleeping, quietly reading a newspaper, or discreetly working on homework for another course.

   - Move around the room! Sometimes, moving closer to the disengaged audience member can catch his/her attention and draw that person back into your presentation.
   - Use attention-getting techniques like asking participatory questions, telling stories, sharing interesting statistics/facts, etc.
   - Localize the material of your presentation to your audience; try to increase the relevance of your speech content to your classmates.
   - Strive to make your delivery more dynamic by strategically altering your volume, speech rate, or vocal inflection.

2. **Tangential Audience Member:** This person asks questions that are unrelated to the speech.

   - Acknowledge the question (to show that you are listening) and attempt to link it back to the content of your presentation.
   - Politely explain that the question falls beyond the scope of your speech. If desired, you can offer to address this audience member's question at a later time.
   - If needed, politely explain that question falls beyond the parameters of your specific presentation and solicit questions from a different audience member.

(continued)

3. **Participatory Champion Audience Member:** This person dominates question-and-answer sessions. Although very well-informed and asking thought-provoking questions, he/she is preventing other students from participating.

   - After answering one or two of his/her questions, thank the audience member for his/her participation and interest. Then suggest it would also be useful to hear the perspectives of others and solicit questions from other audience members.

4. **Disruptive Audience Member:** The behavior is outwardly disruptive—answering a cell phone during the speech, socializing with another audience member, loudly sorting through his/her school bag, or leaving/entering the classroom during the presentation—and is distracting other audience members.

   - Use attention-getting techniques (e.g., asking a participatory question) to redirect his/her energy and focus to your presentation.
   - Politely identify the problematic behavior, empathize, and then redirect the behaviors in a positive manner.
   - If the disruptive behavior is fairly mild and not distracting other audience members/yourself, you can opt to ignore it. Alternatively, you can address the problematic behavior with the audience member *after* the presentation (to avoid embarrassing him/her in front of others).

5. **Hostile Audience Member:** This person has clearly rejected the speaker's central idea and uses his/her nonverbal behaviors to openly dismiss and reject the speaker's message.

   - You can decide to ignore the hostile audience member, especially if he/she is not being outwardly disruptive or distracting.
   - Acknowledge that some audience members seem to disagree with the main point. Encourage them to listen to the supporting evidence before rejecting the idea.
   - If the audience member poses a hostile or loaded question, repeat or paraphrase his/her question. This can prevent a potential misunderstanding between you and the audience member. It may also give you a moment to collect your thoughts and to organize your response.
   - Try to determine the underlying motives for the hostility by asking questions. Do they disagree with a particular section of your presentation?
   - Provide more evidence and sound arguments to support your position from research you didn't include in the presentation because of time limitations.

—Lisa Hanasono
Assistant Professor
Bowling Green University

Communication Apprehension.   Throughout the last three chapters, we have given you advice about how to reduce ***communication apprehension.*** Fear of public speaking is perfectly normal. Most people, including ourselves, get butterflies in the stomach or slight nausea or heart palpitations. Through careful planning and preparation, most of these symptoms will subside once you begin your presentation.

However, there is a small percentage of the population that suffers from extreme communication apprehension. These people may be so fearful of communication events that they cannot raise their hand in a class, call for a pizza, or engage in interpersonal communication. For many people, their fear may be localized to one of these situations. For others, they may experience extreme apprehension in all of them.

If you are not extremely apprehensive, then you can skip the rest of this section. But if you feel that you fit the description, there may be some tips to help you. I (KSY) taught a special section of oral communication at The Pennsylvania State University that was designed for students who had severe apprehension. The program was developed by Gerald M. Phillips, who published prolifically in the communication field for over 40 years. During the 1980s, Penn State had to offer three sections of the course every semester because of the number of students affected by severe communication apprehension.

The program encouraged students by having them first set a goal and then brainstorm scripts of communication encounters. For example, if Judy is afraid to call and order a pizza, she would set a goal ("I will call Joey's Pizzeria and order a pizza") and a date for when the event would take place. She would write what the person on the other end of the phone would most likely ask her and what her answer would be:

Judy:	Hi, I'd like to order a pizza.
Pizza place:	What size pizza would you like?
Judy:	Medium.
Pizza place:	Toppings?
Judy:	Yes, pepperoni please.
Pizza place:	Crust?
Judy:	Thin.
Pizza place:	Pick up or delivery?
Judy:	Pick up.
Pizza place:	Name?
Judy:	Judy.
Pizza place:	It'll be ready in 20 minutes.
Judy:	Thank you.

Once the script was brainstormed, Judy would practice reading it out loud over the next couple of days, employing the help of friends if possible. Phillips believed that communication apprehension would be reduced by practicing the words that would be used over and over again. For someone who is not severely affected by communication apprehension, this may seem to be a simple and tedious process, but it is effective and necessary for those who suffer from this debilitating condition. There are other theories for reducing communication apprehension, including meditation or systematic desensitization.

Critiquing Another Person

The idea of critiquing the performance of a classmate may seem intimidating at first. Think of the critique as an opportunity to help others (and yourself) improve their public performance. Written/verbal feedback is the only way an individual can assess whether their research, organizational, and performance skills are where they need to be. If you learn the concepts discussed throughout this book, you will be able to offer helpful suggestions for an effective presentation and to identify areas that need improvement. Remembering how others have criticized your work, as well as what you wish they might have said, will help you take personal feelings into consideration when selecting your comments to help others. A critique should be a positive way of making others better communicators.

Solid critiquing is a learned skill that requires practice and works best when facts are drawn from a speaker's performance. Objective language rather than subjective language allows someone to read your comments without becoming defensive. It pays to approach the critiquing experience with the idea of reaching out to help someone. This positive mental approach will guide your word choices. Remember the information about "I" messages. Critiques that begin with "I found your main points hard to follow" are less confrontational than "You didn't state your main points." But be honest. Giving a good critique when the performance was poor does nothing to help the speaker.

Make sure to critique only the behaviors and choices that the speaker can change. For instance, some women get a royal red flush on their necks when they speak. There is nothing the speaker can do to control that physical reaction to nerves other than wear a turtleneck. Therefore, focus on things that the speaker can do something about—particularly their content, organization, supporting material, citations, etc.

Although you may find doing a critique difficult at first, it is useful to remember that performance reviews (critiques) are used in the workplace to determine continuing employment, bonuses, and advancement within organizations. Not only will you receive constant critiques about your work in the years ahead of you, but you may also be expected to critique others. Professional communication improves your life as well as the lives of others through the analysis of facts.

We have provided a basic critique form to help beginners master the task.

Speaker Name _____

Questions	Your Comments
Was the introduction exciting?	
Did it contain an AGD, connection step, credibility statement, and preview?	
Identify the key	
Identify the 3 main points of the speech	
What was the most interesting piece of supporting material?	
Did the conclusion include a review, restatement of need, and strong concluding statement?	
Were there any delivery skills that distracted you?	

Your Name _____

Professional Perspective

First of all, when the occasion arises for you to speak, it is very important that you stick to the point and do not ramble; otherwise you will lose the audience, and they will stop listening to what you have to say. Second, it is equally important for you to be aware of your nonverbal behaviors. Maintain eye contact with the audience; this behavior reflects your interest in what you are doing. This is very important in U.S. culture. For example, when I first came to this country from India and started interviewing for jobs, I would not look the interviewer in the eye; as a result, my credibility and honesty were questioned. I was unsuccessful in getting a job. The negative turned into a positive; it prompted me to study differences in communication styles between various cultures.

Pehali baat yeh hai ki jab bhaashan dene ka samay aye, to ye dhyaan me rakhana bahut jaroori hain ki aap mudde pe baat karein, nahin to sunnewale sunna band karenge. Doosari baat yeh hai ke, aapko apne haav bhaav ka bhi dhyaan rakhna chahiye, jaise ki sunnewalon ke saath aankh se aankh mila kar baat karna, is se yeh pata chalta hai ki aap is mudde per dilchaspi rakhtein hein. Is desh mein (U.S.) is baat ka bahut dhyaan diya jataa hai. Udaharan ke liye, hum jab pehali baar is desh main aaye aur naukari dhoondh rahe the, to naukri dhoondte samay, parichay ke samay main hum sawal poochne wale ke taraf aakh uthakar bhi nahi dekhte the. Iske vajah se, mujhe naukari nahin mili, lekin acchi baat yeh hui ki isi kaaran, hum is kshetra mein dilchaspi lene lage ki alag sanskriti ke logon ka bol-chaal aur haav-bhaav ka tareeka kaise fark hota hai.

—Dr. Aparna G. Hebbani, Lecturer
School of Journalism and Communication, University of Queensland
Brisbane, Australia

Summary

Many people fear public speaking initially, but they learn that it can be mastered. You need to follow the speech design instructions given to you by a teacher or an executive, give yourself adequate time to prepare, know your information well, and practice out loud to sound natural for the audience. Your butterflies may never go away completely, but you can gradually learn to appear calm and to be confident in public speaking situations. Like anything else in life, it takes time to improve. Make sure you take the time to practice.

KEY WORDS

articulation
communication apprehension
delivery style
extemporaneous style
grammar
impromptu style
inflection
manuscript style
memorization style

practice
projection
pronunciation
rate
traditional visuals
visual aids
visual technology
vocalized pauses

DISCUSSION/ACTIVITIES

1. Describe a speaker whose delivery style is excellent. Explain.

2. Are certain visual aids more appealing to you than others when you listen to/observe a speaker?

3. List the visual aids you use when speaking to an audience. Why are you comfortable using those aids?

4. Which vocalized pauses are the most annoying to hear a speaker use? Why?

5. What elements of a speech critique do you find to be the most helpful? Why?

6. Which articulation, pronunciation, or grammar errors do you hear in others that distract you from what they are trying to say? Do you possess any of these errors yourself that you can correct?

7. Do you expect a speaker to make eye contact with you during a presentation? How often should this occur to keep you interested in them as an audience member?

8. Listen to one of your teachers during a lecture. How much time do you think they took to prepare for the lecture? Why do you feel that way?

9. How much preparation time do you require to feel comfortable in front of an audience? Remember, the same experience is present when you Skype or web conference. Technology is not any more forgiving of delivery errors than the "live" audience experience.

ten

Understanding the Principles of Persuasion

OBJECTIVES

After reading this chapter, you should be able to:

- Define persuasion *Process that involves a communicator who tries to influence the attitudes, beliefs, values, or actions of another individual. The message design & delivery (formally/informal)*
- Explain the idea of perceived choice
- Explain the difference between informing and persuading
- Identify the 4 contexts of persuasion
- List the three types of persuasive speeches

Adam and Megan are newly married. They have lots of gadgets in their spacious house: food dehydrators, a vacuum-sealing machine for food and clothes storage bags, etc. They own hundreds of pieces of jewelry and every tool in the world, all ordered from online shopping sites. They even possess name-brand cereals, sneakers, clothing, dishware, perfumes/colognes, and furniture. In addition, they rarely take overtime opportunities at their jobs to earn extra money because their friends constantly persuade them to go out partying. They are living the good life.

In reality, Adam and Megan are also in serious credit card debt. They can't resist persuasive messages. They use their credit cards freely rather than analyze the messages that influence their spending behavior. Although their lifestyle makes them appear very successful, Adam and Megan are living on dream power rather than actual earning power. Persuasive messages in our culture are quite powerful. It's important to think critically about media and social messages before you react to them. *You* are responsible for your financial behavior—not the media, family, or friends.

Throughout this chapter we will discuss the basic concepts of persuasion. In chapter 11, we will take you through the persuasive speech design process.

Defining Persuasion

Persuasion is a process that involves a communicator who tries to influence the attitudes, beliefs, values, or actions of another individual through message design and delivery, both formally and informally. Basically, a persuader tries to change or influence someone's opinions or behavior with well designed language and nonverbal stimuli. Persuasion happens in both public speaking (parts of school lectures, religious lectures, press conferences, electronic news, and corporate blogs and websites) and interpersonal communication (family gatherings, peers, and chat rooms) situations. For public speaking, each element of a persuasive message is crafted to influence others. If a message is designed well, it supports the audience's basic beliefs, values, and personal needs. Receivers often accept persuasive messages without thinking critically because they are constantly bombarded by them. On the interpersonal front, we use persuasion on a daily basis to influence the people around us to believe as we do, to do something with us, or to behave in a certain way. A simple comment like, "Let's go to the movies" is persuasive because you are targeting another individual and trying to get them to perform an action that benefits you.

If you take a semester-long course in persuasion, you'll find there are many variations of its definition. For our purposes, we limit the discussion of persuasion to messages designed with persuasive intent. In other words, when someone is persuaded by information, we don't label that as a persuasive message. This is basically the difference between *indirect persuasion* and *direct persuasion*. With indirect persuasion, you can be persuaded by facts. Think back to your round of informative speeches. You may have heard a speech on rock climbing. If the speaker followed content guidelines properly, it was strictly an informative speech. However, by hearing the information about rock climbing, you may have been influenced to try this activity during your next vacation. The speaker gave an informative rather than a persuasive speech, yet you were persuaded by the information to consider rock climbing. Another example of pure information affecting behavior is when a student changes his or her major after taking a course in a particular academic discipline. An instructor is usually not actively looking for new majors and using the course to persuade. But when the instructor presents facts and the student finds the information interesting, the student could decide to change majors. While the end result was persuasion, we do not consider this situation to be an example of a direct persuasive message. You design direct persuasive messages with intent to alter the beliefs or actions of another person.

Ultimately, receivers decide the effectiveness of the persuasive message. Receivers are in control and, therefore, must think critically about the persuasive messages they receive from friends, parents, bosses, advertising, news, and other media. You do not have to accept persuasive messages (such as your parents' political views) blindly unless you choose to do so. Some parents give their children a sense of family, set an example for personal standards and moral values, encourage them to study and succeed, and share their beliefs on many topics. As children mature, read, and reflect on various issues, they may find themselves at odds with some of the messages they have received from their parents. As adults, we are responsible for what we say and do—not our parents. Therefore, it is important to decide whether we are persuaded by a particular viewpoint, rather than accepting it without question because we have heard it so often. It is acceptable to change your views based on your own analysis of society and culture. "The ultimate power rests not with the source but the receiver, to attend or ignore, accept or reject, remember or forget, act or not act on the persuasive effort" (Benjamin, 1997, p. 12).

The definition of persuasion includes an actively designed message (i.e., opinion and reasoning are included), a perceived choice on the part of the listeners, and a goal of influencing the audience's attitudes, beliefs, values, or actions. Our definition also includes the concept that persuasion is a receiver-oriented phenomenon. People decide for themselves which messages will influence them and what actions they will take.

TRY IT!

List five examples of interpersonal persuasion you've seen or experienced in the past 24 hours.

_____

_____

_____

_____

_____

Informing versus Persuading

We talked about informative speaking earlier in the book. Informative and persuasive speaking have different basic goals. The goal of informative speaking is to get the audience to remember specific, factual information. With persuasive speaking, however, you add the personal element of drawing conclusions about the factual information you are sharing in order to get the audience to believe something or do something. As a receiver listening to an informative speech, you only need to assess the factual information. With persuasion, however, you must critically analyze the factual information as well as the communicator's reasoning to arrive at the conclusion. A persuasive speech attempts to get the audience to believe a specific point of view and sometimes to act on that point of view.

TRY IT!

Write an informative statement about food. _____

_____

Write a persuasive statement about food. _____

_____

_____

It is useful to know what's happening in our country and the world, and it is also important to remember your unique position in both of them. Media is a form of public speaking. It is your job to listen critically, analyze the information, and then alter your beliefs or actions based on sound judgment. It is equally as important to realize that we don't get all of the facts about any story unless we go looking for them. A lot of cultural persuasion occurs when people are complacent about obtaining all of the information necessary to make an informed decision.

TRY IT!

What kinds of stories on the news make you fearful? What are the chances that those events could happen to you?

_____

_____

_____

_____

_____

Reality ✓

Is the nightly news informative or persuasive? While we are taught to think that the news simply gives us the facts about what is going on in the world, we would be naive to think that it is unbiased information. Just as we filtered the information presented in this textbook and chose to focus on choices and consequences, a news producer is responsible for framing the information broadcast as well as the facts that were omitted from the story.

Broadcast news spotlights a limited number of events. Let's say the news reports an anthrax incident or a shark attack. Do you immediately think, "What percentage of the population is involved in such incidents?" Why not? Just because a story is reported does not mean that it influences your life in any way, so why worry about it?

Unfortunately, we do tend to focus on what is in the news. After 9/11 there were a number of reports of anthrax attacks. The number of people who died from those attacks numbered less than 20, yet many people were fearful and opened their mail with rubber gloves. At the same time, we rarely hear about intimate partner violence (IPV). These are assaults that occur between two people who are in an intimate relationship—not random, violent attacks. According to the Centers for Disease Control (2011), "women experience about 4.8 million intimate partner related physical assaults and rapes each year. Men are the victims of about 2.9 million intimate partner related physical assaults." And yet how much time do we spend fearing that we'll end up in an intimate relationship where that kind of horrible violence would take place? Chances are, you never think about it, because it is rarely brought to our attention.

The next time you watch the news, think of it as a persuasive presentation. What is the news channel trying to persuade you to believe about the world in which you live?

Perceived Choice

There is a fundamental distinction between persuasion and coercion. Persuasion, as defined above, is influence with a ***perceived choice,*** whereas **coercion** is perceived force. Many people argue that we have choices in every situation, and we agree. However, we may not always perceive that there is a choice.

For example, Kathleen turns in the first draft of a paper. She includes information and an analysis she believes is accurate. She draws a conclusion about the information and feels great conviction that her analysis of the subject is correct. However, the instructor returns her paper, questions her analysis, and does not agree with her conclusion even though it was supported by evidence she presented. The instructor tells her to rewrite the conclusion in a specific way. Kathleen does not agree with the teacher's decision, but she knows this instructor assigns failing grades to people who don't comply. She decides to change the conclusion of her paper according to the teacher's wishes.

In this case, Kathleen has not been persuaded that her analysis is incorrect; she has been coerced to change it. Coercion means there is no perceived choice in a specific situation. We label it a *perceived* choice because Kathleen does have choices, even if they include undesirable outcomes. She can disregard the instructor's comments and write what she believes to be the appropriate conclusion to her paper knowing her grade might be lowered. She can also discuss the conclusions with the teacher again and hope this time the teacher will approve the original analysis. However, because she needs a good grade in the class, and the teacher has a reputation for being closed-minded, Kathleen doesn't perceive she has a choice in this situation. Therefore, she is coerced to alter the paper's conclusion.

Coercion — you think you have no choice

Coercion can frequently occur in interpersonal relationships with siblings, friends, and intimate partners. It takes time to realize that you always seem to do a lot of things for other people, and they rarely make themselves available to you. Our siblings usually know nearly everything about us because we shared our lives with them growing up at home. Some of you may have had pleasant sibling relationships, while others of you did not. Regardless of which category you fall into, did a sibling ever use coercion to get you to do a task for them with the threat that they would tell your parents what you did or said? This is a common communication challenge in childhood, and yet it is coercion at a time in life when you aren't prepared to analyze the request and you don't perceive that you have a choice.

Friends use coercion to control our behavior by reminding us of what they did for us the last time we asked them to do something, so now it's our chance to return the favor. There is occasionally a payback theme to coercion, but it isn't a valid reason to do something for someone else. The emotional bond in this type of interpersonal exchange is usually applied to get the appropriate results. Even intimate relationships can display coercive techniques at times. One example of this type of coercion is family holiday visits. Which set of parents do you visit on which holidays? This discussion is always interesting with newly married couples, and the "traditional" visits are normally set before children enter the picture. If one individual is uncomfortable with their actions in an interpersonal situation, the action itself is probably the result of coercive messages. However, that person may have perceived that they had no choice in the matter when, in fact, they could have collaborated to achieve a different result.

Effective persuasion occurs when two people explore the options, share their reasons, look at all the information, and come to an effective agreement. One person will have persuaded the other to see their point of view, but each person should recognize that they have a choice.

Persuasion Comes from Many Places

Some efforts to persuade are easy to recognize, such as when your roommate persuades you to turn out the lights because she needs sleep

---

Professional Perspective

Some people always seem to get what they want. Other people only get what others want them to have. We need to ask, "Why?" The answer is, "Persuasion." In sales, like all other walks of life, persuasion is the difference between success and failure. Because so much depends on "making the sale," some agents are tempted to do *anything* in order to close a deal. This is an unfortunate, unethical implication of persuasion. Sales agents can become so skilled that they coerce or force a person into buying something that may not be suitable for them. In the world of investments and financial planning, for instance, an effective communicator must construct a range of persuasive appeals and arguments that can ethically be adapted to a range of clientele with differing needs. The ethical communicator constructs messages that accurately describe the rationale, the advantages and disadvantages, and the short-term and long-term implications of investment vehicles, recognizing that the needs of every client are unique. Ethical communicators use their persuasive abilities to construct messages that are based in truth and accuracy, allow the listeners to decide for themselves what action is best, and effectively demonstrate the implications of any decision for their clients.

—Barry McCauliff
Account Executive
The Investment Center

---

prior to a big test the next day. Or, you are out shopping with a peer, and they say you should buy something because you'd look good wearing it. You decline, but they continue telling you that you are worth the expense and haven't had anything new in a long time. When you went to the mall, you had no intention of buying anything. However, the persistent persuasion of your friend convinces you to purchase the item you don't need on your credit card bill without thinking twice. Do you regret the decision when the credit card bill arrives? Or, an organization in which you are a member is raising money for some cause. The cause may be worthwhile, but you don't have a particular interest in it—yet you hand over your money to support it.

These scenarios are reminders of how constant persuasive messages are in daily life. We often react to them without thinking about our actions or their financial toll on our budget. It may be time to think critically and then actively support those causes and values in which we truly believe.

Media projects numerous persuasive messages, whether through programming or advertising. Its messages are strategically aimed at all levels of culture. Did you ever look at the set and prop design background in your favorite program or ad? Does your family live in a home like the one your favorite characters inhabit? Do you have the same furniture and room decorations? Probably not, but they make a subtle impression on you to make decisions about your own color and style. You could decide to purchase similar items because you believe they will make you happy or that they will make you look more sophisticated. What about the wardrobes or hairstyles of your favorite celebrities? Do you stop to think that media talent have stylist/designers working with them to create the best look for them as individuals, or do you assume you'll look equally good if you style your hair similarly or buy clothing to copy a look? If you buy into the message, your money supports the advertisers and retailers promoting their products. It's possible you aren't even aware that your buying habits are shaped by media's overt and covert messages.

The media can shape our views as well. Gender communication theory looks at the pervasive persuasive messages designed to show us that women should look a certain way. The size of women that you see on TV is far smaller than the average-sized female in the general population. Typically women in sitcoms are a size 0–2, whereas the average American woman is somewhere between a size 12–16. Women you see on the covers of magazines and in advertisements have been made-up and then airbrushed and their image manipulated by a computer. In some instances the images are computer generated altogether, and there is no real person there. When we look at a person in an advertisement for cosmetics, the intended message is that we will look like that if we buy the product.

Our culture also generates a multitude of persuasive messages. If you are born in the United States, you receive persuasive messages about the importance of being an individual from the day you are born—from family, friends, and the media. You also learn the importance of money to buy "stuff." We'll examine just one more example: Bigger is better. This message dominates American culture—houses have expanded, cars are larger, etc. In England, the closets in homes are quite small because British culture encourages individuals to have a few things of very good quality rather than a lot of stuff. Americans, on the other hand, desire huge walk-in closets because bigger is better. The more you have, the more successful you are perceived to be.

As you experience daily persuasive messages, you need to think critically about each message and whether you are willing to be influenced by it. But in order to think actively through your choices as the receiver of a persuasive message, you need to recognize that you have a perceived choice.

TRY IT!

Take a quick look at how American culture has persuaded you to have more. Count up the number of items you have:

Pairs of shoes _____

Shirts _____

Electronic/digital gadgets _____

Contexts of Persuasion

We've already alluded to the different contexts of persuasion in some of the examples of the previous sections. However, it is a good idea to be very clear that persuasion does indeed happen in four separate contexts: intrapersonal, interpersonal, mass interpersonal, and mass persuasion. The analytical process you use in any one of the contexts can influence the decision making in others.

Intrapersonal Persuasion

Intrapersonal persuasion is the psychological analysis/discussion going on in your mind on a daily basis. Internal discussions weigh the visual, aural, and nonverbal stimuli confronting you against your previous experiences, standards of conduct, ethical convictions, and moral values to determine an appropriate response. For example, you believe that you don't give money to people who beg for it in public places. Yet one day while walking down the street in a city you are visiting, you spot an older citizen sitting on the cement in a doorway looking at the people passing by with an expressionless gaze. He appears hopeless and doesn't have a sign asking for money or reach his hand out as you walk past. You find yourself reaching into your pocket, pulling out a dollar bill, and walking back to hand it to him. He thanks you, and you turn and keep going, feeling better about your deed. You recognize that you just broke your rule about giving strangers money, but you feel good for doing it. There was something about that older citizen that persuaded you to act; your action evolved from indirect intrapersonal persuasion.

Interpersonal Persuasion

Everyone uses interpersonal persuasion daily. You can be a persuasive sender of a message or the receiver of a persuasive message. In either case, it is helpful to recognize what you are asking someone else to do or what they are asking you to do as the persuasion persists. It is important for you to be comfortable with your actions and to take responsibility for them even when a situation is rather simple.

For example, your roommates want you to go with them to a movie because they do not want to go alone. You and your roommates are close friends, and you decide to go to the movie even though you have a final examination in one of your classes the next day. You're sure you will be back before midnight, so you can stay up all night studying for the test. You hit the books once you return to the room. An hour into your studying, you fall asleep at the desk. You manage to wake up just in time to race to the final but perform poorly on the test. Your roommates engaged in a simple form of persuasion, but you are the one who took the risk of not doing well in one of your classes by not studying as you should have. Simple persuasive efforts happen daily, and it is important to analyze the pros and cons of each action or you may regret the consequences.

Critical Thinking

How often are you persuaded to do something that benefits someone else, but may harm you? Think about the example of a roommate asking you to turn out the lights. If you have a paper due the next day, how will you handle this? Do you cater to the needs of someone else while ignoring your own situation? Or do you find a solution that works for both of you, such as taking your laptop out of the room and going somewhere else to write so she can sleep?

There are many ways that we try to gain compliance from people. Parents try to get their children to follow rules. Managers try to get employees to work hard. Tamara Golish and Loreen Olsen (2000, p. 297) discuss ways that students try to use power in order to gain compliance from their instructors. They share some examples of antisocial behavior alteration techniques that we think are worth noting. How effective do you think these interpersonal persuasion strategies are when trying to get your professor to change a grade?

Blaming the Professor: "You graded this too hard. The material was too difficult."

Complaining: "I have too much to do in other classes."

Emotional Displays: Attempting to look really sad when discussing the grade.

General Excuses: "My grandparent died," or "I got the flu."

Punishing the Teacher: "This will reflect poorly on your evaluation."

Reference to Higher Authority: "I will talk to the dean or chair of the department."

Verbal Force/Demand: "I deserve a grade better than the one you gave me."

Have you ever used any of these? How effective were they? Look at this prosocial behavioral technique. *Honesty-Sincerity:* "I wish I had an excuse, but I just didn't get it finished." Do you think that would work better? How about the neutral ones below?

Pleading: "Please . . . I need this grade to graduate."

Play on Teacher's Ability to Relate: "Remember back when you were a student?"

Public Persuasion: Purposefully request a change in front of another student reasoning that it will be more difficult to say "no."

Stress/Overload: "I have a lot of tests right now . . . I am stressed out."

What you may find is that even some of the antisocial techniques may work on certain people. However, they do reflect on your character. For instance, threatening to report a teacher to a dean might work on an insecure teacher, but do you want to be known as someone who uses threats? And if your teacher is not insecure, you will lose all credibility by attempting this technique. Many of us have had instances where a student has said that, and, knowing we were in the right, we simply respond, "Go right ahead."

Mass Interpersonal Persuasion

The phenomenon of mass interpersonal persuasion "brings together the power of interpersonal persuasion with the reach of mass media . . . this new way to change attitudes and behavior is the most significant advance in persuasion since radio was invented in the 1890s" (Fogg, p. 1). B. J. Fogg lists six components of mass interpersonal persuasion:

1. *Persuasive Experience:* An experience that is created to change attitudes, behaviors, or both.

2. *Automated Structure:* Digital technology structures the persuasive experience.

3. *Social Distribution:* The persuasive experience is shared from one friend to another.

4. *Rapid Cycle:* The persuasive experience can be distributed quickly from one person to another.

5. *Huge Social Graph:* The persuasive experience can potentially reach millions of people connected through social ties or structured interactions.

6. *Measured Impact:* The effect of the persuasive experience is observable by users and creators (p. 4).

Mass interpersonal persuasion is being felt in today's society through social networking. The digital age presents one-on-one feelings to thousands and millions of people (fans/friends) globally. Each thought (factual or emotional) is sent into the cyber world with instantaneous responses from acquaintances and strangers alike who try to support you or put you down with their responses. For example, you post to your contact list that you are doing a walk/run to raise money for a specific cause. In addition, you include basic information with your post about the cause or add a hyperlink for those interested in reading more about the event. As a result of your post, you receive financial pledges for the cause. You may have thought you were sending information about your participation in a worthwhile cause, but your post generates money to support the cause and comments to support you. The financial contributions are the result of mass interpersonal persuasion. Your fans/friends like you while others like the cause more, but in either case, the message gets results.

Mass Persuasion

Mass persuasion involves messages designed to reach thousands or millions of people. These messages are usually developed by political groups, governments, businesses, or religious groups. It takes money and planning to coordinate messages that can convince, reinforce, or actuate thousands or millions of people. "Mass media persuasion takes three primary overt forms: *commercial advertising* (of consumer products and services), *pro-social advertising* [charities, advancing health care goals] and *political advertising*" (O'Keefe, n.d.). The designed messages are usually visual, aural, or a combination of both. The critical thing to remember when listening or viewing persuasive material is that you need to check the facts being presented against other reliable sources prior to being influenced by them. It's not always easy to check facts on every message, but that doesn't mean you should totally believe everything someone tells you or sends you either. Some of the greatest satisfactions in life come from making the effort to find the truth about facts. It may take time, but persistence will uncover the truth.

What Does It Take to Be Successful?

While we would hope every persuasive message we design ultimately leads to total audience/receiver change, that isn't a realistic goal. So let's start thinking in terms of a persuasive speech. How far must an audience shift in its attitudes, beliefs, values, or actions for you to be considered a good persuader? We will argue that if you get even one person in the audience to think about what you've said, you have been somewhat successful. Persuasion happens over time. Most people aren't persuaded to change their beliefs on major topics in a five- to ten-minute speech.

Sometimes your persuasive goal does not come to fruition for many years. For instance, if people are unaware of a specific issue, they may become more interested once they are better informed. If you don't know that dust mites grow in unwashed sheets, simply showing you a picture of the mites along with the information of how often sheets should be washed and at what temperature will be all the information you probably need to get the audience to take to action immediately.

Some people are persuaded by repetitive messages over time. For example, in the 1980s organ donation became a topic of public discussion, and college students used the topic for their persuasive speeches. The first time I (KSY) heard about this program, I thought, "Well, that is interesting. I ought to think about that." I didn't initially change my actions, however, but the thought was introduced. In subsequent semesters, I heard more speeches on the topic. As time passed, I finally decided to sign a card, but I made sure to list all kinds of exclusions, such as my corneas and other various body organs. After a few more semesters of hearing the message and processing the information, I became a full-fledged organ donor with no exclusions.

Other people may not change their beliefs until there is a personal connection. For example, health care organizations in the United States try to get the population to eat less sugar and sodium and lose weight to stave off diabetes. Even if you are overweight and eat poorly, you may not be affected by that message in the least until you find out that your mom or dad has developed Type 2 diabetes. Now the message is more urgent to you, and you might be more receptive to the persuasive messages to eat right and lose weight yourself.

No matter how well crafted the persuasive argument is, there are some people who will never be influenced by the message. Think about die-hard smokers who are perfectly happy to die with the cigarette in their hand.

Critical Thinking

What have you tried to persuade your parents to think about or do that took a number of attempts before you were successful?

_____

_____

Types of Persuasive Messages

There are three types of persuasive messages. Whichever one you choose to use becomes your goal statement for a persuasive speech or the basis for your interpersonal message. You must decide whether you are trying to convince, to reinforce, or to actuate with your communication. A message to **convince** targets the audience's attitudes, beliefs, and values. With this message, your goal is change. In a speech to convince, your audience disagrees with you or is neutral about your topic.

A message to **reinforce** also targets the audience's attitudes, beliefs, values, and actions. What makes this speech different is that the audience already agrees with you or is performing the action. You are strengthening the audience's convictions on the topic or reinforcing their motivation to continue doing the action.

A message to **actuate** is for people who are not *doing* an action you want them to do. A speech to actuate is best for listeners who are not hostile to your topic. You are more likely to get the audience to perform the action if they are already convinced the topic has merit or if they are neutral about the topic but simply lack the motivation to take action.

TRY IT!

These three goals also apply to interpersonal persuasion. Come up with examples of persuasive messages you have received or have used on others in each of these categories:

Convince _____

_____

Reinforce _____

_____

Actuate _____

_____

Let's look at the topic "Using a campus tutoring center." Think about realistic goals for a speech to an audience consisting of typical first-year college students. If the audience believes the tutoring service offers no benefits for them, you could *convince* this audience they should use the tutoring center. The end goal would be to change their belief that the tutoring center is not useful. If you found that most of your audience is already using the tutoring center, then you might design a speech to *reinforce*. You want to strengthen their belief that the center is helpful and motivate them to keep going. If the audience felt they could benefit from the tutoring center, but didn't have the motivation or knowledge to use it, then you would design a speech to *actuate*. The end goal would be to get audience members to make appointments at the tutoring center. As you can see from this discussion, audience analysis is imperative in deciding on the type of persuasive speech to present.

TRY IT!

For the remainder of this chapter and in chapter 11, we will use the following scenario for the Try It! boxes. Let's say you are a straight-A student who reads your textbooks each and every time they are assigned. You decide your goal will be to persuade your audience to do the same thing. Using this reading topic, what type of speech will you be designing?

Reality ✓

Have you ever heard anyone say, "You are preaching to the choir!"? What they are saying is, "Hey stop trying to convince me. I already believe your message!"

Summary

Although understanding persuasive messages seems quite simple, we often fail to apply our reasoning skills to the constant persuasion around us. You need to listen critically to every message you hear. Without analyzing persuasive messages, you could find yourself in a financial situation like the example of Adam and Megan at the beginning of this chapter. They were actuated to purchase items they did not need and could not afford. You may think you can avoid their circumstances, but poor judgment for just a moment can place you in a similar situation.

Persuasive messages can be positive. For example, think of the emotional reinforcement you acquire from a weekly religious service or the thrill you get when you finally convince your parents you are right about something. On a daily basis, you need to find people to go with you to dinner, lend you some money, and take you places. Persuasion is the tool that accomplishes these daily goals.

Know your beliefs and values well so you can recognize whether persuasive messages match your needs before you take an action. Avoid reacting to messages unless you are thinking critically. Question everything and discover significant reasons why you should believe certain philosophies or hold certain values. This intrapersonal discussion makes you a stronger communicator and increases your ability to persuade others so you can help them. Persuade by example. Be ethical in all the roles in which you find yourself—within the family, the community, and your chosen profession. Responsibility for your behavior and actions is an indication you are becoming a good communicator.

KEY WORDS

on paper

~~actuate~~	perceived choice
coercion	persuasion – on paper
~~convince~~	~~reinforce~~

DISCUSSION/ACTIVITIES

1. Describe a situation where you used coercion to achieve a specific goal.

2. Name a commercial advertisement for each of the three persuasive goals: convince, reinforce and actuate. Analyze each choice.

3. Discuss a situation in which you feel you had a perceived choice not to follow instructions but failed to act individualistically.

4. Describe an incident where you did not give in to peer pressure. What was the result of your decision?

5. Analyze how many messages you receive via technical channels to be persuasive: indirect or direct.

6. Discuss which mass persuasive appeals attract your attention. Do they also get you to send money or actuate behavior? Why?

7. Discuss an incident where you wasted your time going somewhere with another person. What did you learn about yourself and how did you alter your behavior?

eleven

Constructing the Persuasive Presentation

O B J E C T I V E S

After reading this chapter, you should be able to:

- Develop a reasonable goal
- Write purpose statements for three types of persuasive speeches
- Explain how audience analysis helps the persuasive presentation
- Explain credibility and logical and emotional appeals
- List the types of claims and write examples for each
- Explain the five steps of Monroe's Motivated Sequence
- Identify other organizational patterns for persuasion
- List the types of reasoned arguments and write examples of each
- List and recognize the fallacies of reasoning
- List emotions that can be targeted

In the last chapter we covered the basic concepts of persuasion. In this chapter we take a look at the construction of formal persuasive situations/arguments. The examination of persuasion allows you to be more effective in analyzing external stimuli and your personal response to them as well as shaping your own statements to be more effective in obtaining the reactions you desire from others. This chapter will take you through the process of designing your persuasive presentation.

Preparing for Persuasion

Before you begin planning a persuasive speech, it is a good idea to think about your personal feelings about the topic you select. You need personal conviction in order to be a successful persuasive speaker. If you haven't reflected on an issue and carefully evaluated why you believe what you do, then you won't be able to discover appropriate reasons and psychological motivations to persuade others. For example, if you automatically accept your parents' opinion on an issue, you lack the necessary conviction to focus on critical thinking. You need to carefully analyze your reasons for believing in a topic or doing a particular action as you design a persuasive speech. Careful analysis will help you discover what motivates you, the reasoning that convinced you to hold your position, and the language that will help you motivate others.

Critical Thinking

What topic do you really feel strongly about? If you could get the entire world to believe as you do, what would you argue for?

_____

_____

_____

_____

_____

As you select your topic, it is essential to consider the ethics of the persuasive situation. Your ultimate goal is to change beliefs, values, attitudes, or actions, which entails ethical responsibility. You must absolutely believe your message is reasonable before you attempt to convince an audience to agree with you. If you are planning to ask the audience to perform an action, you must first perform the action yourself. We hope you don't ask why. But if you do, there are two reasons. First, you are believable only when you sincerely hold your opinion. An informed audience can hear the difference. Actors are trained to portray themselves as other people, but speakers don't usually possess such skills. Second, it is unethical to construct messages to influence your audience to do or believe something you yourself don't believe or practice. This is the equivalent of lying, and most people would agree that lying is wrong.

If an audience learns you lied to them, you lose credibility. For instance, Jerome constructs a wonderful persuasive speech about giving up red meat. He gives numerous statistics, emotional appeals, and well reasoned arguments. Fred is really moved by this speech and thinks he might try to give up red meat so he can be healthier, as Jerome suggested. Later in the week, after two days of meatless meals, Fred notices Jerome in the window of a fast-food restaurant wolfing down a triple burger. Fred now knows Jerome lied to him during the speech. He feels angry and betrayed because he believed Jerome was telling the truth. Fred now finds it difficult to believe anything Jerome says to him. Jerome's credibility is gone.

ETHICAL CONSIDERATIONS

What ethical considerations should you make about yourself and the audience when you proceed with your speech on reading all assigned textbooks?

_____

_____

_____

_____

_____

Reasonable Goals

Your best approach to a persuasive message is to have **reasonable goals.** Think for a moment about things that you have a strong opinion about: abortion, euthanasia, gun control, or capital punishment. Could a 6-minute presentation get you to change your mind and/or perform an action on any of these topics? It's highly unlikely.

To keep your goals reasonable for a persuasive speaking assignment, follow these guidelines:

1. Choose a topic that is *not* a *national debate*. We already have strong views on topics like immigration and the legalization of marijuana. These topics are incredibly complex, and unless you have three days to speak, it is unlikely you can even begin to develop the details of the subject in a meaningful way.

2. Choose a topic that is *not* a *national campaign*. Persuading people to stop speeding, to wear a seat belt, to exercise regularly, and to eat right are national campaigns with multimillion-dollar budgets and marketing plans. If these persuaders, a loved one, or the police can't get the audience to change, we doubt you'll be successful. Plus, we already know the recommended behaviors for these issues; so unless you can provide new information on these topics for an audience, select another topic.

3. Choose a topic to which *you have a personal connection*. Find something you are involved in or you feel strongly about. Unless you have a personal connection with a topic, you do not have the moti-

vation necessary to project sincerity. We all know that we should donate blood. We all know where and when, but we don't do it. Why? A story about a little girl who needs blood isn't enough to persuade a college audience to donate. We have witnessed over 50 donating-blood speeches. There was only one truly effective speech. A young college student with leukemia presented it. He had the personal experience of needing blood and sitting in a hospital waiting until they found it. Because the audience of college students could relate to him, the speech was effective. Also, don't ever attempt to persuade us to do something that you don't do. It is unethical.

4. Choose a topic that is *easy for the audience to comprehend and to do*. For instance, one semester a student tried to persuade us to volunteer to work with people with intellectual disabilities. But it wasn't until the question and answer period, when she stated we could do something as simple as send a card, that we felt helping was within our realm. She might have had more success if she had selected an easier and more tangible topic: "I want my audience to send a card to Alicia or Kevin at the facility where I work."

5. Choose a topic most people don't do because *they don't know about it*. We all know we should floss, but do we know to change our toothbrush every three months? That is a bit more unique, and most of us don't think about it. However, be careful to avoid topics people would find trivial—or discover a way to persuade the audience that the subject is, in fact, important. Think about everyday things you do that you feel other people should do and go from there.

6. Choose a topic that can be *phrased as a positive*. You need to tell us something to do rather than something not to do. Rather than tell us not to use Q-tips to clean our ears, give us the alternative, "You should use a washcloth to clean your ears." The audience will react better if you suggest an action rather than a prohibition.

TRY IT!

Which criteria are useful as you try to keep your goals reasonable when persuading friends, family, and significant others?

_____

_____

_____

_____

_____

Purpose Statements

In chapter 10, we explored the three types of persuasive messages. A speech to convince seeks to alter someone's beliefs, attitudes, or values. A speech to reinforce seeks to strengthen someone's beliefs, attitudes, values, or actions. And a speech to actuate intends to call someone to action. As you build a persuasive speech, you need to have a purpose statement.

Convince: I want my audience to believe that. . . .

Reinforce: I want my audience to believe more strongly that . . . or
I want my audience to continue doing X.

Actuate: I want my audience to. . . .

Convince: I want my audience to believe that the tutoring center could help them.

Reinforce: I want my audience to believe more strongly that the tutoring center is useful.
or

Reinforce: I want my audience to continue using the tutoring center in their second year of school.

Actuate: I want my audience to schedule two appointments at the tutoring center.

Notice that depending on which type of speech you choose, the focus is totally different. Once again, your first decision involves the audience. What reaction do you want from your audience? Do you want the audience to believe something, believe something more strongly, or do something? If you want them to do something, then you don't design a speech to convince.

TRY IT!

Think about your speech to actuate students to read their textbooks. What is the purpose statement you should design?

Audience Analysis

What should you know about the audience? In persuasive speaking, there are three main things you need to know. For a speech to convince, it is imperative to find out whether the audience agrees with you, is neutral, or disagrees with you (sometimes called a hostile audience). Obviously, if the audience already agrees with you, you do not need to convince them. If you are constructing a speech to actuate, you need to know whether the audience is always doing the action, doing it sometimes, or not doing it at all. In addition, you must know how much the audience knows about the topic. We are neutral about some topics. Sometimes we don't perform an action because we don't possess the necessary information. Some college students don't wash their sheets as frequently as once a week, nor do they think that it is important. The subject of clean sheets can become a good topic for a speech to actuate. Once students hear about the millions of dust mites that grow in sheets and crawl on their bodies at night, most of them will be quick to agree washing sheets is important. This makes it extremely easy to persuade them to action. This is a good example of how to examine the environment around you to find a clever way to actuate an audience.

The following continuums will help you with audience analysis.

POSITIVE				NEGATIVE
	Agree	No Opinion	Disagree	
	Always Do Action	Sometimes Do Action	Don't Do Action	
	Know a Lot	Know a Little	Don't Know	

We recommend the 50-percent rule of audience analysis for a persuasive speech: at least 50 percent or more of your audience should oppose your position on a topic to make the speech worthwhile.

Let's say you want to persuade your audience to exercise five days a week. As noted in the reasonable goals section, a national campaign is not a reasonable topic for a short persuasive speech. Nonetheless, you think you could use time as your key argument to convince students that they have enough time to exercise at the university fitness center. Is time an appropriate key argument? Probably not. We have polled college audiences numerous times, and we found that only 20 percent of the audience does not exercise because of lack of time. Some do not exercise because they are admittedly lazy. Others do not exercise because they hate exercising. Many don't exercise because they don't think they need to or don't see the benefit. Many feel uncomfortable in the university fitness center because at some schools the climate is one of a sweaty singles' club. Still others don't do it because they are on a sports team, and they exercise elsewhere. Many exercise at home. Some may be ashamed of their body type and feel uncomfortable exercising in public. Thus, there is no solid target for your speech; the audience is too fragmented in terms of their reasons for not acting. If you find out through audience analysis why at least 50 percent of the audience doesn't believe or do an action, then you have an appropriate approach to the topic. Look once again at the reasonable goals section. The discussion is not a reasonable goal, but many college students persist in trying.

Tracy's best friend was killed by a drunk driver. She wants to give her speech on drinking and driving. So, she designs a speech to convince her audience drunk driving is wrong. Tracy makes a crucial mistake. Think about the audience for a minute. What do you suppose the audience's current belief is about drinking and driving? Do you imagine the audience believes drunk driving is right? Not a chance. Tracy argues with her instructor, "But people still do it!" OK, that is true, but that isn't a speech to convince. So, Tracy decides to actuate her audience to stop drinking and driving. Well, once again, while this is a morally wonderful goal, it doesn't fit the audience. With strong evidence of tragic consequences and stiff penalties for violating the law, 50 percent of your audience doesn't drink and drive. Most people use designated drivers.

If Tracy persists in using this topic, she needs to find a new angle. At one time, a speech to actuate the audience to take keys away from others worked. But even that topic rarely meets the 50 percent rule anymore, since most college students already perform this action. Another possibility for an approach might be to persuade people in the audience to never get in a car with someone who has had even one drink. You'd have to do an audience analysis to see whether this meets the 50 percent rule, however. Many people don't have the personal strength to find another way home if their driver has had only one or two drinks. People still get in the car. This speech would focus on our personal responsibility to keep ourselves alive as more important than the possibility of offending a friend by refusing to accept a ride.

Remember, drunk driving is a national campaign. There are messages everywhere, and people who choose to drink and drive aren't going to stop based on a brief presentation. The only unique approach to this topic we have ever seen was a 23-year-old student who was widowed after her husband was celebrating a promotion at work and was then killed in a drunk-driving accident. The personal connection and the shock of her circumstances gave a compassionate edge to the speech that made it successful. So once again, unless you have a unique angle, you should stay away from topics such as this one.

TRY IT!

What audience analysis questions would be important to ask in order to design an effective speech on reading the textbooks? You should be able to generate at least eight good questions that will help design the focus for this speech.

_____

_____

_____

_____

_____

_____

_____

_____

_____

Aristotle defined the three building blocks used in a persuasive message: *credibility* (ethos), *logical appeals* (logos), and *emotional appeals* (pathos). Credibility is constructed through the use of citations and testimony. Logical appeals are constructed from facts, figures, and reasoning. Emotional appeals are constructed with stories and examples.

Building Block #1: Credibility (Ethos)

We talked about **credibility** in the informative speaking section. It always amazes us when students ask, "Do we really have to cite sources in a persuasive speech?" Our answer is, "Of course!" **Citations** are what make you appear to be knowledgeable. Without citations, your entire speech is nothing but opinion. If the audience is going to be influenced by your message, you must first convince them of your credibility. If you have not researched your topic and discovered experts who agree with your position, your ability to persuade an audience member approaches zero.

TRY IT!

Find a citation for your speech about reading assigned textbooks.

_____

_____

_____

In addition to citations, you can build your credibility in other ways. Robert Gass and John Seiter (2011) note that people who are perceived as trustworthy enhance their credibility. Having goodwill toward the audience also will influence the audience's perception of credibility. Secondary dimensions of credibility include being extroverted/dynamic, composed/relaxed, and sociable. Therefore, if you can establish a rapport with the audience so that they believe you have their best interests at heart, that you are presenting both sides of the argument, and that you are open-minded and ethical and sensitive, they will tend to believe you more readily.

An audience perceives a speaker to be credible through the entire package of a prepared speech and good delivery. There is no way to persuade without credibility.

Building Block #2: Logical Appeals (Logos)

The term **logical appeals** refers to all of the structure and reasoning you build into a persuasive presentation. In the following sections, we discuss types of claims, persuasive organizational patterns, and types and fallacies of reasoning.

Types of Claims

As you design your persuasive message, you will choose your claim. A *claim* is what you want the receiver to do or believe. In persuasive speaking, there are three types of claims: fact, value, and policy. The type of claim you choose will influence the organizational pattern. Your claim should also relate to the persuasive goal you have chosen for your speech.

A **claim of fact** attempts to convince the audience (or reinforce existing beliefs) that a certain piece of factual information is true. For instance, you may claim that tuition at your school will rise by 6 percent in the next five years because of a new fitness center being built on campus. Since no one will know for sure what the actual percentage increase will be until the five-year interval ends, you need to provide evidence for your claim of 6 percent.

A **claim of value** attempts to convince an audience (or reinforce existing beliefs) that one thing is better than another. A speaker may try to convince an audience that a Mediterranean diet is better than a low carbohydrate diet. Because of the word "better" (an opinion word), this is a speech of value. Sometimes speakers get confused here because they believe their opinions are factual. The statement, "The Mediterranean diet is the best" is a claim of value, not fact, no matter how much you believe it to be factual.

A *claim of policy* attempts to move someone to action. A speaker could try to get the audience to buy a product, sign a petition, go someplace, join a demonstration, or attend events on campus. Any time your goal is to promote action, your claim is a policy claim. Usually, a claim of policy statement includes the word "should," i.e., "You should. . . ."

So let's review:

Choose your claim carefully so that it connects to your goal. In the next section, we'll talk about how your claim is related to your organizational pattern.

Persuasive Organization

Depending on your topic and your audience, you need to choose your organizational structure carefully. Use statement-of-reasons and comparative-advantages structures for speeches to convince or reinforce. Use a problem-solution structure to convince your audience that someone else should act. Use Monroe's Motivated Sequence to persuade an audience to perform an action themselves.

STATEMENT-OF-REASONS

In a *statement-of-reasons* structure, a speaker reveals the persuasive claim at the beginning of the speech and follows the claim with a number of reasons why the audience should accept it. For example,

> I want my audience to believe *Everybody Loves Raymond* was the best sitcom ever.
> - It was a top-rated show for CBS.
> - It had excellent comedians.
> - It's the most talked-about show in interpersonal conversations.

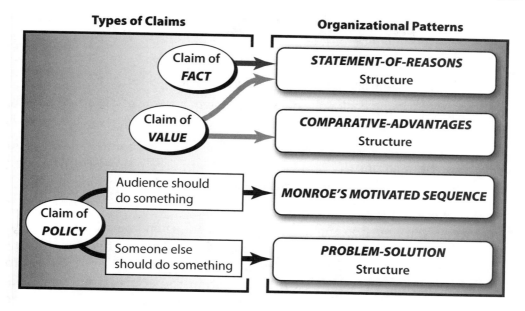

Notice the reasons are presented in order of strength. You can document the first reason with statistical evidence. You can document the second reason by citing expert opinion. Unless someone has done research, you can only document the third reason as a personal observation, making it the weakest of the arguments. Each of these reasons would be a main point in the body of the speech.

COMPARATIVE-ADVANTAGES

The **comparative-advantages** structure is similar to statement-of-reasons because the speaker states the persuasive goal first. The main points in this speech demonstrate the advantages this goal has over any other option. For example,

> I want my audience to believe cotton underwear is preferable to silk underwear.
>
> • Cotton material breathes better.
> • Cotton material cuts down on urinary tract infections.
> • Cotton material is cheaper.

In this speech, you would document each of these advantages, giving the audience reasons to agree with your proposition. Notice you aren't persuading anyone to buy the underwear. You simply want them to agree that cotton is superior to other fabrics.

PROBLEM-SOLUTION

A **problem-solution** structure is useful if you want to convince an audience someone should do something. In this structure, your main points are (1) the problem, (2) the solution, and (3) the advantages of the solution. For example,

I want my audience to believe that Anytown University should build a parking deck.

- Parking is a problem at Anytown University.
- The administration should build a parking deck.
- A parking deck will solve the problem and make the student body content.

This is essentially a policy claim, but you want someone else to do something about the problem. In the next speech structure, Monroe's Motivated Sequence, you want the audience to do something.

MONROE'S MOTIVATED SEQUENCE

If you are choosing a speech to actuate, then you will probably go with **Monroe's Motivated Sequence (MMS).** This is a five-part organizational pattern that is appropriate if the audience is not opposed to your topic—they just lack the motivation to perform an action. This structure is more complex than the previous ones because you are attempting to get the audience to take action rather than simply agree with you. You need to ignore the statement-of-reasons structure to be successful with MMS. You are no longer stating a claim and giving reasons why someone should do something. With MMS you must describe a problem for the audience so they will be motivated to take action.

MMS moves an audience through five steps (German, Gronbeck, Ehninger, and Monroe, 2010). All five steps are important, and we will cover each step in detail.

Attention Step: You first need to get your audience's attention. The attention step in MMS is similar to the attention getter in an informative speech. After hearing this step, the audience should say, "I want to listen!"

Showing the Need/Demonstrating the Problem: In this step you must convince the audience there is a problem that affects them. The first thing you do is state the problem; be clear and specific. To prove to your audience that this is indeed a problem, you will need to include lots of evidence in the form of supporting material. It is not enough just to say a problem exists—you must prove it. Obviously, some problems require more evidence than others. If you want to prove your audience is stressed, it will not take much convincing. However, if you want them to believe there are pollutants in their air, you may need a lot more factual evidence and emotional appeals to accomplish your goal.

Be careful not to reveal your claim in this step. The idea is to convince your audience that they face an urgent problem (air pollution). You will show them what to do about it in the next step (buy houseplants). Note the problem is air pollution. If you say the problem is that the audience doesn't have houseplants, you are building a circular argument.

Don't forget to link the problem with your audience; they must believe it is *their* problem. Think of the commercials for starving third-world children. You know it is a problem, but how many of you send money to help? If you don't, chances are the reason is you don't feel connected to the problem. It is something that happens "over there" and doesn't affect you personally other than the fleeting emotion you may feel when you see the commercial.

Satisfying the Need: You reveal your claim in this step. You tell the audience what it is you want them to do. There are five parts to this step. You must first *reveal the action* you want them to perform in a clear and concise manner. Second, you *explain the details* of what you want them to do. In some speeches, you will need a lot of explanation. In others, you will not. If I want my audience to buy houseplants to clean the air, I don't really need to explain what houseplants are in more detail other than to say, "By houseplants, I mean indoor plants like snake plants and spider plants." In your textbook example, however, you will need to explain precisely what you mean by reading the textbook. "Many of you may think reading simply means to drag your eyes across the lines of text. However, when I say read the textbook, I mean you must examine all of the chapter headings and see how they fit together, read and comprehend each paragraph well enough to write a small summary note in the margin."

The third part is to explain *how the action you want them to do solves the problem* you outlined in the previous step. You must use strong reasoning and factual support here. In the houseplant example, provide evidence that snake plants and spider plants remove 87 percent of air pollutants in the first 24 hours they are in the room. The fourth part contains *evidence that the solution has actually worked* in real life. You might use personal testimony, research studies, and citations by expert authorities to prove this point.

Finally, the fifth part is designed to *meet imagined objections*. Keep in mind you can't persuade people if they are arguing with your claim intrapersonally. In this part of the satisfaction step you need to refute any potential arguments the audience could be composing. Here is where a thorough audience analysis comes in handy. You need to know why they aren't currently doing the action. If you chose stress in the need step and then propose a $2,000 cruise to Bermuda over spring break as the action, a discussion about how safe Bermuda is as a place to vacation and assurances that the audience won't be sucked into the Bermuda Triangle would totally miss the mark trying to meet imagined objections. Safety is irrelevant; students would be thinking, "Oh sure, like I have $2,000!" By the time you complete the satisfaction step, your audience should realize that executing your claim will solve their problem and that there are no barriers to prevent them from doing so.

Visualization: In this step, you want to show the audience how their world will be a better place if they perform your action. You can do this by describing how things will be better if they do the action, how things will be worse if they don't perform the action, or you can include elements of each.

Requesting Action: In this step, you convince the audience to begin the action. You need to give them every detail they need in order to do so. In our houseplant example, you would need to explain where to get them, how much they cost, and how to choose the right one. It is often extremely effective to give something out during this step. You might give them a handout with the info they need. You might give them a sample of the thing you want them to try. We find audiences are much more receptive to an action when they get a free product. Be careful, however, of the method you choose to distribute your aid. In many cases you can give your handout or product at the conclusion of the speech, but it is acceptable to alert the audience in the action step that they will get something. Think creatively here.

We have outlined the MMS sequence below (German et al., pp. 236–241).

Monroe's Motivated Sequence

I. Attention Step
[*Use an effective attention-getting device here*]

II. Need Statement
   A. Make a definite, concise statement about the problem (avoid a circular argument!).
   B. Use one or more examples explaining and clarifying the problem. Be sure to include additional examples, statistical data, testimony, and other forms of support.
   C. Show the extent and seriousness of the problem.
   D. Make it clear that the problem affects the audience.

III. Satisfy the Need (Explaining WHY it works)
   A. State the action you want the audience to begin (or stop).
   B. Explain your proposal thoroughly.
   C. Demonstrate with reasoning how your proposed solution meets the need.
   D. Refer to practical experience by supplying examples to prove the proposal has worked effectively where it has been tried.
   E. Forestall opposition by anticipating and answering any objections that might be raised against this proposal.

IV. Visualize

    A. Describe conditions as they will be in the future if the solution you propose is carried out; or

    B. Describe conditions as they will be in the future if your proposal is not carried out; or

    C. Use both the negative and positive potential results.

V. Request Action

    [Explain HOW to do it; tell the audience every detail they need to know in order to perform the action.]

Recently, a student gave a speech to actuate. She wanted the audience to use ginger for nausea. Following MMS, she did not mention her topic until the satisfaction (third) step. She built the problem that her prescribed action would solve by demonstrating that popular over-the-counter antinausea medications are potentially dangerous drugs.

In the need step, she built the problem that most of us take these products when we are nauseated. She cited a source that states using a particular over-the-counter product can result in ringing in the ears and a black tongue. She also stated that according to J. Jamison Starbuck (2000), "drugs like Dramamine work on the Central Nervous System, depressing the body's reaction to movement stimuli." By the time she was done with the need step, we were all appalled at the side effects or potential dangers of both of these products. We were left wondering, "What can we do?"

As she approached the satisfaction step, she told us ginger was an alternative approach for the condition of nausea. She cited evidence that there was no danger to humans from this natural root and cited studies that proved its effectiveness. She talked about the personal success she had with the product. She also met potential objections of expense and dislike of the taste.

In the visualization step, she created a hypothetical story about driving on vacation and missing everything because of sleeping due to the side effects of the drugs the audience would normally take for nausea.

In the action step, she showed the alternative products you could use, including ginger tea, ginger candy, ginger drops, and crystallized ginger. She told us where in town we could get it. And she handed out ginger drops to all audience members to try the next time they experienced nausea.

Now it's your turn. Using your speech to actuate students to read a textbook each and every time it is assigned, fill in a brief keyword outline of what you would do in each step of the sequence.

REMEMBER: You cannot talk about reading textbooks until the satisfaction step. You must build a problem in the need step that reading assigned textbooks will solve.

Attention

_____

_____

Need

_____

_____

Satisfaction

_____

_____

Visualization

_____

_____

Action

_____

_____

Reasoned Argument

Once you've decided on your goal, your claim, and your organizational structure, then it is time to support your claims with reasoning. **Reasoning** refers to taking facts, analyzing them, and drawing conclusions from them. If you take a logic class, you will learn various logical appeals. For the purposes of introductory speech building and for critical consuming of the persuasive messages you receive, the following three types of reasoning are generally sufficient: inductive reasoning, reasoning from analogy, and causal arguments.

INDUCTIVE REASONING

When you use *inductive reasoning*, you take some facts and draw a conclusion based on them. For example, it is a fact Ben failed geometry. It is a fact that he failed trigonometry. Ben also failed calculus. What general conclusion could you draw about Ben and math? Probably it would be a safe bet to say that Ben is mathematically challenged. Let's look at another example. Jana ate kung pao chicken and got sick. On another day, Jana ate chicken and snow peas and got sick. Recently, Jana ate chicken and cashews and got sick. With these three facts, what conclusion can you draw? Well, you can quickly see that there are a number of conclusions you can draw from these facts. Jana may be allergic to MSG—a common ingredient in Chinese food. Jana may have developed an allergy to chicken. Jana may be visiting a restaurant that is not following FDA requirements for food safety and preparation.

When you hear an inductive argument, you should always ask yourself

- Whether enough specific facts were documented to support the conclusion.

- Whether the examples presented were typical of the situation or simply an exception.

Let's look at an example. Anytown, USA declares a medical emergency. Three people die from an unknown virus. It is reported in the national news, and people in your community become concerned they could be susceptible to the same virus. However, your community is on the opposite side of the country from the original incident. Your local mayor makes a statement that all residents should follow five precautions. He is using inductive reasoning. He thinks because three people died, the general population in his community is at risk. How logical is his argument? Do three deaths in a distant community warrant a conclusion that you are at risk? Thinking about the question of typical instances, you may want to research information about the victims. If the three people who died were elderly people who had compromised immune systems, then they are not representative of the general population. As a receiver of this message, you would ask for more information.

REASONING FROM ANALOGY

When you compare two concepts saying that what is true of one will be true of another, you are *reasoning from analogy*. Let's say someone uses the argument, "If you liked Boston, you'll love Washington, DC." What they are saying is that these two cities are so similar they can make this comparison. When you design or hear an argument from analogy, you need to ask yourself

- Whether the two cases are similar enough to be compared.

Are Boston and Washington, DC similar enough that we can make this case? It depends. If you are enthralled by a variety of restaurants, then yes, those two cities are very similar. However, if you like Boston because of its colonial history, then your analogy fails because Washington, DC doesn't have that history.

Have you ever heard the expression "comparing apples to oranges?" The expression refers to poor arguments based on analogy—the two things being compared are too dissimilar to be linked. Whenever someone presents reasoning from analogy, think carefully about what is being compared and the facts presented.

CAUSAL ARGUMENTS

Reasoning from analogy compares two concepts, but a *causal argument* puts two concepts together stating one concept is the cause of the other. For example, "A college education leads to success" is a causal argument. The cause-to-effect reasoning is that if you get a college education, you will be successful. We know there are some flaws with this argument. When you hear a causal argument, you should ask yourself

- Whether another cause might produce this conclusion.

It may not be the college education that produces individual success; it may be the professional connections you make during your college experience. It may be that your work ethic makes you successful. It could also be your maturity after four additional years of growing up that helped you to focus and become successful. A roommate's parent or someone you met on the college campus could offer you a job. Or it could be the college education itself. You get the idea—there are many possible causes for success after college. Causal arguments are very hard to prove because there are so many potential causes for various phenomena.

TRY IT!

Now that you are familiar with three types of arguments, try to write one of each for your speech on reading textbooks.

Inductive:

_____

_____

Analogy:

_____

_____

Causal:

_____

_____

_____

Fallacies of Reasoning

A *fallacy* is an error in reasoning. If you take a logic course, you will study this concept in much more depth and with different parameters. In basic communication, be aware of the following fallacies: ad hominem, hasty generalization, false cause, bandwagon, circular argument, appeal to authority, and irrational reasons. All of these fallacy names are derived from Latin. However, only ad hominem is still commonly known by its Latin name.

Ad Hominem: This fallacy happens whenever there is an attack against a person rather than against a concept. Alexander says to Rita, "Don't choose Professor X for this class. She dresses like a hippie. She is horrible." This is a personal attack. The argument rests on the clothing choices of the professor and has nothing to do with the quality of her teaching, her teaching style, or her knowledge of the discipline. Therefore, it is a personal, irrelevant attack. As a critical consumer of com-

ETHICAL CONSIDERATIONS

What are the ethical implications when you design a biased argument?

_____

_____

_____

_____

munication, Rita should recognize this fallacy and ask some follow-up questions, such as, "Why does the professor's appearance matter?" or "How knowledgeable is she in the discipline?" "What teaching style does she use?" "Does she relate to her students?" These are excellent critical-thinking questions.

Hasty Generalization: Hasty generalizations happen when communicators draw conclusions from insufficient facts. Think about the arguments we talked about above. In which type of argument would hasty generalizations happen?

Sue says to Bia, "I swear, men cannot fold laundry. My husband has a PhD in engineering, but the man cannot fold a T-shirt without wrinkles." At another table in the cafeteria, Raule says to Christopher, "I swear, women can't drive. I came to school today and a woman was swerving all over the road." In both of these cases, Sue and Raule are guilty of hasty generalizations. Just because one man can't fold laundry and one woman can't drive straight does not mean they can generalize about the entire population of men and women. Think how often you hear hasty generalizations in daily conversation. Again, it is your responsibility to ask questions. "Do you have other specific instances of this event?" "How often does it occur?" "Are studies available that support your conclusion?" would be some initial questions to ask to determine if someone is making a premature generalization. Think how offended you might be if a teacher made a hasty generalization that all students are cheaters because one student was caught cheating on the last exam.

False Cause: False cause occurs in causal arguments when a different cause could have produced the phenomena. Let's say Shirley did very poorly on the test because she was out all night partying and didn't sleep properly. This statement could be false because it is possible she didn't read any of the chapters during the semester, didn't understand any of the material, or didn't go to class. All of these things could have caused her failure on the exam, or she might have failed because she was out late one night. Think how often you hear a friend say he failed an assignment because the teacher didn't explain it properly. Is it really the teacher's fault? What if everyone else in the class completed the assignment properly? Be careful of drawing false-cause arguments in the workplace or in interpersonal relationships. These types of arguments are rarely accepted, and when bosses or friends hear them, it's the type of fallacy that breeds bad feelings. In our society, placing blame on false causes is becoming more and more prevalent. If you are the type of person who builds these arguments into your everyday speech, you may want to assess whether it is a behavior you need to change. Listen carefully for these arguments as well, so you aren't drawn into reasoning by false cause.

Bandwagon: Reasoning that you should be allowed to do something because everyone else is doing it is the bandwagon fallacy. Think about the times in your teenage years when you said, "But Mom! *Everyone* is going to the party," and Mom replied, "If everyone were jumping off a bridge would you do that too?" What Mom knew, and you didn't, was that your argument was an error in reasoning. She knew that just because other people are doing something does not mean that the action is good. Think of the advertisers who use the bandwagon approach. Everyone who is anyone has product X; if you want to be liked, you need to buy product X. You are targeted with messages that imply you must have the latest clothes, electronic products, or body adornments because everyone else does. Is this a valid argument? Of course not. Be alert to the bandwagon fallacy so you do not get persuaded to do something that is not good for you.

Circular Argument: You are guilty of a circular argument when your conclusion is the same as your statement. Think about a child who comes down to dinner, and the parent says, "Wash your hands." The child says, "Why?" The parent replies, "Because you haven't, and I said so." The parent is arguing in a circle, saying that the reason something should be done is because it isn't being done. No reason is given in this argument, making it a fallacy. As a child, you simply do what you are told, but when you are older, you need to ask questions. You will also be expected to give solid reasons for your assertions in the workplace or at school. When a teacher asks for your opinion on a speaker, you may find yourself saying, "I just didn't like that." When the teacher asks "Why?" and you reply, "Because it wasn't any good," you are using a circular argument. The teacher may press you for additional details about what you specifically didn't like. Some students cannot articulate what they didn't like and reply, "I don't know; I just didn't like it." This is a serious flaw for a competent communicator. If you suffer from this problem, start the process of change now. Think about why you are making the statements you make.

Irrational Reasons: This fallacy occurs when we use unrelated or irrelevant reasons to support our conclusions. It takes a little practice to recognize this fallacy. Tom comes in to see his instructor. He waits until his last semester to take his oral communication course. He just failed his first speech and is terrified he won't pass the course. He tells the instructor, "But there is no way I could fail this speech. I practiced eight times." The instructor refers him to her comments on the grade sheet that indicate the problems with the speech, including items such as a missing bibliography, missing citations, no attention-getting device, information that is not targeted to the audience, inability to conform to the time limit, lack of transitions, inappropriate organizational pattern, reliance on a manuscript for an extemporaneous assignment, and no eye contact with the audience. The student continues to repeat, "But I worked really hard on this and practiced a lot." You should be able to see how his reasons do not support his conclusion that he should not have failed the speech.

Appeal to Authority: This fallacy is not a common one for beginning speakers, but we include it because it is used in advertising. It is important for critical consumers of communication to realize that messages relying on a celebrity endorsement are actually fallacies in reasoning. Anytime you see a celebrity doing a commercial or supporting a cause, it is important not to buy into that product or cause simply because the celebrity endorses it. Can you find out whether the celebrity actually uses the product? Does he or she really support the cause? Or is the celebrity there because he or she was paid to appear in the commercial? Realistically, you probably won't take the time to research the background of the celebrity, but as a practicing critical consumer of communication, the red flag should go up, and you should question the validity of the argument when you see your favorite celebrity endorsing a product or cause. There are advertising laws to protect the public, so attractive performers say something like: "I'm not a doctor, but I play one on TV, take product X." Advertisers know the public has a tendency to ignore the disclaimer and to identify with the celebrity. You should analyze your reaction to the performer carefully before you race out to get the product.

Once you have determined your claim, type of persuasive speech, organizational pattern, method of argument—and checked your reasoning for fallacies—your speech should come together successfully. You need to use supporting materials effectively and include citations as well. You are almost finished, but there is one more important element for an effective presentation. For the greatest persuasive effect, it is time to add emotional appeal.

TRY IT!

While you should never use fallacies, we think it is a great learning experience to design some intentionally so you will be more familiar with such arguments and, therefore, more able to identify them in a message. Using your speech to persuade your audience to read their textbooks each and every time they are assigned, write a statement for each type of fallacy.

Ad Hominem _____

Hasty Generalization _____

False Cause _____

Bandwagon _____

Circular Argument _____

Appeal to Authority _____

Irrational Reasons _____

Building Block #3: Emotional Appeal (Pathos)

To make credibility and logical appeals work, you need to add an *emotional appeal* that connects you personally with the audience. We know most audiences are not persuaded by facts alone. If that were true, why would so many people smoke? Everyone knows smoking is a dangerous action. Smokers know how many people die annually from related health problems. Those facts are not enough to get people to

---

ETHICAL CONSIDERATIONS

When does using an emotional appeal cross the line from effective persuasion to manipulation or coercion?

_____

_____

_____

_____

stop smoking. If you were going to try to persuade someone, you would need to connect on an emotional level.

I (KSY) often tell my students a true story of a young 23-year-old woman named Teri who was my neighbor when I was first married in the late 1980s. She had her own townhouse and a beautiful new Iroc-Z (a very popular sports car at the time). She was beautiful and had the world at her fingertips. She found out in December she had lung cancer. She was a smoker. By June, she had lost all of her hair and was unable to move about her house without assistance from a nurse. A few weeks later, she died. You may find this true story to be more touching than a statistic about how many people die, even if you don't know me or the person in the story. It's real. The story is emotionally powerful.

TRY IT!

Check out this link that has statistics about texting while driving.

http://www.edgarsnyder.com/car-accident/cell-phone/statistics.html

Are you moved? Now watch this extremely emotional video from Wales that is based on a true story.

http://www.youtube.com/watch?v=R0LCmStIw9E

Is there a difference when you see the message with the emotional appeal?

Types of Emotions

There are many types of emotions to which we can appeal. Think about speakers who make us fearful of something. In regions where tornados occur on a regular basis, students can design an element of *fear* into speeches to actuate the audience to keep a 24-hour emergency kit in their house. The government used to use fear appeals in public service announcements in our rural areas to encourage families to have an emergency plan in case a terrorist event occurs. Emotional connections help motivate an audience to do something or believe something.

Another emotion is *anger*. If we can get an audience angry about something, then we can often get them to do or believe something. You may get an audience to buy used textbooks online from individual sellers by appealing to the emotion of anger. Tell your audience the profit their campus bookstore makes on the used textbooks they buy and sell. You will have everyone's attention. Caution: many bookstores are nonprofit.

Speakers can appeal to happy emotions, too, such as *pride*. Think of a patriotic speech that builds on the pride we have in our country. Freedom is a powerful word, and the emotions it can release when used appropriately will surprise you. Maybe a speaker can also appeal to your personal pride in doing a job well. Most people enjoy doing a job well, and they like to be reminded that a work ethic is important.

Think of a speaker trying to get you to donate five dollars to Habitat for Humanity. He may try to make you feel *ashamed* that you willingly spend five dollars for a latte when there are people without homes.

These are just a few of the emotions that you can target effectively in a persuasive argument. It is important to remember that not all emotional appeals work on every audience member the same way. Some people are persuaded by fact, others by emotion. Some people will be touched by an appeal to shame, others will say, "Oh, for crying out loud—big deal—it's not my problem." Therefore, your best choice is to design a speech with a variety of appeals so you have the best chance of reaching the majority of your audience.

Let's take a quick look at the difference between a strictly factual account of an event and one that uses a carefully designed emotional appeal. Look at the difference between the two passages in the box on p. 238. Which technique would reach the majority of the audience?

Emotional appeals are powerful in persuasive speaking. Without these appeals, it is difficult to persuade. You must, however, be ethical. Using emotional appeals to deceptively manipulate or to take advantage of an audience is no different from coercion. Think of the various companies who used fear appeals after the September 11, 2001, tragedy to sell gas masks and other equipment to protect people from terrorism. These gadgets were overpriced and unnecessary. The companies incorporated fear appeals in their advertising by suggesting the possibility of another attack. They took advantage of a fearful public during a time of national tragedy. As the receiver of emotional appeals, think critically before you act. The act of communicating with others carries tremendous responsibility.

CHOICES AND CONSEQUENCES

Now that you understand the various persuasive techniques, what choices will you make in your daily life relating to your own use of persuasion as well as to analyzing the persuasion of others?

_____

_____

_____

_____

_____

_____

Reality

Factual Account:

The U.S. Department of Housing and Urban Development reports annually to Congress on the counts of homelessness nationwide. The most recent report indicates there are 643,067 sheltered and unsheltered homeless people. More than 6 in 10 were in emergency, while 37 percent were unsheltered. Nearly two thirds were homeless as individuals. The other third were homeless as part of a family; 21 percent of all homeless family members were unsheltered. Seventy-eight percent of all sheltered homeless persons are adults; 61 percent are male; 62 percent are members of a minority; 38 percent are 31 to 50 years old. One of these people could be you. We all need to help the homeless.

Account with Emotional Appeal:

My family celebrates Thanksgiving as its major holiday every year. All of my siblings and their families come home to the house where we were raised. The sight of everyone, the assortment of food, and the stories about growing up make this day very special for all of us. We look forward to it each year. As far as I'm concerned, this is the only way to celebrate the Thanksgiving holiday.

But not everyone celebrates the holiday this way. [pause] My brother didn't come home this year. I was very upset when I didn't see him at the table. Mom and Dad said he called to say he had to work and couldn't make it. The normal glow of the Thanksgiving festivities dimmed because my brother wasn't there. Yes, we all talked, ate, laughed, and enjoyed ourselves, but we wanted to know why he didn't make it for the holiday we all held sacred.

I called him to say happy Thanksgiving from the family. All of us were ready to yell and sing when he answered the phone. But, all that greeted me was his answering machine. The look on my face silenced the excitement in the room. My voice stood alone as I said, "Hi, Jim." The happy Thanksgiving part of my message evaporated and out came, "Are you OK? Where are you? Please call when you can. [pause] I love you."

My phone rang at 2 AM. It was Jim. Before I could say a word, the excitement in his voice caught my attention. He told me his closest colleague at work, a 32-year-old man named Ed, had been fired the previous week. Ed had not managed money well and was being evicted from his apartment because he couldn't pay his rent. He and his wife and three young daughters, Laura, Samantha, and Claire, had no place to go, and he was embarrassed and depressed because they would be on the street for Thanksgiving. My brother invited Ed and his family to move in with him temporarily.

Rather than drive home to be with his family, my brother spent the entire day racing around trying to throw together a Thanksgiving dinner for Ed's family and make them feel at home. He apologized to me and asked me to explain the situation to everyone at breakfast. [long pause] I don't think I have ever been more proud of my brother. He never struck me as a generous person, but like a bolt of lightning, he had done the most unselfish act I had ever known. I had always written checks to help the homeless. But my brother took action. His spirit made me see Thanksgiving properly for the first time.

[Note: Keep in mind that an emotional appeal does not have to be this long, but we have included an extended example to demonstrate the variety of emotional appeals you can use.]

Critical Thinking

From the Thanksgiving story in the Reality Check box, try to identify the following persuasive techniques and how they are used:

Paralanguage:

_____

_____

Language:

_____

_____

Personal Connection:

_____

_____

Emotional Appeal:

_____

_____

Summary

One of the most valuable skills a communicator can learn is to recognize the persuasive techniques others use. All advertising is based on the persuasive techniques we have presented here. Listen to any commercial or infomercial to pick out the parts of Monroe's Motivated Sequence. Does it use emotional appeal to help convince or actuate you? As people construct persuasive messages, they hope you are not aware of various techniques and that you won't think critically as you react to the message. If Adam and Megan in the initial example used in chapter 10 had thought more critically and analyzed their resources, they would not have faced the possibility of bankruptcy.

In addition to analyzing persuasive messages critically, you can use your improved skills in a positive and ethical manner to make changes in your environment. For example, you may be able to convince someone at your school there should be a rape-awareness day. You may actuate the PTA at your child's school to implement an anti-bullying program. You may actuate students on your campus to create a fundraising event for a local charity. Too often, students think their opinions don't matter, or they believe they can't make a difference. Neither is true. All it takes is one determined person with knowledge of persuasive principles to get the ball rolling.

TRY IT!

Analyze the messages on your social networking sites for one day. Do any of the posts fit into the persuasive message category (convince, reinforce, actuate)? Do your findings encourage you to approach your social commentary differently now?

_____

_____

_____

KEY WORDS

citations   fallacy
claim of fact   logical appeals
claim of policy   Monroe's Motivated Sequence (MMS)
claim of value   problem-solution
comparative-advantages   reasonable goals
credibility   reasoned argument
emotional appeal   statement-of-reasons

DISCUSSION/ACTIVITIES

1. Analyze your classmates for similarities and differences in age, gender, academic major, cultural background, etc. What topics might appeal to this audience during a persuasive speech? Why?

2. Analyze a faculty lecture for fallacies in reasoning. Cite the fallacies you heard.

3. What type of persuasive reasoning captures your attention: ethos, logos, pathos? Why? Which type are you the most comfortable using in a speech? Why?

4. Describe a political ad that is a claim of policy.

5. Describe a reasonable goal for a persuasive argument in a speech. Does the impact of a persuasive argument have more influence on an audience when it is in a commercial ad form and repeated hundreds of times rather than a single performance such as a speech?

twelve

Interviewing

OBJECTIVES

After reading this chapter, you should be able to:
- Identify the elements of an effective résumé
- Describe how to spend time preparing for an interview
- Explain how to make a good first impression
- Explain the importance of personal artifacts in the interview
- Explain the concept of behavioral interviewing
- Answer questions using behavioral interviewing techniques
- Identify unique aspects of phone interviewing
- Identify unique aspects of Skype interviews
- Describe the elements of a stress interview
- Understand the importance of communicating after the interview

Interviewing is a process where a person demonstrates effective communication skills to obtain employment or promotion. Why do we cover interviewing in an oral communication textbook? The answer is quite simple. Interviewing (both the oral process and the written résumé) is the most important piece of persuasion in which you will engage when you complete school. Without a persuasive résumé, you will not get to the interview. And many job applicants who look terrific on paper don't make a good first impression during the interview. Your oral and written skills need to be outstanding.

There are no absolutes in the world of interviewing. The most up-to-date interviewing information changes constantly. Tips for effective résumé writing and interviewing vary from profession to profession. Therefore, in addition to the general tips we provide, we strongly recommend you do a thorough Internet search for interviewing tips in your field before you embark on the interview adventure. A knowledgeable faculty advisor is also a valuable resource.

An interview is a conversation to determine if a candidate's skills and experiences are a good match to the needs of the organization. You must prepare appropriately for the conversation. This includes, but is not limited to, ensuring your résumé is accurate (no typos please!), researching the company, and presenting yourself in a professional manner.

Quite frankly, your résumé is a reflection of you. It should be clear and concise, listing practical experience as well as academic success. How you format it is a personal choice, but it should be easy to read without filler. If it has a typo or is not professional, I won't even look at it. A sloppy résumé speaks volumes about an individual.

All too often, I have interviewed recent college grads who responded to my inquiry about their knowledge of the company I represented with an uninspiring answer along the lines of, "I looked at your website when I applied for the job." Simply put, "and . . . ?" Looking at a website career page does not constitute research. To prepare for an interview, learn everything you can about the company—including what they do (products, services, etc.), where they're located (local, regional, national, global), how long they've been around, and if possible, how they're doing.

Once you get to the actual interview, don't blow it by not dressing or acting professionally. Dressing for business is the key, regardless if the company allows a casual business environment. There is a fine line between confidence and arrogance. You should be able to speak to the accomplishments and experience listed on your résumé.

Getting an interview is not easy, so don't blow it by not doing everything possible to prepare.

—Dean De Peri
Director, Human Resources
CIGNA HealthCare

Résumés

Most employers only spend about ten seconds glancing at your **résumé,** which is a written summary of your accomplishments and capabilities. Imagine trying to read a stack of 60, 150, or over 1,000 résumés to fill one opening in a company. The task is daunting. In order to whittle the pile of applicants down to a manageable size, employers look through the stack very quickly to see if they can eliminate any candidates immediately. Think of this as an altered corporate version of the cliché where "your life flashes before *their* eyes." Only in this case, your life is in print. A résumé immediately goes into the discard pile if it is not visually attractive or easy to read.

An effective résumé must:

- Be visually attractive
- Contain no typos
- Showcase your qualities, strengths, and experience
- Follow the format required by your professional area

To demonstrate the quality differences between an ineffective and an effective résumé, we provide two samples on the following pages. Each is a real résumé created by a student (her name has been changed to protect the innocent). Please don't look ahead to the effective sample, but take a look at the ineffective sample and see if you can determine some of the problematic issues.

Wanda Fitzgerald

28 Fuller St., Detroit, Pa 16842
(000) 555-0000
WandaFitzgerald@notcoldmail.kom

Objective   To get a video-editing position

Education   *Mansfield University*
Graduated May 2002
B.S. in Mass Communication

New York Institute of Photography
Currently enrolled for professional certification
Home corespondence course
Expected graduation December 2002

Experience   *Country Ski and Sports*—**Sales / Bike and ski technician**
April 1998–Present
- Sales of outdoor products and services to customers.
- Repair and assembly of bicycles.
- Mounting and testing of ski equipment.

WNQV 104.5 FM—**On-air announcer**
February 2000–Present
- On air announcing.
- Live remotes and engineering.
- Interviews and production of commercials and liners.

Good Vibrations Entertainment—**Co-owner**
May 1998–Present
- Formed mobile disc jockey business with partner.
- Promoting ourselves.
- Building and maintaining our reputation.
- Attracting new clients.

Rossignol Ski Company—**Area Sales Ambassador**
November 1998–Present
- Attracting new customers to the Rossignol Company.
- Promoting the company in the area.
- Assisting the sales reps with product displays and demos.

References available upon request

Critical Thinking

Pretend that you are an employer. Write an assessment of Wanda Fitzgerald's résumé. We advised this student to use a different format for her résumé (see next Reality Check). Analyze the differences.

_____

_____

_____

_____

_____

_____

This résumé does follow the format for her chosen profession; however, it does not highlight her strengths. You'll notice the jobs this student has held have absolutely nothing to do with a video-editing position. This more traditional résumé format places jobs in a centrally focused position. The format does not sell the student. You'll also notice the information is crammed together without bolding or highlighting to differentiate among its sections. As the employer scans the text, typos create an unfavorable impression (did you catch all three of them?). If there are any typos in a résumé, most applicants are disqualified instantly. Employers look at a résumé as your best piece of work. Nothing about this résumé encourages an employer to look at the candidate more closely.

Some résumé requirements that may vary from person to person or from field to field are:

- Whether to use an objective
- What sections to include
- Whether to limit the résumé to one page

Objectives. In reviewing interviewing research, we found that about 60 percent of sources recommend using an objective, whereas 40 percent do not. In making your decision about whether to use one, you should consult with professionals in your field. If you do decide an objective is important, you must keep in mind that this statement is the very first item on the résumé and makes an immediate impression. An objective must be brilliantly written, or you will end up in the discard pile. Everyone knows your objective is to get a job. Don't state the obvious. You must highlight your abilities in the objective.

The best objective uses a format that highlights the applicant's strongest skills:

Objective: An xxx position in an organization where yyy and zzz would be needed.

Xxx is the name of the position you seek. Yyy and zzz are the most compelling personal qualities, abilities, or achievements that will communicate your potential value to the organization and will make you stand out from the other applicants. The research you have previously done to find out what is most important to the employer will provide you with the information to fill in yyy and zzz.

For example:

Objective: A software sales position in an organization where an extraordinary record of generating new accounts, exceeding sales targets, and enthusiastic customer relations would be needed.

The objective is your attention-getting device; it immediately showcases your best skills. When written well, the objective captures the attention of the employer and invites further exploration of the résumé. Consider the difference between the two objectives below.

Ineffective: To get a video-editing position.

Effective: To obtain a video-editing position in a company where enthusiasm, technical skill, and self-motivation are desired.

The effective objective would be a great persuasive statement at the top of the résumé. If Wanda's work experience included a few video-editing jobs, the objective coupled with the job highlights and some effective changes in formatting could be enough to secure an interview. However, because none of her jobs relate to a video-editing career, that format is not to her advantage even with a strong objective. So, let's take a look at a more effective résumé format for Wanda (p. 247).

Sections. This rewrite of the résumé takes advantage of using a proper format to showcase Wanda's skills. It contains the same information, but in a format highlighting the applicant's strengths. The résumé is visually appealing, from the balance of white space to the use of italics and bold. It contains no typos that would immediately disqualify her. This format allows Wanda to put relevant qualifications at the top, selling her immediately. Instead of emphasizing only previous employment, the résumé shows the employer that Wanda has done some professional work in her field and owns her own equipment.

The qualifications section is a great way to showcase your skills, but what other sections should be included on a résumé? Awards and honors should be listed if you have them. You should include special skills such as working knowledge of a computer program. However, refrain from listing the obvious. Everyone knows how to use Microsoft Word. You should not list that as a skill. But if you are familiar with more specialized software, list that ability.

Include community service in the qualifications section. Employers look for people who have gone above and beyond and volunteered their time. If you have been in a leadership position in clubs and organizations, showcase that ability. Fluency in a foreign language is also a valuable attribute.

Page limitations. Check résumé standards in your field for the acceptable length. At one time, résumés were limited to one page. That is still true in some fields. One of our former students wanted to work on Capitol Hill. She sent out 100 copies of a two-page résumé. She was bewildered when she did not get a single inquiry. Then, she did some more research and found the norm on Capitol Hill was a one-page résumé—anything over one page went into the trash immediately. She retooled her résumé to one page and received a number of interviews. A two-page or greater résumé may be perfectly acceptable in certain fields. In these professions, you would not want to limit yourself to only one page if you had enough relevant information to include.

Remember, many large companies scan résumés. This means no human being looks at your résumé initially. Instead, a computer scans each incoming résumé for key words. Be sure to emphasize qualities valued by employers, such as "organized" or "innovative." Keep in mind that fancy formatting and marbled papers do not scan. Those choices would put you immediately into the discard pile. If the company requires electronic submission, in most cases, the text of your résumé must be left justified, with no formatting. Most company websites explain their process and format requirements for résumé submissions.

It is also important to place your résumé in a PDF file. More and more companies are asking for your résumé to be submitted online. By having your information available in a PDF file, you can send the résumé from your computer or handheld device instantly. It is important to print the PDF file on a few different printers to make sure your preset margins print properly. You should use two easy-to-read fonts for the PDF file. Content is what employers are looking for rather than visual creativity (colored or textured paper, underlining, multiple fonts, varied margins, etc.). The speed at which a potential employer receives your material can make a positive impression about your knowledge of technology in addition to a real interest in a position with their company. By the way, you should also have a hard copy of the résumé with you when you go to an interview in case the interviewer requests it.

Wanda Fitzgerald

28 Fuller St. • Detroit, PA 16842
000-555-0000 • WandaFitzgerald@notcoldmail.kom

Qualifications
- Experienced in linear and nonlinear editing procedures. Own Canon XL-1 mini-DV camera. Proficient with AVID and Adobe Premiere 6.0 video-editing software and Cool-Edit BSI, Goldwave, and Multiquence audio-editing software.
- Produced music videos for the bands Backstreet Law and Fourfourteen. Produced promotional videos for Nightwind Studios and Benchmark Audio. Produced various interviews, PSAs, newscasts, and miscellaneous video projects.
- Started own company, Good Vibrations Entertainment. Responsible for inception of idea with partner, self-promoting through marketing, and building the business.
- Experienced in sales, customer service, promoting business, attracting customers, keeping records, and working independently.

Education
Mansfield University, Mansfield, PA
Bachelor of Science—Mass Communication, Broadcasting   **May 2002**
Coursework in TV Production I and II, Writing for Broadcast Media, Television and Radio Announcing

New York Institute of Photography, NYC
Professional Certification   **expected December 2002**
Currently enrolled in home correspondence course

Work Experience
Good Vibrations Entertainment
Co-Owner   **5/98–present**
- Initiated mobile disc jockey business with partner—began with a $20 mixer hooked into a school PA system
- Reinvested to grow the business to approximately 90 jobs per year and own $30,000 of sound and lighting equipment
- Responsibilities include: booking clients, talking to a variety of customers, ensuring customer satisfaction, purchasing and maintaining equipment, handling finances, maintaining web page, setting up, and performing

WNQV 104.5 FM
On-Air Announcer   **2/00–7/02**
- On-air announcing
- Conducted and engineered live remotes
- Produced commercials and promos, conducted interviews

Country Ski and Sports
Sales/Bike and Ski Technician   **4/98–present**
- Sales of outdoor products and services to customers
- Customer service on various levels from greeting customers to handling dissatisfaction and complaints

TRY IT!

Wanda's résumé is still lacking in some important areas. She only shows her work history and qualifications. What other categories should she include on her résumé to help sell herself?

_____

_____

_____

_____

Professional Perspective

As a recruiter who skims through several résumés a week, a potential candidate has about 30 seconds to capture my attention before I'll move on. Some of the more important areas are:

Presentation: Your résumé should look professional and does not need to include fancy fonts, graphics, or a lot of bells and whistles. Often, if you are sending via e-mail or replying via a website, files do not transfer in their original format.

- Use a standard one-inch margin.
- Single space between listings and add additional space between sections.
- Highlight items using bold rather than changing fonts. Items that you want to stand out can be bolded, such as your name, the employer's name, or the name of the institution.
- Use bullets to highlight accomplishments. Limit bulleted items to a few lines. Bullets make a résumé look clean, clear, and crisp.
- No spelling, grammar, punctuation, or typographical errors (a personal pet peeve . . . no interview from me).

Be Brief: More does not mean better. Do not include every detail of your work history; a résumé should highlight your experience and accomplishments. Your finished version ideally should be one or two pages.

Never Lie: Aside from the moral implications, if you are hired and your fabrications are discovered, you can be dismissed.

In the end, for the best results, be concise yet compelling.

—Julie Allen
Sr. Human Resources Specialist
The Summit Federal Credit Union

Once you have perfected your résumé and sent it to a potential employer, you should prepare for the next step. If you have effectively persuaded the employer to contact you, you need to remember the material from chapter 5 on electronic channels. An immature or inappropriate e-mail address or message on your voice mail can halt the interview process. The potential employer looks at the e-mail address on the résumé and may listen to your voice mail message. Everything must be professional. If all goes well, you will receive a call to continue the interview process.

ETHICAL CONSIDERATIONS

What are the ethical implications of making exaggerated statements on your résumé? Is it ethical to say that you volunteered for community service if your fraternity or sorority required that work of you? Is it ethical to imply you worked somewhere longer than you actually did or had more responsibilities than you actually had?

_____

_____

_____

_____

_____

Interviews

Once your résumé attracts an employer's attention and leads to an interview opportunity, you must diligently prepare for the interview. Some students think they can just talk and be themselves. This casual attitude is not what an employer desires. Employers prefer concise, logical answers to their questions.

To be effective in an interview, you must:

- Spend time preparing for the interview
- Make a great first impression
- Be able to answer questions effectively
- Be prepared for phone interviews
- Be prepared for Skype interviews
- Be prepared for stress interviews
- Communicate effectively after the interview

Spend Time Preparing

Once you get the interview confirmation, there are a number of things you can do to plan for success. Make sure you have a correct address and directions for exactly where you need to go. If possible, make a test run before the day of the interview. If you have a GPS device, use it. While usually reliable, there can be problems. Use one of the Internet mapping services (MapQuest or GoogleMaps, for example) to check potential routes; print the maps. If you have a current street map, you can use it to orient yourself if you make a wrong turn. You should plan for where you are going to park your car as well.

Remember to take the phone number along in case you have an unusual complication. Don't hesitate to ask questions of your contact person at the organization. You are in much better shape if you overplan than if you get lost.

Another question to ask the contact person is whether you will be interviewing with an individual or a group. Ask for the name(s) of the people with whom you will be interviewing. Consult the company website to see if it profiles those individuals. They will seem more familiar, and you may learn valuable information for use during the interview. Keep in mind that names don't always reveal the sex of a person. Don't assume that people are male or female just because they have a certain name. You don't want to look shocked when the person you thought was going to be a man is actually a woman.

Research the company so that you know all of the basic information about it. We once had a job applicant who arrived for an interview and asked how many students were enrolled at our institution. That immediately told us the person had not done any preparation for the interview.

If it has been a few days or weeks since the interview was scheduled, it is a good idea to phone your contact the day before to confirm the details of your appointment. Also be prepared for corporate or personal emergencies that arise; it is possible that you might arrive for the interview and be asked to come back another day.

Be aware that anything can happen. A colleague told us about an unusual circumstance. Her friend arrived at a job interview, and the interviewer asked her to drive them to lunch. She was horrified because her car was littered with fast-food wrappers, coffee cups, and multiple personal items strewn on the floor and back seat. What would the perception of the interviewer be after that short ride?

Finally, remember that you are "on" the entire time. From the moment you step out of your car, people may be watching you. The same scenario applies to your departure. Until you are safely down the highway, you should be a visual model of a responsible employee.

Making a Great Impression

The **first impression** is extremely important. Think back to chapter 2 on perception. Most people decide in the first minute whether you are competent, whether they will like you, and whether you belong in their company. The way you look when the interviewer first sees you, the way you move as you enter the room, and how you shake an interviewer's hand can affect your chances of being successful.

You must choose your personal artifacts carefully. For example, Maurice walks into an interview with an advertising agency in a crisply pressed, jet-black suit. He has a silver dress shirt and black silk tie. His shoes are shined to reflect the light. His belt is black leather with a silver tip. Maurice's appearance places him two steps ahead of his competition when he is introduced to the interviewer.

Anita, however, has not learned the importance of nonverbal symbols such as artifacts. While she can afford much more expensive clothing than Maurice, she has made some unwise choices. She chose a flowery dress in a fabric that wrinkled while driving to the interview. Her shoes have open toes and heels. The tattoo around her ankle is visible through her nude-colored panty hose.

CHOICES AND CONSEQUENCES

You have choices as a college student. You need to think ahead to the consequences. A female who gets a tattoo around her ankle and then wants a corporate job will have a limited wardrobe choice since the tattoo will be seen unless she always wears slacks and opaque stockings. Men may believe tattoos will be covered, but think about going to the health club with other people in your company. As soon as you change in the locker room, your tattoos are visible to others. While tattoos may be widely accepted by your peers, the people who are hiring and promoting you are usually at least a generation ahead of you. Remember attribution theory? Interviewers may assign a negative meaning to people who get tattoos and body piercings, thinking they are easily influenced by fads and cultural trends. Therefore, the interviewers may draw the conclusion that the interviewee cannot think or act independently.

Maurice communicates success and confidence. There is nothing in his appearance an interviewer could interpret as objectionable for a potential employee in the advertising field. He sticks to the basic principles of the corporate dress code. He realizes, however, if he were interviewing in a more traditional corporation, he should wear a dark suit, a white shirt, and a conservative tie. Anita is clueless. A flowery dress is simply too casual. Her visible tattoo gives the employer personal information that could be interpreted in a negative manner. (It is quite possible that Maurice has a tattoo, but it is covered by his suit and not visible to the interviewer.) The best choice is to analyze the company and be as conservative as possible.

Attire and overall appearance are essential to your success in the interview. You may not be able to afford expensive fabrics, but you can choose colors and styles that make you look good. Be careful with jewelry. Long bangles, enormous watches, multiple bracelets, etc. will call attention to the artifacts and may create an unfavorable impression. Accessorize carefully and tastefully. Employees in many companies have a specific look, and you must find out what it is. In some cases, the dress code is casual, and you may look out of place in a formal suit. Research the dress code for that specific company.

TRY IT!

Do a quick Internet search to find three specific recommendations about clothing, jewelry, or appearance for an interview that have not been discussed here.

_____

_____

_____

Get comfortable with dress clothing and begin building your professional look while you are still in school. If you and your family do not have a lot of money, ask for items such as shoes, ties, scarves, and belts for holidays and birthdays.

TRY IT!

Do an inventory. List what pieces of interview attire you already own.

_____

_____

_____

List what you still need to acquire.

_____

_____

_____

Make a plan to acquire these items by your senior year in college.

_____

_____

_____

Clothes are important. You must look the part. While you may enjoy being an individual by wearing green hair and face hardware now, that look will not be accepted in most companies. You must also look like the people who have the job you desire. In most companies, the dress code is conservative. Your first impression will make or break you.

Remember to select clothes that complement your body type. Here are some of the fundamental rules for conservative interviewing.

Dos

- One earring per ear (no earrings for men)
- Either a necklace or a bracelet
- One ring per hand
- Shined shoes
- Plain, conservative tie (no cartoon characters!)

Don'ts

- No open-toed/open-heeled shoes
- No sleeveless outfits (women), no short-sleeved shirts (men)
- No gaudy or noticeable makeup
- No work boots/sneakers

Professional Perspective

Preparation for an interview is just as important as the interview itself. One of the most important things you can do before an interview is to organize a professional black folder with several things. First, you will want information about where you are going. Maps and phone numbers to your destination should be easily accessible. Second, you will want to have information about the company. Companies hate it when you ask them obvious questions that you could easily answer yourself if you looked! Third, you will want to have a list of questions to ask during your interview, or while you are being shown around the company. Finally, you will want to make sure you have a pen and some blank paper for notes on information you will need to remember.

Planning also extends to personal items. Ladies, bring extra panty hose; you never know when a nasty snag will appear! Also, bring nail glue in case a fake nail comes off or nail polish in the event that your nail polish chips. Ladies and gentlemen, bring extra deodorant; some people perspire more when they are nervous. Bring a lint roller to get rid of those ugly fuzzies.

—Sarah Loher
Graduate, Mansfield University

Once the interviewer sees you, you have made your first impression. But it doesn't stop there. As discussed in chapter 4, your handshake will add or detract from the first impression. A firm handshake sends the nonverbal message of confidence—a quality desired by most interviewers. Wiping sweaty hands on your pants or fumbling with papers so you can extend your hand for a handshake sends a message of incompetence and lack of professional interpersonal experience.

The requirements of making a good first impression vary with culture. For instance, in U.S. culture, business cards are exchanged after a meeting is completed. In some cultures, however, business cards are exchanged as you meet someone for the first time. If you don't know

Professional Perspective

An important lesson I learned in an organizational communication class was that your handshake is a great way to make a good first impression. My professor in college would not let us leave the classroom until we had successfully completed a professional handshake, which was classified as a firm grip while looking straight into the other person's eyes. It took a few tries to get it right, but I am still using this technique in my professional environment. My company had an open position where many candidates who were recent college graduates applied for an entry-level position. One candidate in particular had a handshake like a cold, dead fish. This was an instant turn off for me. I immediately considered him to be weak and untrustworthy. This impression carried through the interview, and I was uncertain whether he would be an asset to our team and company. He did not get the job. My first impression of him through his handshake was never proved wrong through his responses to questions. In a professional setting, a firm handshake is necessary for a good first impression; you cannot afford to make into a bad impression.

—Angela Dickson
Senior Coordinator of Communications
American Architectural Manufacturers Association

the culture, you could ruin an interview in the first few moments. If you do any business travel or have the potential to meet someone from another culture in this country, you should research the culture carefully to determine what you need to do to make a good first impression.

Professional Perspective

In Japanese culture, the handling and presentation of business cards are paramount because they are an extension of one's self. When meeting a Japanese executive for the first time, the business card should be skillfully removed without fumbling and presented to the executive by holding the card in front of you with two hands. The executive will always take the card with his two hands, grabbing the card by the lower ends with two fingers. Accept a card from the Japanese executive using the same procedure.

Once you have accepted the card, you will talk to the executive by holding the card in front of you at chest level. Never look him in the eye. In Asian cultures, this is considered aggressive and threatening behavior.

The business card should be placed in a respectable place only—a cardholder or breast shirt pocket. Placing a card in a wallet or a money clip is considered very insulting. When working with any internationally based organization, it is a worthwhile activity to understand the culture of the home country.

—Robert. H. Christie
Senior Vice President, Corporate Communications
The New York Times Company

Answering Questions Effectively

Once you have made the first impression, you need to be able to sound intelligent when you speak. You must be aware of nonverbals such as volume, rate, and inflection. Some people speak very loudly or very quickly when they are nervous, which can be annoying to others. You should also work on the coherency and uniqueness of your answers to questions.

It is essential that your answers to questions demonstrate that you have a basic understanding of the company. Research is imperative. Let's say you are interviewing for a job at a famous ice-cream company and you ask, "So what kinds of ice cream do you manufacture?", or "How many employees are in your company?" The immediate impression is that you aren't prepared. The interviewer would obviously think, "If you can't take the time to look up simple facts, why should I consider you for this job?"

A common concept in interviewing is called behavioral interviewing. In a **behavioral interview,** employers expect interviewees to provide detailed information that demonstrate competence for the job in a meaningful and memorable way.

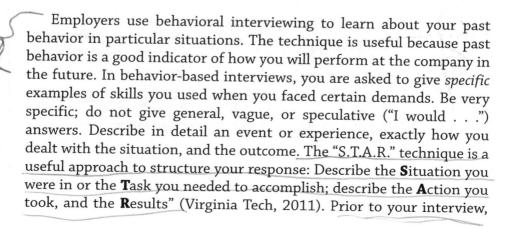

Reality ✓

Behavioral interviewing is used to weed out "polished" people who interview well without saying anything. Companies use this technique to find the candidate who can offer specific examples of the skills they possess. Behavioral interviewing requires candidates to respond with specific examples of past experiences rather than generalized or hypothetical responses. While behavior-based interviewing is not a panacea for complex recruitment and retention challenges, it is a time-tested methodology for improving hiring results. It has been studied, evaluated, and practiced for more than 30 years and is a central component of selection strategy at some of the world's best known companies (Kursmark, 2007).

Employers use behavioral interviewing to learn about your past behavior in particular situations. The technique is useful because past behavior is a good indicator of how you will perform at the company in the future. In behavior-based interviews, you are asked to give *specific* examples of skills you used when you faced certain demands. Be very specific; do not give general, vague, or speculative ("I would . . .") answers. Describe in detail an event or experience, exactly how you dealt with the situation, and the outcome. The "S.T.A.R." technique is a useful approach to structure your response: Describe the **S**ituation you were in or the **T**ask you needed to accomplish; describe the **A**ction you took, and the **R**esults" (Virginia Tech, 2011). Prior to your interview, review the skills, abilities and characteristics required for the job. Think back to occasions when you demonstrated these attributes so that you can discuss them factually and specifically in the interview.

If you answer the question, "What is your greatest strength?" with "I'm very calm under pressure; I can really get the job done; I don't sweat the small stuff," you haven't said anything. The interviewer will not remember these clichés. There is no way you can make an impression with that answer.

Instead, when Veronica is asked that question, she answers with a one-minute story about a personal experience.

> Well, I'm very calm under pressure. For example, when I was working at the ice-cream shop, a customer received a cone that had a hole in it. It was a small hole in the bottom, but the ice cream began to drip through because it was a hot day. The woman was so irate that the ice cream had dripped on her suit, she came up to me and threw the ice cream in my face. I had to stand there in front of other customers and handle the situation without losing my cool.
>
> My first reaction was to get really angry and say something I would have regretted, but I bit my tongue, wiped off my face, and said very nicely, "Is something wrong?" And with that, all of the other customers turned their heads and stared at her. Once the focus was on her rather than on her actions, she stormed out of the ice-cream shop. While I was disappointed I couldn't make her happy, at least the other customers complimented me on the way I handled the situation.

Note that this is a 1–2 minute answer. It meets all of the criteria of storytelling in that it has characters, a plot, a climax, and a resolution. It paints a visual picture the interviewer is not likely to forget. And it answers the question. This type of answer will make Veronica memorable to the interviewer and much more likely to get the job.

Some of the basic questions you should be prepared to answer are:

1. Why should we hire you?

2. What is your greatest strength?

3. What is your greatest weakness?

4. What accomplishment has given you the greatest satisfaction?

5. What motivates you to put forth your greatest effort?

6. Why do you want to work for our company?

However, as more and more interviewers are looking for behavioral interview answers, you may find that they will present you with statements calling for a response describing previous behavior:

7. Tell me how you handled your last conflict.

8. Tell me about a time when you had to work on a team.

9. Tell me about the last time you had to handle a really stressful situation.

As you create your answers to these questions or statements, keep your interviewer in mind—just as you think about your audience in public speaking. If you answer, "Why do you want to work for our company?" with "Because I really need a job," or "Because I find this company to be prestigious," you are not thinking about your audience. Your answer is egocentric; you should respond with information that is useful for the company. Show how your greatest strength can benefit the company. A personal story about your dependability and how that quality will benefit the employer can work to your advantage.

As you get ready to create your stories, it will be helpful for you to prepare a list of your skills and personality traits. Skills are competencies you've learned, such as computer programs, problem solving, or speaking a foreign language. Personality traits are desirable qualities you possess, such as being dependable, energetic, and detail oriented. Once you have developed your list of skills and personality traits, you can then describe events that highlight them. Good narrative explanations will make you stand out.

TRY IT!

Take one of the six interview questions and write an answer that includes a true story from your personal life. The story should have characters, a plot, a climax, and a resolution.

_____

_____

_____

_____

_____

_____

_____

_____

_____

Sometimes the interviewer is looking for your ability to think creatively. The interviewer may ask a **_brainteaser_**—an open-ended hypothetical question that tests the problem-solving ability of a potential employee and necessitates a factual, logical, descriptive answer. Brainteasers are common in interviews for creative jobs. "Why use logic puzzles, riddles, and impossible questions? The goal . . . is to assess a general problem-solving ability rather than a specific competency" (Poundstone, 2003, p. 20). Here's an example of a brainteaser: "How much does the ice in a hockey rink weigh?"

Brainteasers are also used in noncomputer-related industries, such as those that deal with the public or the law. The goal of this type of interview question is to test your experience with problem solving as well as your ability to remain calm under pressure. Many brainteasers do not have a correct answer. Your verbal ability to piece together logical thoughts in an impromptu manner is important. The brainteaser differs from behavioral-interviewing answers. The details and sequential logic in your answer must impress the interviewer.

Illegal Interview Questions

There are a number of illegal interview questions. It is illegal for interviewers to ask these questions, but sometimes they do anyway. You'll need to decide ahead of time what you will do if an employer asks you an illegal question. The following questions are from *HR World* (2010), and the article gives in-depth explanations about why each of these is illegal.

1. Are you a U.S. citizen?
2. What is your native tongue?
3. How long have you lived here?
4. Which religious holidays do you observe?
5. Do you belong to a club or social organization?
6. How old are you?
7. How much longer do you plan to work before you retire?
8. What is your maiden name?
9. Do you have or plan to have children?
10. Can you get a babysitter on short notice for overtime or travel?
11. What do your parents do for a living?
12. If you get pregnant, will you continue to work, and will you come back after maternity leave?
13. We've always had a man/woman do this job. How do you think you will stack up?
14. How do you feel about supervising men/women?
15. What do you think of interoffice dating?
16. Do you smoke or drink?

17. Do you take drugs?
18. How many sick days did you take last year?
19. Do you have any disabilities?
20. Have you had any recent or past illnesses or operations?
21. How far is your commute?
22. Do you live nearby?
23. Have you ever been arrested?
24. Were you honorably discharged from the military?
25. Are you a member of the National Guard or Reserves?

If an interviewer asks an illegal question, you are in a difficult situation. You can point out that it is an illegal question, side step the question, or simply answer it. None of those three choices yields particularly good results. While you can prepare yourself for the possibility of an illegal question, the best procedure may depend on the specific situation—meaning you may need to decide what you want to do when the question arises.

PHONE INTERVIEWS

Phone interviews add an interesting dimension to the interview process. This is a good news/bad news situation. The good news is you don't have to worry about your attire or posture. You can use interview notes with answers to potential questions and lists of skills or qualities that you don't want to forget. The bad news is your vocal technique, vocabulary, and verbal style is all an interviewer hears. Therefore, you must concentrate on your grammar and the completeness of your thoughts. Stand up while you talk so you have the best breath support for energy and vocal quality. You can tape your notes and résumé on the wall. Above all else, make sure you have good cell phone service. There is nothing worse than having difficulty with your phone connection.

Also remember you will have no nonverbal feedback. You cannot tell whether the interviewer is smiling and nodding or looking disgusted. Think positive thoughts. A positive image of the interviewer will help you remain calm.

SKYPE INTERVIEWS

Companies have begun using the Internet to conduct preliminary interviews through services like Skype. Skype allows the employer to see you through a webcam in addition to hearing you react to their questions. This technical platform is extremely useful to an employer when they wish to fill a position quickly and can screen a candidate as though they are sitting in the same room. Do not forget however that you are being seen by a total stranger, so your appearance is important,

---

Professional Perspective

As a nontraditional student I felt confident in the interview process because I already had work experience and an extensive résumé, but I got a rude awakening recently. I went through all of the formalities of the job process including: submitting an online application, a résumé, a cover letter, and I was involved in an exchange of e-mails, but I still had to do a phone interview in the end. The interview seemed to be running smoothly until I was asked a salary question. I did not feel that the question was appropriate in the phone interview setting, and I may have made a mistake by voicing my opinion about the question.

I felt that it was a trick question, since it is one of those questions designed to get me to either say an amount that was too large or too small. I was raised to not discuss money in this type of context and that belief affected my interview. I did not feel that it was wise to answer the question with a dollar amount. What is the best answer for this type of situation? There really is not a correct one.

The most important thing I learned was, you can be well rehearsed and prepared for an interview, but there is always the chance that something will come up that catches you off guard. It is important that you let each question resonate with you for a second before you make your response. Answer the questions honestly, but remember, some of the questions may be designed to elicit a certain response. It is important to practice your interview skills now, before you find yourself in an awkward situation. Remember, you only have one chance to make a first impression, and you do not want it to be the wrong one.

—Michael Southard
Graduate, Mansfield University

---

as is the background seen by the camera. Therefore, it's useful to practice setting up your computer a few times to check your image, to become comfortable talking into the camera, and to check what is visible by the camera. Make sure the lighting is good and there is nothing distracting in your picture. You want to try to have a good facial shot—not too close, but not too far away. If you have a Skype account, place the address on your résumé and business card along with your home address, phone number and e-mail address.

STRESS INTERVIEWS

Another situation you should be prepared to handle is the stress interview. In a **stress interview,** the employer will test you to your limits. I (KSY) had an accounting major who went for an interview to be a financial planner. The interviewer looked at her and said, "OK, Heather, here is a stack of travel brochures. I'll be back in 20 minutes, and I expect you to have a persuasive presentation ready for me concerning where I should go on vacation." He exited the room. When he got back and heard her presentation (using Monroe's Motivated Sequence!), he immediately launched into questions. She was not allowed to use any material twice for her answers to 16 questions. When he asked her what her greatest weakness was, she paused for a brief moment, and he badgered her with, "What's the matter Heather, do you think you are perfect?" In this situation, the employer is trying to see how she will hold up under stress. Although this may seem unfair, a job as a financial planner entails dealing with very unhappy customers when the stock market goes down, and the employer needs to know she can handle pressure.

One of my (HPT) students who had a degree in broadcasting interviewed for a video-editing position. When the student arrived at the studio, he was handed video clips from a breaking story aired earlier the same day. He was given 30 minutes to cut his own version of a news package for the station. He was given no training or explanation of the company's equipment in the editing suite. He finished creating his version of the story within the time limit. The supervisor thanked him for his time and said the senior producer would contact him upon screening the package. No further questions were asked. The interview was over.

A third example of a stressful interview situation is the group interview. There are times when all applicants are brought into the same room and asked to answer questions in front of one another. We know of two people who have reported being asked to answer the question, "Why should we hire you instead of the specific person on your left?"

Thinking about the three scenarios above, it is important to find out what the interview norm is in your field. Are you likely to run into stress interviews? Make sure you can do what you say you can do on your résumé, because you may be tested on the spot. Any hesitation on your part in performing a task or answering a question may give the interviewer a bad impression. Be prepared and remain as relaxed as possible to handle whatever question the interviewer throws your way.

Reality ✓

Many companies now give spelling tests during the interview. If a job you are seeking requires a lot of writing, be prepared for a spelling test on words commonly used in your profession. Typing tests for speed and accuracy are also given. Employers may ask you, especially if you are applying for a teaching job, to hand write an essay so they can check your ability to spell and the clarity of your writing. You may experience writing tests on a computer in the corporate world.

Communicating after the Interview

It is essential that you use the utmost caution when writing to a prospective employer in ***post-interview communication.*** While handwritten thank-you notes should be sent, one misspelling in a thank-you note or e-mail will reveal additional information about your writing ability. Be especially sure to get the correct spelling of the interviewer's name and title. You can always type a thank-you note in a word process-ing program to check your spelling, and then hand copy it onto an appropriate note card. It is also wise to write your e-mail the same way.

Professional Perspective

A former intern contacted me regarding opportunities for future employment. The student was graduating from a prestigious East Coast university and had been reliable and hard working throughout the course of the summer.

The intern was extremely excited about two possible opportunities I could offer, so I contacted my associates. The positions were in competitive fields; without my assistance, it would have been difficult to obtain an inside contact. My associates asked for a résumé and letter of inquiry to be sent to their e-mail addresses.

I expected the intern's transmittals would be forthcoming, but my colleagues did not receive any e-mail from the intern for nearly two weeks. When I finally received an e-mail from the intern, the intern had decided to inquire about only one of the positions. I had expected the intern to con-tact both of these individuals regardless of the intern's preferences and as a professional courtesy to my colleagues and myself.

When the intern finally drafted a letter to my associate, I received a call from this colleague who was shocked at the typographical errors and lack of formality in the intern's e-mail. The intern also did not send a résumé. The opportunity was lost.

When attempting to make a virtual impression on a potential employer, carefully draft and proof your letter of inquiry, résumé, and any follow-up e-mail, always address your potential employer with a professional tone and formality, and promptly respond to any messages regarding the opportunity.

—Anonymous
A member of the Professional Staff at a Large Museum

As a student, you may not think about the personal implications that are present when someone agrees to give you a reference or to help you make a professional connection. Rather than just providing a criti-cal assessment of your skills, the person is putting his or her reputation on the line. Inappropriate or unprofessional behavior on your part dur-ing the interview process reflects poorly on the person recommending you. Many professors and professionals are extremely cautious about giving recommendations because they have been burned by students and other colleagues after giving them a recommendation. A recom-mendation is a transaction involving mutual respect. If Professor Smith gives Dominick a contact person, Dominick is obligated to con-tact that person and to let Professor Smith know he has followed through. Additionally, it is respectful to keep Professor Smith informed of the process, since she put her reputation on the line to help Domi-nick. A thank-you note to Professor Smith would also be in order. All of these details reflect favorably on Dominick's credibility.

Summary

Remember that interviewing communication is a package deal. Your written material allows you to be selected for a job interview. But once you walk into a corporate environment, the employment pendulum swings away from your writing to your appearance and verbal communication skills and style. You must concentrate on verbal and nonverbal messages throughout your exposure to a potential employer. Everything you do and say is remembered. Practice and improve your written and oral skills while you are still in school. Remember to concentrate on your vocal technique during phone/Skype interviews. Electronic interviews focus on only part of the communication package. Vocal technique and use of paralanguage become your selling points. It is important to develop your communication skills early. Sell your ability during an interview in a warm and friendly way. Your future depends on consistent communication skills and style.

KEY WORDS

behavioral interview	post-interview communication
brainteaser	résumé
first impression	Skype interview
interviewing	stress interview
phone interview	

DISCUSSION/ACTIVITIES

1. Identify the career you seek after finishing school. Jot down the skills and activities you need to possess to be a good candidate for the career.

2. Describe your "brand." Does it match your career objective?

3. List the personal skills you plan to write on your résumé. Why do these skills sell you to an employer?

4. Conduct an interview with a classmate as though you are a human resources person. Critique each other when both interviews are completed.

5. Participate in a behavioral interview exercise. Give students 5 questions in advance. Students are asked to prepare a 1–1½ minute story response for each question. During the exercise, each student stands in front of the class while one of the questions is asked. Critique the exercise when the entire class is finished.

6. Write a brief follow-up note thanking an interviewer for their time.

thirteen

Working in Teams

OBJECTIVES

After reading this chapter, you should be able to:

- Explain the organizational elements of an initial team meeting
- Describe the importance of discovering the needs of team members
- Describe the importance of a team contract
- Describe the five styles of team leadership
- Explain how to select a leader
- Define task versus social elements of teamwork
- Explain how to keep proper records
- Identify ways to motivate team members
- Identify elements of effective planning for meetings
- List the six steps of The Standard Agenda
- Explain why The Standard Agenda is effective for problem solving
- List three types of team presentations

Groups are integral to modern life. Everyone congregates in groups during family functions, at school, during community or religious events, as well as in corporate life. At other times, we are assigned to work in groups. Groups help people to accomplish social and professional tasks that benefit their family, community, religious establishment, and business organization.

Groups are composed of individuals with similar ideas or goals coming together to complete a task or to solve a problem for a common good. **Teams** do exactly the same thing, but they go one step further. What makes a team different from a standard work group is the sense of cohesiveness they experience while working together for a brief period of time. An ideal team becomes cohesive as team members work to accomplish their task. This cohesiveness can be seen and felt by other people who aren't even part of the team. There are many facets to good team problem solving because you must work on a task and deal with the intricacies of interpersonal differences at the same time. Only when you combine effective task work with effective interpersonal skills do you have a true working team. Some groups never achieve team status.

There are many task groups in the workplace, but many are comprised of people who don't feel a sense of belonging, don't support a common goal, and don't worry about their interactions with each other. This is not a team. Some corporations use the team concept in the workplace successfully. By using the word "teams," corporations encourage a spirit of family, cohesiveness, and productivity. However, some corporations promoting the team philosophy still do not achieve their goal. Many employees never actively contribute to this spirit even though they do their work. These members hold the group back from becoming a team. Everyone must fully cooperate with other members throughout the duration of a task to achieve the team label. Forming a team is an ideal goal for any small group working together on a task.

An Effective Beginning

So how do you become a team? The first few minutes of interacting with a new group of people present the same challenges as a first impression in an interpersonal relationship. Members may like or dislike each other based on their appearance or their nonverbals or preconceived notions about each other. The group must become cohesive quickly and forget their differences in order to be effective and complete the task.

For example, you walk into your oral communication class on the day the teacher is starting to talk about communicating in groups. Then, the teacher announces you will be doing a group project and assigns students to specific groups. You immediately think this isn't fair, but the teacher is actually preparing you for a potential team experience. You soon discover you are working with Tony, Nancy, Juan, George, and DeShara. Your disappointment mounts quickly because Tony is in your group. He hasn't come to most class sessions all term. When Tony is there, he is obstinate and argumentative. You are not looking forward to dealing with him. You are somewhat thankful, however, that DeShara is in your group, since she expresses her opinions in a positive way.

You meet with your group for the first time. If you don't know the people in your group, it makes it more difficult to talk to them effectively. Spend some time getting to know one another. The next task is to assess everyone's skills, goals, and needs. Groups often fail to talk about the skills each member brings to the task; this is an error that may prevent a team from ever forming. An initial skills assessment is

CHOICES AND CONSEQUENCES

Describe the most difficult person you've had to work with.

_____

_____

What choices did you make?

_____

_____

What were the consequences?

_____

_____

What would you do differently now?

_____

_____

necessary to determine who is good at research, writing, editing, proof-reading, and visual and oral presentation. Once you know who can do what, members can be assigned to the right tasks. It is obviously self-defeating to assign the final draft randomly to someone who can't write. Assess member skills immediately.

As your team members talk about their skills, you discover the following:

- Tony says he is good at computer layout and graphics. He likes to make information look good on paper.

- Nancy says she is an excellent writer and editor. She pays a lot of attention to detail.

- Juan says he is creative. He likes to do original research, think of new approaches to material, and come up with unique ideas. He also enjoys talking to people.

- George says he is very task oriented. He likes to lead a group and make sure they are progressing through the task. He likes to pre-plan and is interested in being the group leader if no one objects.

- DeShara says she is a good critical thinker. She likes to analyze ideas and find flaws and positive qualities in arguments.

- You are a little shy. You want to be involved, but you can't see yourself confronting Tony and DeShara. You like to take notes, and so you offer to record all of the ideas and minutes for the group. You also enjoy research, so you can work on your own. But if anyone needs a hand, you offer to help.

ETHICAL CONSIDERATIONS

What are the ethical considerations of telling the group that you are strong at something when you really are weak?

_____

_____

_____

_____

All group members should work together to understand the goals of each member. What does each person want out of the experience? Are some members excited about working hard to achieve an A on the project? Do others express the desire to do minimal work for an average grade? If so, you already have conflicting goals. An initial conversation about goals can save a lot of misunderstandings and hard feelings later. In the workplace, you can be assigned to committees that have an important task, and everyone commits to doing their best. On other committees, the task may be "busywork" where everyone knows no one will ever look at their work and evaluate it. In that case, you may decide to finish the task quickly without putting a lot of effort into it. The more clearly the members state their goals, the more cohesive the group will be—and the closer they will be to ideal team status.

Everyone says they will do whatever it takes to get an A on the project. You are skeptical, however, because you know Tony and Nancy have not done stellar work in the class so far. DeShara says, "Tony, you are never in class—are you sure we can count on you to do quality work?" Tony says, "Yeah, I just don't like going to class, but my computer work is spectacular. I'll bring in a copy of a report I did in high school, and you tell me if you've ever turned in anything that looked that good." DeShara says, "You're on! Make sure you bring it to the next meeting."

In your first meeting, everyone begins with the premise that the group would like to do well as a team. Whether it will actually happen is up to the long-term efforts of each member. Doing an inventory of members' skills is essential, but it does not guarantee success. If a member fails to follow through with a commitment, simply knowing what he or she is good at doing doesn't do the group much good. How-

Critical Thinking

Typically, what are your goals for a group project?

_____

_____

_____

ever, an honest assessment during the members' skills inventory can be an effective beginning to bringing the group together as a team.

Members' Needs

To facilitate your group becoming a team, it is a good idea to talk about and analyze each ***member's needs.*** It's easier to work interpersonally if you understand one another. Some people need a lot of encouragement; they need to hear people say they are doing a good job. People with high self-esteem could find comments like "good idea!" to be condescending. Some people need to be in charge. Others have a high need for organization. And others just want to goof off. The more you know about people's needs, the better you can interact with them. If all members choose to interact effectively on an interpersonal level, your group will be well on the way toward a team feeling.

George suggests everyone should make a statement about his or her personal needs, but his nonverbals suggest he isn't sincere. Nancy looks at George and says, "You think this is stupid, don't you?" George replies, "Well, sort of. I've never had to do this with other people before. It is weird to talk about my needs. But as I think about projects I've done before, I've been disappointed in the lack of feedback by group members regarding the research I've collected. I'd like to know what they think is good or bad."

Tony says, "I know what you mean George. Every time I get a paper back, the teacher says, 'The ideas are not written well, but the layout is great.' I sure wish they'd explain why it isn't written well."

DeShara says, "It is important to me that you listen when I talk. I get really irate when people don't look at me and pay attention to my ideas. A simple 'good idea' once in a while would be nice too."

You know it is important for you to feel valued and included in the team. But because you are shy, you don't feel that you can say this to everyone. So, you don't share your feelings. This decision is not a wise one because the other members of the group don't know how to support you properly during the task.

Critical Thinking

List two personal needs you have that will be important for you to share with your group:

_____

_____

_____

_____

Tony, George, and DeShara have provided valuable information to other team members. DeShara's simple statement lets every team member know it is important to make eye contact and to pay attention to her when she is talking. Think about the hard feelings this team avoids later by simply having this small piece of information about DeShara.

Professional Perspective

International differences might make the meeting challenging until you understand how everybody communicates.

In the United States, people change their reactions to others based on age, but only slightly. In Korea, if you are around anyone who is older, there is not much contact with them. If the older person speaks, you don't look at them. There are specific verbs and nouns used to signify that you have respect for them. You will never go against what an older person has to say. You can't express disagreement with their opinion unless you know them extremely well.

It would be easy to see how an American entering a Korean group would be seen as rude and/or arrogant when s/he offered a conflicting viewpoint. At the same time, a Korean who enters an American workgroup might not be willing to share a point of view and be seen as incompetent for not having an opinion. By doing what each has been trained to do through social communication, they will actually be giving a poor impression to group members even though they believe themselves to be acting in an effective manner.

—Hyun Mook Kim
Former International Student
Mansfield University

Team Contract

You may want to think about a written **team contract.** While this may not happen in the business world, we find it is extremely useful for students. The purpose of a contract is to outline what the working expectations are for each team member. You might also talk about penalties for not meeting individual obligations. In this way, there should be less misunderstanding on an interpersonal level as the task stages develop.

One example of a team contract has six sections:

1. A team goal

2. A list of what each member will do

3. A list of what the members will not do

4. A list of penalty points for each of the items in numbers 2 and 3: For example, "For each missed meeting, a member will lose five points for an excused absence (defined as . . .) and 10 points for an unexcused absence (defined as . . .). Think ahead for potential problems.

5. A list of the roles of team members (include the leader, secretary, and others)

6. A list of the strengths of each participating member

The contract is particularly important if you have a peer-grading element for the project. If you critique group members at the conclusion of the project, it will be easier to assign points later with a solid contract. It is important to have a peer critique after any team project. Even if you don't have the opportunity to grade one another, you can still do a contract and share your reviews verbally or in writing once the project is completed.

Styles of Leadership

Before you discuss who will be the leader, everyone should decide what style of leadership works best for him or her. Leadership models have evolved over the years. There are three types of leadership: authoritarian, laissez-faire, and democratic. **Authoritarian leaders** tell people what to do. They don't ask a lot of questions and don't get input; they make all the decisions and expect people to follow their orders. **Laissez-faire leaders** are laid back. They are "hands off," letting the group do as it pleases. They are not involved in much decision making and don't synthesize needs and ideas. **Democratic leaders** are characterized by their ability to solicit and synthesize ideas, attend to

---

TRY IT!

Based on the descriptions in the text, which group member in our example would be the best

Authoritarian leader _____

Laissez-faire leader _____

Democratic leader _____

people's needs, keep the group on task, and reach decisions that consolidate the concerns of each member of the group.

James MacGregor Burns (1978) introduced a new perspective on leadership. He compared traditional leadership, which he called transactional, with a more complex style that he called transformational (Hackman and Johnson, 2009). ***Transactional leadership,*** as implied by its label, involves exchanging rewards for desirable outcomes. The leader tells you what needs to be done and rewards you for doing it. Transactional leadership essentially maintains the status quo. Good performance is rewarded; poor performance is corrected. Burns believed that ***transformational leadership*** was both empowering and inspirational, creating more than a mere exchange.

Professional Perspective

In my opinion, a leader is someone who leads by example. A good leader is honest, hardworking, and has the ability to inspire the work ethic of his or her colleagues and peers. Leaders are listened to, respected, and have a take charge attitude. Leaders get things done and make things happen.

Prior to continuing my education, I had the opportunity to work with an influential leader, Christopher S. Decker, Professional Engineer and Vice President of an international corporation. Chris has always lived and worked by the following two beliefs: "A good leader will always know when to lead and when to follow" and "do not ask for more than you are willing to give."

—Eric J. Schmidt, Nontraditional Student
Mansfield University Graduate
May 2011

The best leader for most discussion/task groups is going to be the one who can be flexible with all of these styles. There are times when the leader needs to back off and let the team run with an idea. At other times, the team may be unmotivated, and the leader should move into authoritarian mode, telling people what to do. The democratic approach works well most of the time because the leader is soliciting ideas and synthesizing feedback. In all teams, it is important for all members to articulate clearly which leadership type is most effective for them. In this way, whoever becomes the leader can adapt to the needs of the members. It is much more difficult for a leader to be effective if she doesn't know how you like to be treated. If you are the one who is selected to be the leader, you will need to finesse your skills. Try to move out of your normal comfort zone if you rely on only one of these styles. Be fair to everyone and use the appropriate leadership style at the right time. You need to help your group feel that you care about their success and well-being.

Professional Perspective

The single most important skill one needs to perfect in order to be successful in a team environment is learning how to listen. It's very easy in chaotic, high-stress situations and corporate meetings to stay focused on what you as an individual have on your mind. Inevitably, everyone in your group falls into that trap, and it becomes almost impossible to make any forward progress. In addition, most people get caught up in being vocal about their own ideas with no one actually listening to what is being said. Lots of time, energy, and good ideas get lost. The trick to listening successfully and effectively in a team environment can be summarized in three steps. First, absorb what is being said by the other group members. Second, incorporate the good ideas and thoughts you hear with your own. Finally, present your clear and concise ideas on how to accomplish your team's goals to the rest of the group. If you follow these steps, you will consistently be seen as a valuable leader within your team.

Apprendre à écouter aux autres est le talent le plus important à développer lorsque l'on considère le travaille en groupe. Dans un environnement chaotique, bruyant et tendu, et aussi dans les rendez-vous incorpores, il est facile de rester fermé sur soi plutôt que de se tourner vers les autres. Il est inévitable, alors, pour chaque membre de l'équipe de rester dans son propre monde et tomber dans ce cercle vicieux où il est impossible d'aller de l'avant. De plus, tout le monde a tendance à parler uniquement de ce qui le préoccupe individuellement sans avoir personne à l'écoute. À maintes reprises, les idées intéressantes se perdent dans l'aliénation du groupe, et l'énergie de chacun est gaspillée. Pour apprendre à écouter de façon efficace, on peut utiliser une astuce simple qui se déroule en trois étapes: d'abord, absorbez ce qui vient d'être dit par les autres membres de l'équipe. Ensuite, rassemblez les bonnes idées et les pensées intéressantes que vous venez d'entendre et les synthétiser avec les vôtres. Finalement, exprimez vos idées de façon claire et précise à votre équipe, et expliquez sereinement les étapes nécessaires pour atteindre les objectifs que le groupe s'est fixé. Si vous suivez ce procédé, votre équipe vous considérera invariablement comme l'une des têtes pensantes les plus compétentes au sein du groupe.

—Robert C. Weigand
Senior Manager, Project Planning and Administration
ABC

Selecting a Leader

Leaders can be appointed, or they can emerge. There are always situations where you end up becoming the leader whether you want to or not. Think about the problems that occur when a group or a supervisor selects a person with the wrong skills as the leader. Imagine if you, the shy person, are appointed as the leader. Will the group function in the same way if either DeShara or Tony is appointed? What will be the dynamic between George, who has the organizational skills and wanted to be the leader, and any other team member who is elected? If tasks are assigned to the wrong people, member hostilities arise.

It is important to choose a person with the right skills to be the leader. This person should desire the leadership role and provide evidence of leadership experience. Skills without desire don't yield effective leadership. Those who want to lead but have no evidence of appropriate skills are not effective either.

Professional Perspective

The best leaders are passionate about their chosen field and are prepared to make the commitment needed to succeed. In addition to management skills, a leader must also impart:

- **Character:** Words, actions, and ethics define the character of a leader and the way people respond to them. Admired leaders give and receive the respect needed to succeed. You must be willing to do what is right.
- **Vision:** A vision is much more than a good idea. It creates a long-term perspective. Innovative leaders break with tradition and embrace change. You cannot be inhibited by a fear of failure.
- **Motivation:** It is imperative to learn how to listen and ask the right questions. This will enable you to understand and address individual needs and strengths when seeking support.

Not everyone can be, should be, or for that matter, wants to be a leader. The decision to be a leader is a matter of balancing your proficiency skills with professional and personal goals.

—John W. Nichols
Executive Director
The Art Museum Partnership

As you select a leader, review the group's skills list. Some groups try to shirk the responsibility of choosing a leader. However, having a leader is important. Think about the teams you've experienced. How often have individuals pulled their own weight? How often has there been no conflict? How often has everyone simply known what to do instead of needing someone to delegate tasks? How often has everyone been able to meet at a convenient time? The chances are your answers to these questions indicate the necessity for having a leader.

ETHICAL CONSIDERATIONS

You are leading a group that has put together a proposal. Your efforts are highlighted in a newspaper article; however, the article discusses the proposal as something that you have done. There is no mention of a committee. What should you do?

_____

_____

_____

_____

Your group decides to select George because he wants to be the leader, and he offers evidence of having led other groups effectively. As he talked about his previous experiences, his communication style provided evidence that he thinks in an inclusive manner, and he appears to be direct and warm. In addition, he is the only member of the team who made direct eye contact with every member while he was explaining his background. The first thing George does after being selected is to thank everyone for the opportunity to lead the group. He begins with a brief motivational statement about the project, working together, and the group's mutual goal.

Critical Thinking

Pick a group member other than George. Write a description of what would happen if that person were selected to be the leader.

_____

_____

_____

_____

_____

_____

Task versus Social Elements of Teamwork

As you begin the task, it is important to remember that teamwork involves task and social elements. **Task elements** relate to the project on which you are working. **Social elements** include chatting with one another, asking if people are doing well, and joking around. Some people are very social all of the time, and nothing gets accomplished. Other people are so task oriented they can't even say hello. They call the group to order immediately, get to the business of the day, and then get angry when someone cracks a joke. Neither of these approaches works well. In order to work effectively on a team, you need to have a good mix of task and social elements.

Critical Thinking

Where do you fall on the task-social continuum? How will this help your team?

Task Oriented   **Socially Oriented**

1	2	3	4	5

_____

_____

_____

As the meeting progresses, George says, "First we need to exchange phone numbers and e-mail addresses. Then, we need to set up a schedule for meeting times. After that, we need to decide on our group roles. Finally, we can start working on the project." George asks you to record this information and to e-mail it to the rest of the team. You tell the other members they will receive their e-mails by 10 PM. As secretary, this will be your first test of credibility with the team. If you fail to e-mail the information by the deadline, they will know they cannot count on you. Your follow-through is critical.

Reality

Some of the types of people you will encounter who perform task and maintenance actions are as follows:

TASK

Information giver

Initiator—the person who gets things started

Clarifier/Summarizer—the person who synthesizes what has already been said or decided

Information and Opinion seeker—the person making sure that everyone has a chance for input

Recorder/secretary

MAINTENANCE

Harmonizer—the person who soothes irritable people

Tension releaser—the person who lightens the mood when necessary

Encourager/supporter—the person who acknowledges other people's contributions

NONPRODUCTIVE

Monopolizer—the person who is always talking and never listening

Bully—the person who always has to be right at any cost.

Nonparticipant—this person is there, but does not participate or help the group in any way

Reality

Tony doesn't meet a deadline, so George and DeShara no longer trust him. They begin to do his work, because they are afraid it won't get done. Their decision subdivides the team. George and DeShara are more focused on the grade and the quality of the project than on the cooperation of team members. This begins a downward spiral for the team. When Tony comes to the next meeting with work in hand, he finds that George and DeShara have already done the work. Tony feels excluded from the group and begins to withdraw. Meanwhile, George and DeShara begin to complain they have to do all the work.

This is a perception problem. Often when we have heard students complain about doing all of the work in a group, we hear from other team members that those people wouldn't allow them to do any work. In order to be successful as a team, you must find ways to trust, to encourage, and to motivate each other.

Motivating Team Members

Before getting to the task, George says he wants to discuss **motivation,** the spark that causes a person to act. Team members have already shared their individual goals. George says he will do his best to keep everyone motivated and on task, but members are also responsible for motivating themselves to get their assigned work completed. If everyone works diligently, the group will be satisfied with the final product and have interpersonal harmony. Juan, being creative, says he is motivated by pizza. The team laughs. But rather than let it go, he says, "No really, in my computer programming task group, we ordered food, and everyone was much happier and less cranky after they snacked."

Motivation can come in many forms. Some people are internally motivated. Others are motivated by a break in routine, food, or the comments of team members. It is important for team members to discuss motivational ideas and decide what might work for everyone. Those who think they are already motivated and don't need this discussion are fooling themselves. Teams can lack motivation at some point

---

Professional Perspective

Motivating Young Leaders

I was hired for my first professional position when I was 24 years old. I had just finished graduate school and was working in student affairs, mainly advising fraternities and sororities at a moderate-sized college in southern Pennsylvania.

Performing my job well required a unique balancing act. I had to appear credible in front of, and earn the respect of, two very different audiences. First, there were my fraternity and sorority students whose average age was 18–23. Although I was not much older than many of these students, it was now my responsibility to direct the development of their community and get them to buy into it. My second audience was my colleagues, whose experience ranged from other new professionals to veteran student affairs professionals, tenured faculty, and university administration.

During my first year I struggled with this balance, but I eventually found success in falling back on learned communication behaviors. I paid attention to my appearance, always dressing professionally at work. I volunteered for committees where I was able to meet employees outside of my division. I paid attention to what was going on in my field. When it was time to recommend some changes in University policy I researched different options and developed my point of view; scheduled meetings with key administrators, advisors, and students; and presented my ideas.

After my initial hard work resulted in success, I came to the conclusion that neither your age nor your experience is as important as the verbal and nonverbal messages you deliver through your work. A strong work ethic that values consistency and prompt decision making based on updated research makes an impact on both seasoned colleagues and young leaders. Time spent on preparation will pay off later. Developing your communication skills will provide you with a strong foundation from which to face new challenges.

—Emilee Danielson
Assistant Dean of Students and Director of Fraternity & Sorority Life
Shippensburg University

Critical Thinking

What motivates you when you are working on a team?

_____

_____

_____

---

during a project and for a variety of reasons. The initial discussion regarding motivation should be revisited whenever motivation dips.

Planning for Meetings

Planning is part of effective teamwork. A team member must be responsible for coordinating the details for the meeting site. In selecting a space (whether a room in the library, a meeting room on campus, or some other space), make sure it contains the technology your team needs. For instance, some university classrooms have computers and projection equipment that allow the team to watch as another member is typing information. As the team discusses and develops ideas, all members can observe the process. Everyone should be comfortable in the meeting space. There should be space to set things—a large table that allows you to display information for the meeting. You need to make sure the lighting is sufficient for everyone. Are there enough electrical outlets to plug in any equipment you may need? Is there air-conditioning? Will it be too cold? Are you in a place where Juan can have his pizza? Don't forget record keeping as you make these plans. It may be important for you to have a university receipt stating you have reserved the space. This can save you a lot of time if others challenge your right to be there or if you need to have a door unlocked.

As an individual member, make sure you are 100 percent prepared for whatever is scheduled on the agenda. You should have read the minutes of the previous meeting, so you can identify corrections and can vote to approve them. You should have reviewed the agenda, so you know what is planned. Be sure you have prepared a concise, accurate report for your portion of the task. You also need to have completed all of your assignments. Team members get irate quickly when individuals make excuses for why their work is not done. This shows great disrespect to your team members and is rarely tolerated in the corporate world. There are often severe consequences for not being prepared in business.

The team approach to working together requires diligence in interpersonal skills. Members must be honest in sharing their needs with others and responsible for competently completing their assignments related to the task. It is also important to develop a sense of group pride in the quality of work generated. Everyone must be self-motivated and held together by a firm, yet positive, leader. Team members become role models for each other when they display excellent verbal and nonverbal skills. Team moments happen, and when they do, they become memorable. Once interpersonal skills unite the team, it is ready for problem solving. However, if the team is not united, the problem-solving process will be more difficult.

Keeping Proper Records

How do you keep **proper records?** Most groups start with a meeting agenda. The agenda can be formal or informal depending on the team. Most agendas include the following items:

- A start time
- Correction and acceptance of previous minutes
- Announcements
- Reports from team members
- Unfinished business from previous meetings
- New business that must be accomplished
- An ending time for the meeting

Surely, you have attended meetings where nothing was accomplished. The leader began with, "What are we doing today?" and no one remembered what had been decided previously. An effective leader creates an agenda; this shows respect for team members because the leader is organized, prepared, and unwilling to waste their time. This is a test of credibility for the leader. If the leader can create, distribute, and stick to an effective agenda, the leader will earn every member's respect. If you finish the meeting early, the leader can dismiss the group. In this way, members who wish to socialize may do so, but others may choose to leave. Sticking to an agenda shows respect for everyone's time.

You should always have a formal record of decisions the team makes. You will find, even in working on a class project, keeping notes of decisions will save you a lot of time and future conflict. In order to keep proper records, the secretary should have the date, a list of who attended the meeting, what time the meeting was called to order, a notation of every item discussed, who initiated the idea, and what decision was reached. The secretary may also keep a record of every vote. The secretary concludes minutes with the phrase "Respectfully Submitted" and signs his or her name. If the minutes are distributed by e-mail, keep a signed original copy for the records.

The secretary should make sure minutes are formally written, with no abbreviations. All names should be spelled and recorded correctly. In business, use only last names. The secretary should proofread the minutes carefully before submitting them to the team. Remember, minutes are a legal document of the proceedings. Everyone should take responsibility for reviewing and correcting the minutes before approving them. We will say more about correcting minutes in the technology and groups section.

Some miscellaneous tips for record keeping include keeping a file folder of all agendas, all copies of the minutes, copies of all e-mail correspondence, copies of all memos, and copies of any handouts from team members. You should also put a date on all information you receive so you know when you received it. The secretary's goal is to keep all information concerning the project in one file.

Reality ✓✓

There are times in the workforce when your notes and conversations from a group meeting are considered to be confidential. You will need to be careful to adhere to the policy or agreements related to confidentiality that your team or organization establishes. It is common for people who do not comply with a confidentiality agreement to be fired.

Meeting Dos and Don'ts

While there is no comprehensive list of what you should and should not do in group meetings, we offer these suggestions:

- Be on time.
- Stick to the topic.
- Leave personal issues behind.
- Be prepared.
- Have handouts ready, if appropriate.
- Give an update of where you are on the project.
- Be positive when you ask questions of other members.
- Keep in mind that the goal is to stay on task.

- Remember the difference between being critical of an idea and criticizing an idea or person.

- Don't keep a critique to yourself to appear to be popular.

- Use the proper tone when being critical of an idea.

- Be honest about what you can/can't do.

- Follow through.

- Express as early as possible any difficulties you are having so other members can help you.

Professional Perspective

The foundation of team building lies in good communication. I take a group of 20–30 people who may or may not know each other and ensure that over a limited period of time (1–3 days) they function as a team. In live television, details are critical. A lot of pieces must come together properly and in the correct order for a live remote to be successful. I provide my crews with a detailed written plan of the project.

You must preplan well, share all information with team members, and remain calm to be effective in building a team.

—Jim Benson
President
Vision Quest Productions

Technology and Groups

Technology is making the workplace more collegial while heightening the skill and time sensitivity requirements of every employee. Businesses use various software protocols from outside vendors to promote a healthy working climate for everyone. Internal departmental communication as well as managerial communication is accessed online via security passwords. Many meetings are also conducted online.

As students, you can prepare yourself for collaborative online work while still in school. **Google Docs** and **wikis** offer you training in preparing reports and documents in the virtual world. Google Docs is a free web-based application for creating, editing, and storing documents and spreadsheets online. All you need to access the files is a computer with an Internet connection and a web browser. Users can import, create, edit and update documents and spreadsheets in various fonts and file formats, combining text with formulas, lists, tables, and images. Wikis allow users to create and edit web pages using any web browser. They support hyperlinks and have a simple text syntax for creating new pages and cross-links between internal pages.

Google documents or wikis can be used for the group reports you are assigned to do. Each member of your group can post research from their computer any time of the day and be able to see and edit the work of other group members as well. Your report can come together faster using technology rather than trying to get every member to meet at a specific time and place to work together. The group should still meet face to face at some point in the process of doing the project, but the document/assignment itself can be seen and developed online from the moment it is given to the group.

Group minutes and virtual agendas can be posted online as well. A group leader can set a virtual meeting date on a document and members of the group can post agenda items directly onto the meeting document. Virtual group documents also give members the time they need to proofread minutes and ok them without a face-to-face meeting. The simple incorporation of this new technology into your preparation for the business world can assist you to be ready for the challenges ahead of you in virtual communication.

The Reflective-Thinking Process

The *reflective-thinking process* is derived from John Dewey's (1910) classic work, *How We Think*, in which he described five basic steps in scientific reasoning. The reflective-thinking process has been adapted into a variety of problem-solving models. Gerald Phillips developed The Standard Agenda—"the most complete, the most flexible, and a time-tested method for problem-solving discussion" (Young, Wood, Phillips, & Pedersen, 2007, p. 11). The Standard Agenda has six steps that take the group through the reflective-thinking process (similar to the conflict-resolution model we talked about in chapter 6).

Let's take a common problem—parking on campus, for example. Most students would agree parking on campus is a problem. So what is the first thing you hear people say when you tell them we need to solve the parking problem? Build a garage! Make more spaces! Take out the flower beds! These are all solutions, but it is possible none of these suggestions will solve the problem.

The purpose of the reflective-thinking process is to influence the type of communication that takes place during problem solving. There are a few key steps in the use of reflective thinking that must be followed to allow a group to arrive at an optimal solution. The group members must understand the procedure. They must also be flexible enough to work back and forth between the steps. This process improves the natural process of decision emergence.

Step 1: Understanding the Charge

Group members must understand their assignment. We have seen numerous groups, both at the student and professional level, begin problem solving before the members realize what it is they are supposed to accomplish.

Understanding the charge means being able to answer the following questions: What is the goal of the group? Who formed the group and why? What resources are available to the group, including financial, material, technological, and human support? When must the group make its final report? What form must the report take? Who gets the report?

TRY IT!

The instructor says she'll give your group $50 to go out for dinner. You must use The Standard Agenda to solve the problem of where you will go. Write the charge and answer the questions in step one.

_____

_____

_____

_____

_____

_____

Step 2: Understanding and Phrasing the Question

Once the group members understand their mission, it is time to define the problem. Often group members assume everyone understands the problem—after all, who doesn't understand the parking problem on campus? Well, think again. What is the problem? Often the dialogue runs like this:

Yip: What is the parking problem?
LaKeesha: There are no spaces.
Yip: There are plenty of spaces on the far perimeter of campus.
LaKeesha: Okay, there are no spaces close to my classroom.
Yip: If you get here at 7 AM, you can park as close as you want.
LaKeesha: Okay, there are no spaces close to my classroom at times convenient to me.

And so it goes. So what is the problem? If we simply said lack of spaces, then we might build a parking garage at an astronomical cost to students and faculty. Maybe if the problem had been better defined, we could have solved it with less expense. Consider the example that there are too many classes scheduled between the hours of nine and twelve. If we redistributed those classes more evenly, perhaps there would be less people on campus at those times, thereby eliminating the parking problem.

So, in this phase the group must determine exactly what the issue is that requires a decision. To do this effectively, the members should establish a discussion question. Discussion questions are usually phrased in the following manner: Who should do what about what? So an effective discussion question could be:

What recommendation can we make to ensure convenient parking for all students and faculty?

An effective discussion question sets the foundation; it does not offer a solution. An *ineffective* discussion might be:

What recommendation can we make to increase parking spaces?

TRY IT!

What discussion question will your group use for the dinner problem?

_____

_____

Step 3: Fact Finding

During *fact finding,* members should collect as much relevant information about the issue as possible and exchange the collected information with each other. To achieve these goals, interactions must focus on (1) critical examination of the facts by all members, (2) whether the facts should alter the phrasing of the original discussion question, and (3) whether enough information has been gathered to proceed.

To be effective problem solvers, you must collect all the necessary facts. It is often difficult to determine when you are actually finished with this stage. Let's continue with the parking example and look at the questions we need to ask to find the necessary facts.

How many spaces are available?
How many people need them?
How many people park illegally?
How much money is available for a solution?
What are the causes of the problem?
Are there any limitations?

List all of the facts you need to examine in order to solve the $50 dinner problem effectively.

_____

_____

_____

_____

_____

_____

Step 4: Establishing Criteria

By now members are usually ready to jump to a solution, but there is an additional critical step. Criteria are the standards by which we judge things. Everyone uses criteria; you have standards by which you judge restaurants, movies, music, and so forth. Instructors have standards by which they judge speeches, assignments, papers, and exams. Instructors cannot just put a "B" on a paper because it "feels" like an above-average paper. Instead, they need to know what they are looking for and how they'll know it when they see it. Criteria tell us how we know a good solution when we see it.

The standard form for criteria is "Any solution must. . . ." You would substitute words for "solution" as necessary. Instructors say, "In order to receive an A, any paper must . . ." and they would finish with a list of criteria:

> Have fewer than three punctuation errors
> Cover all of the concepts assigned
> Be written well

Note the difficulty with one of these criteria—how do instructors define "written well"? The first two criteria are objective; the third is subjective. Let's go back to our parking example. "Any solution must . . ."

> Go into effect by January 2015
> Be acceptable to faculty, staff, and students
> Cost less than X (be sure to define X!)

Do not move on from the criteria step until you have defined and prioritized all criteria. Definition is important so we have objective, concrete statements. Prioritization is important in case more than one solution generated in step 5 meets the same number of criteria. So you need to have your criteria set up in terms of priority—in this case we may say that cost is first because without the money, we cannot do it. Acceptability is next because we are concerned about morale on campus. We are more concerned with acceptability and cost than with the start-up date, so that becomes criterion number three. Different solutions will be rated higher depending on how you set up and prioritize your criteria.

TRY IT!

List and prioritize the criteria for solving your dinner problem.

_____

_____

_____

_____

_____

_____

Step 5: Discovering and Selecting Solutions

In this step, you will brainstorm a list of solutions and select the best one. Notice that we do not even mention the idea of solutions until this step. You must gather your facts and set up your criteria before you consider the solutions. After those steps have been completed, brainstorm solutions. In our parking example, we might come up with: build a garage, provide a shuttle, provide a health campaign giving students a bonus for walking from a parking lot a mile away, pave lawns to create more space, and so on. Remember, no idea should be evaluated while brainstorming.

Next, we systematically evaluate each of our solutions against each of our criteria. It is often useful to make a chart.

Solutions ➤	Garage	Shuttle	Campaign	Pave Lawns
Criteria Any solution must . . . Cost less than $40,000				
Be acceptable to all				
Be in effect by 2015				

At this point, the group needs to discuss whether or not, and to what degree, each solution matches each criterion. Take criterion 1; would a garage cost less than $40,000? No. Would a shuttle? Yes. Would a campaign? Yes. Would digging up and paving over lawns? No. The group would need to provide facts to account for these conclusions.

Once the group has applied the criteria to all the solutions, it should become evident which solution is best. Let's assume the group made the following assessment after careful deliberation.

Solutions——▶	Garage	Shuttle	Campaign	Pave Lawns
Criteria Any solution must . . . Cost less than $40,000	N	Y	Y	N
Be acceptable to all	Y	N	N!	Y
Be in effect by 2015	N	Y	Y	Y

It becomes obvious the shuttle is the best solution. The garage only meets one criterion and does not meet our first-ranked criterion of cost. The next two are equal. However, when we look at the strength of the matches, we find people are significantly more opposed to walking a mile than they are to taking a shuttle.

Keep in mind there are numerous ways to evaluate criteria. For one project, a group of students used the reflective-thinking process to find the best gas station in town. After collecting the facts, they developed a list of criteria by which to evaluate the stations. Note their criteria are in order of priority, so the ones higher on the list get more points than the ones lower on the list.

Gas Station Criteria Evaluation System

Price of Regular Unleaded Gasoline—10 points
  10 points = $3.85–$3.90
   7 points = $3.91–$3.95
   4 points = $3.96–$4.00
   2 points = $4.01–$4.05
   0 points = higher than $4.05

Acceptance of Checks
   9 points = Yes
   0 points = No

Number of Pumps
   8 points = 8 or more pumps
   6 points = 6 or 7 pumps
   4 points = 4 or 5 pumps

3 points = 2 or 3 pumps

0 points = 1 pump

Atmosphere

7 points = Outstanding (how would you define this?)

4 points = Fair

0 points = Bad

Roof Over the Pumps

6 points = There is a roof

3 points = There is a partial roof

0 points = There is no roof

Clean Bathroom

5 points = Would actually use the bathroom

2 points = Would only wash your hands

0 points = Would not use the bathroom or no bathroom available

Window Cleaner

4 points = If available

2 points = If available, but the water is dirty

0 points = If not available

Car Wash

3 points = Good condition, clean, and usable

2 points = Fair condition, moderately clean, and usable

0 points = Bad condition and not usable or not available

Air Pump

2 points = If available and there is no charge

1 point = If available and there is a charge

0 points = If not available

ATM Machine

1 point = If available

0 points = If not available

Using points is just one method for evaluating solutions with the criteria established in step 4. There are many other ways in the reflective-thinking process to measure solutions by the criteria.

List the dinner solutions and evaluate them against your criteria:

Solutions ⟶				
Criteria Any solution must . . .				

Step 6: Preparing and Presenting the Final Report

The last phase is reporting your findings. The report will be in the format requested by the person who formed the group. If you must submit a written report, please refer to the appendix. Group presentations will be discussed later in the chapter.

When Does Reflective Thinking Yield a Bad Solution?

Do not be lulled into a false sense of security. The Standard Agenda helps people to make the best decisions possible through systematic thinking. However, there are times when a group doesn't use The Standard Agenda effectively. Beware of these pitfalls:

Members do not accurately assess the problem
Members do not gather all the necessary facts
Members do not accurately analyze the facts
Members fail to construct a good set of criteria
Members do not systematically apply the solutions to criteria

Types of Group Presentations

There are a number of group presentations, but we will mention four: symposium, roundtables, panels, and forums. The *symposium* refers to a presentation in which the group is in front of an audience, and each person gives part of a prepared speech. There should be an introduction, a conclusion, and transitions between the speakers. The speeches should all be approximately the same length and should flow so that they appear as part of a greater whole. Everything that was discussed in the chapters on informative and persuasive speaking apply in this type of presentation. You need to think of the entire presentation as a whole with each person presenting a main point or section. Therefore, in a group of five, for instance, one person might give the introduction, the next three people would each present the main points, and the fifth person would present the conclusion.

The **roundtable** discussion consists of a moderator and group members having an actual discussion. The moderator can be a group member but can also be someone from outside the group. In a symposium, members prepare their remarks on a portion of a topic; in a roundtable, participants must be prepared to discuss the entire topic. A roundtable discussion is similar to a polite discussion among knowledgeable peers; there is generally no audience. This is a popular television format for journalists discussing topics of national interest (in this case, there is an audience, of course, but not in the studio). A roundtable discussion may be used for focus-group research, where there is a set of prepared questions and a moderator who leads the discussion. Focus-group research is designed to get information from a group of people concerning their opinions or knowledge on a particular topic. It is commonly used in market research for advertising.

A **panel** discussion consists of expert panelists in a roundtable discussion of a topic for an audience. Participants must enter the discussion fully informed about the topic. A moderator is used to keep the discussion moving, usually with preplanned discussion points. The panelists hear the reaction of the audience as they speak. Some panel discussions allow questions from the audience near the conclusion of the presentation.

Forum discussions involve the audience. Any talk show that you see usually has a forum component because the host asks the audience for input or questions. You can add a forum to the above presentations as well. Therefore, you may find a presentation advertised as a symposium forum, meaning there will be a prepared presentation given by multiple people, but when it concludes, they will take questions from the audience. Panel forums do the same thing. Forums are also known as town meetings. Political campaigns often use town meetings, as do organizations and universities.

Tips for the Presentation

There are numerous tips that can make your presentation stand out. Every member should be in professional attire and dressed in similar colors. Dressing alike has definite psychological advantages because your group appears united. Be aware of your nonverbals during a group presentation. If everyone is in front of the audience, it is essential that every member's attention is riveted on the speaker. As soon as members doodle, talk to one another, or fidget, they compromise the credibility of the entire group.

Be sure to practice the presentation. Many groups have each member design a portion of a presentation. If you don't plan this as a team, members often look unorganized and unprepared when they repeat the same information. The verbal and physical transitions from one member to the next should look polished, reflecting good teamwork. It is extremely difficult to work individually and make a presentation look like a synthesized project. A post-analysis critique is essential during this phase. If everyone just presents and then says "great job," no one really listened critically for the flaws in the others' presentations. Remember, just because you deliver information does not mean the presentation has been successful.

Follow the guidelines in chapters 7–9 for public speaking; visit the actual space where the group will be presenting. Learn where the electrical outlets are and the best way to use the space so there will be no mistakes during the presentation. Sometimes team members find they have differing definitions of professional attire. You should have every member practice in their professional attire. Shoes may make noise, blouses may be too low cut, and ties may not be tied properly. Eliminating these nonverbal issues before the actual presentation will help everyone to remain calm and professional during the actual presentation.

Summary

Teamwork can often be problematic. It takes skill and patience to solve problems and integrate personalities into a cohesive team. There are occasions when it will seem difficult to accomplish a task by work-

---

Professional Perspective

The personality traits best suited for teamwork involve a sense of the greater good of the project over your own personal comfort or gain. Retaining this focus is not always an easy thing to do, especially when ego is involved and much of the production process is subjective. But whether you're talking about the production process or building a house, I think the universal traits that everyone needs to succeed as members of a team who are striving for a common goal are focus, commitment, and the ability to see the forest for the trees. In other words, what's the endgame? You need to keep your eye on the prize and not let setbacks and distractions knock you off course.

You also need to have the ability to really listen to people. I mean really listen so you can read what's going on between the lines. It's hard to resist putting forth your own opinions and visions, but sometimes you have to put those aside, buy into the vision of the group, and go for it! A sense of humor also helps.

—Gene R. Sower
Vice President, Production
West Glen Communications, Inc.

ing in a group instead of working on your own. However, at many points in your career you will have to work in a group. Learn the necessary skills to have a good team experience. Once you make effective choices and are committed to a team and the task, you should have a solid, rewarding experience.

KEY WORDS

authoritarian leaders
democratic leaders
discovering and selecting solutions
establishing criteria
fact finding
forum
Google Docs
groups
laissez-faire leaders
member's needs
motivation
panel
planning
preparing and presenting
   the final report

proper records
reflective-thinking process
roundtable
social element
symposium
task element
team contract
teams
transactional leadership
transformational leadership
understanding and phrasing
   the question
understanding the charge
wiki

DISCUSSION/ACTIVITIES

1. Divide the class into groups. Give each group a campus-wide issue or university policy to discuss and improve. A spokesperson from each group will give a 1–2-minute presentation of their solution to the problem in the final minutes of the class.

2. Describe a positive group/team experience. Analyze what made that particular collection of people so effective in problem solving?

3. Discuss a leadership style that would make working life enjoyable. Why?

4. Select the leadership style mentioned in #3 and discuss an individual from world history who represents that ideal.

5. How can the reflective-thinking process benefit individuals working in a diverse team project?

6. Give groups of students an outside-of-class, problem-solving session. The group will present their solution to the problem in class. Each member of the group submits their own record of the meeting(s) as though they are the recording secretary.

fourteen

Final Thoughts

You'll never really know what I mean and I'll never know exactly what you mean.

—Mike Nichols

Can you remember leaving for your first day at school and how you felt as you lost sight of your parents' faces? The butterflies in your stomach as you faced the unknown? You probably were an emotional mix of excitement and anxiety as you walked away from your home environment to face new people, a new situation, and new information. Whom would you meet? Would you like them? Would they like you? Would you be able to adapt to this new learning experience? All of these childhood concerns may seem light-years away now and possibly a little silly in hindsight when you compare that memory to what you have accomplished since then. And yet, that early experience was the foundation for every communication encounter in your life.

Each person you meet, each move you make, and each business that employs you will take you back to that first memory. Of course, the rules of communication are more complex as an adult, but the new situations you constantly encounter can be compared to your going-to-school experience. There are thousands of interpersonal moments to absorb and challenges to face throughout life, but a communicator who adapts to personalities and environments can effectively handle any situation.

Your self-confidence and fundamental nature are rooted in your home and your home community. This environment gives you a set of attitudes, beliefs, and values with which you can develop personal standards of conduct. As you advance in maturity and career, some adjustments in your fundamental nature may occur. These are decisions you must make as you meet a diverse culture you never imagined facing when you were a child. Success is rooted in personal accomplishment, and your self-confidence grows as you find yourself capable of reaching various goals.

Communication errors are made throughout life. You take calculated risks each time you speak publicly, write, or meet strangers. Other people interpret everything you do (just as you judge other people by your own standards). Their interpretation of your communication abilities helps them decide if they want you as a friend, a colleague, or an employee. We can misjudge others through verbal and nonverbal channels just as they can misjudge us. It is for this reason that our fundamental nature may need some adjustment as we move forward in life.

As you read about and study a topic, you soon discover how much information you never knew. The key to better communication is making good decisions about new facts and information. If research convinces you a belief you hold is incorrect, then don't be afraid to change your mind. Rather than hold onto old beliefs because they are comfortable, embrace change. This is where learning helps you adjust your fundamental nature. A good communicator is truthful and adheres to the basic premise that he or she should be honest with every receiver or audience.

Nonverbal adjustments in adult behavior take appropriate thought, patience, and practice. For example, when we are young we don't give a great deal of thought to our appearance. Once we begin to focus on a possible career, however, we begin to make adjustments to our personal appearance, including our wardrobe and physical movement. Our role models become the heads of companies or departments we want to work in, and we find a way to adjust our appearance to be accepted. This adjustment is not always a complete makeover. It is important to communicate your own personality, but there may be some nonverbal elements that should definitely change, so you can be perceived by decision makers as someone who has experience at their level. Your adjustment can be as simple as a new hairstyle or a different color scheme for your wardrobe. These are nonverbal commitments you make to become successful in your career.

Let's say you aren't as well organized as you could be with your personal effects. At work, other employees may think you are messy when they see a cluttered desk or office. They may think you project a poor image for the company and decide clients should not see your office space. This may not be a fair perception about you, but they make this value judgment anyway. Nothing is ever said about it, but their reaction colors their interactions with you. This could hurt your future with the company if one or more of the people holding this perception are in decision-making positions. You need to be self-critical. Engage in intrapersonal communication and make adjustments that will assist you in being seen as a professional. Each nonverbal move you make is seen and judged in some way by other people. Take risks—but also assume responsibility for the reactions created by your behavior.

Perception checking is a critical skill. Whenever you wonder why someone did something or said something, ask a question. Do not attribute meaning to another person's actions, because your perception may be incorrect. Don't waste your time and energy worrying about hypothetical possibilities when a simple question can provide an answer. If the paralanguage of an answer still bothers you, ask another question. Why add stress to your life by imagining possible answers? Don't be afraid to ask questions and discover the truth. It's better to clarify your perception of an incident, so you can move forward to other issues.

Your pursuit of an education should excite you to explore the meaning of words in our culture and in global cultures. As an educated person, you are responsible for the effect your communication has on others. The more you read, the better you will be at using the proper words to explain your thoughts clearly in both spoken and written forms of language. However, words need to be examined as part of a complete thought. A complete thought tells a listener or reader what your message means. When you are the listener, don't isolate a word

Professional Perspective

You never know the hand life will deal you, so you never know what words you'll need to know. In the age of the Internet, all the planet's population is a click away. No borders, no boundaries, no separation by country, race, sexual orientation, etc. If you don't understand what people are saying, you can never really know what they mean or understand the unsaid words lying beneath the surface of the sentence. Without the words you never know how to feel—or what you feel is inappropriate more times than not. Without the words you're obeying a master who uses them to his or her own purpose. Words allow you to distinguish between lies and truth, love and humiliation. Words allow you to understand yourself.

Words took me from New York City's South Bronx to Spain, Colombia, England, the Hawaiian Islands, Puerto Rico, France, Germany, Austria, Hollywood and Beverly Hills, China, Egypt, Greece, Italy, Mexico, Belgium, Switzerland, and San Marino. Who would have thought? Who would have known? Dream.

Nunca sabes lo que te espera en la vida, así que nunca sabes que palabras vas a necesitar. En la edad del Internet la población del mundo está a un clic de distancia. No hay fronteras, ni limites, no hay separación por país, raza, orientación sexual, etc. Si no entiendes lo que la gente dice, jamás podrás saber lo que verdaderamente quiere decir, ni podrás comprender el significado de lo que se deja entredicho. Sin las palabras, no puedes saber qué es lo que sientes, o lo que sientes no es apropiado la mayoría de las veces. Sin las palabras, te sometes a la voluntad de un amo que las usa para su propio fin. Las palabras te permiten distinguir la verdad de la mentira, el amor de la humilación. Las palabras te permiten entenderte a ti mismo.

Las palabras me llevaron del Sur del Bronx de la ciudad de Nueva York a España, Colombia, Inglaterra, las Islas Hawaianas, Puerto Rico, Francia, Alemania, Austria, Hollywood y Beverly Hills, China, Egipto, Grecia, Italia, México, Bélgica, Suiza, y San Marino. ¿Quién lo hubiera pensado? ¿Quién lo hubiera sabido? Hay que soñar.

—Edward Gallardo
Playwright

and react to it out of context. You must listen to a message and analyze its impact once it's complete. To do otherwise is unfair to a communicator or reveals an inability to listen and follow an argument.

Learn to express yourself effectively within your profession. Remember to eliminate any jargon if you speak to audiences who are not familiar with the language of your profession.

There is another important decision to make about words as you mature professionally. They need to be pronounced properly. You need to analyze the speech patterns you absorbed in your childhood. The pronunciation and grammar you learned make you a part of that community. As you move beyond that community, you may need to adjust your articulation of some local sounds and develop more standard pronunciation to be understood. This is a decision only you can make, but it is an important one. The phone is a common channel for employment and business communication—a receiver of your voice should not be able to identify you by region or ethnic background. You don't know what a stranger is thinking as she hears your voice. Don't give anyone the opportunity to form prejudicial impressions based on your speech. By simply mispronouncing a word in a conversation, a listener could think you are not well educated or are not experienced in your field. Of course this is unfair, but you allow this decision to be made against you by not modifying your speech pattern. Perceptual decisions are made in seconds. Don't give anyone the chance to consider you unqualified because of vocal habits you can adjust but fail to recognize. When teachers or colleagues make suggestions for vocal change, think about what they are saying. Word pronunciation is easy to check in a dictionary. The choice to change is yours. Choose wisely.

Spoken words are interpreted as others listen to you. Therefore, the quality of your voice, its energy and pace, plus your articulation and pronunciation, influence others' reactions to your message. People enjoy listening to others who speak well. The spoken form of communication is extremely important, but, you also must master using words well in written communication. It is important to have a solid writing style that makes you easy to follow as people look at your words and think about them. Clarity in your writing is absolutely critical. Just think about all of the technical channels you currently use to convey a written message: memos, IM, e-mail, reports, articles, evaluation forms, and employment forms. How is your spelling? How is your grammar? Do your word choices connect properly with the receiver?

Once your thoughts are written, receivers can reread the material as many times as they wish. This is why you must proofread every message for accuracy, clarity, and style. We take the time to proofread and analyze material in a report or an article knowing it will be in print. But occasionally we fail to recognize that electronic writing needs the same high degree of critical analysis before hitting the send button. Typos and incomplete thoughts can lead to improper understanding of a message. Even more damaging, they can cost you your career in many professional areas. There are individuals who refuse to read anything with a typo. Electronic messages are not private. They are stored in corporate electronic archives and can be retrieved by anyone. Unintended receivers can read your thoughts and messages. Therefore, keep your written thoughts professional and accurate.

Handwritten notes, application forms, memos, and thank-you notes do not have the automatic security of spell-check to alert you to errors. You must know how words are spelled. It is embarrassing to have colleagues discover you don't know how to spell when they read your handwritten notes and suggestions on reports. Even if you plan to use word-processing software and think all of your bases are covered with spell-check, a power failure could force you to write a report by hand to meet a deadline. In addition, spell-check corrects only misspellings, it won't tell you if you have used "here" instead of "hear." If there are spelling errors, you will have created an impression that will be remembered and difficult to change. This affects your credibility. Remember that you do not determine whether you are credible or not; other people make that decision about you. One mistake and your credibility is at risk.

The greatest challenge in using words effectively is to succeed in having other people understand your message as you intended it to be understood. Language should always be appropriate and organized to convey your message. You should also choose the best channel to send a message to another person or group of people. The intent of all communication is to help a receiver comprehend your analysis of a topic. Spoken speech is an extemporaneous exchange; you only have one opportunity to make the message clear. Your vocal pace, quality, and delivery are critical. In written language, receivers can review your thought process as many times as necessary to understand your meaning. This gives written language an advantage over spoken language for audience comprehension. An inattentive reader can review your thoughts again, but a lazy listener misses your point entirely. Spoken and written communication should work together in helping you reach your audience; you need to build a strong foundation in both skills to be perceived as an excellent communicator and colleague. As Ralph Waldo Emerson stated, "It is a luxury to be understood."

We receive feedback about our behavior, thought process, use of language, and knowledge. The choices we make in selecting which pieces of information to accept or reject in adjusting who we are and what we want to become are very important. The external world seems to impose suggestions continuously about what we should do and what we should think. It is up to us, however, to make choices about our communication abilities and make the necessary adjustments to be successful. The consequences of our choices influence our future. This is not a frightening thought at all. It simply reminds us to take seriously how we communicate and how we listen to the external world.

Our lives appear to get more complicated as our careers advance and family responsibilities increase. The best solution is to learn to manage time more effectively and to set priorities regarding life's important issues. One way to use time better is to know how to listen effectively to messages and then pick an appropriate way to react to those messages. Some messages can be ignored; other messages require action. Experience helps us to select the right words and behaviors to respond to a message, plus it helps us to select the appropriate channel for a response.

Social media are immediate and broadcast our messages to diverse audiences. For those very reasons, you need excellent judgment in deciding when and how to use the channels. For public figures—and for others—there are contradictory rules. James Poniewozik (2011) cautions: "Be provocative but not offensive. Be authentic, but don't alienate people. . . . The very qualities that make someone popular on Twitter (mischievousness, authenticity, a quick wit) can backfire when taken to an extreme (offensiveness, oversharing, lack of impulse control)" Poniewozik noted astutely that thus far he has had the common sense not to tweet anything ghastly but also asked if he has common sense all the time—does anyone? He observed that the instant feedback from social media can be intoxicating but also warned that one lapse of judgment can cost a person his or her reputation or career. (Remember the example in chapter 5 of Gilbert Gottfried, the voice of the Aflac duck.) As emphasized throughout this book, we do have choices—and there will be consequences. Electronic channels amplify those consequences.

We strongly support the use of face-to-face interpersonal communication for very important personal messages. When you take the time to see others and congratulate them on a job well done, console them, listen to them, or explain a difficult issue to them, you send a message of caring about them. What do you think about an employer who sends you a memo or e-mail saying your employment has been terminated versus an employer who takes the time to explain the issue to you directly? The consequence of the communication remains the same, but at least the person-to-person meeting expresses respect and some concern for you as a person. It is important to recognize the need for voice and physical presence in your communication style. Yes, it requires more of your time, but it also tells people you care about them. This is an important personal choice to make as an effective communicator.

Listening is a vital skill for personal growth. Don't respond without really listening to a family member or colleague because you feel pressed for time. You owe it to other people to evaluate their ideas fairly before you respond to them. This is what interpersonal communication is all about. Do your best to analyze what they would like you to do or think and then find the proper words to respond to their needs. Family dialogue is stronger and business dialogue is stronger when we listen critically and evaluate a proper course of action prior to responding to another communicator's message. We are rarely alone in decision making. Compromises are usually necessary, but everyone must feel good about their compromises in interpersonal and team efforts for relationships to remain strong.

You have a greater chance for long-term personal success if your communication style can blend into a business culture that is globally diverse and a world that is becoming much smaller through cyberspace.

We talked about the word *adjustment* earlier. Adjustment requires that you research various topics. There are times when you need to

---

Professional Perspective

These are skills and insights I have developed and come to understand as necessary when dealing with clients in the music-promotion business as it pertains to achieving airplay at radio stations. I come across many, many different situations and people. I try to incorporate all of these insights into my conversations and presentations when dealing with clients.

1. ***Know what you believe.*** Have total belief, conviction, and knowledge in what you are communicating. Don't simply articulate a brief summary or outline of your skills. Go into great depth and detail about what you have to offer. Give examples of your successes. Illustrate how your skills will benefit a person/business and how they benefit your current company, business, etc.

2. ***Be an optimist.*** If you are upbeat and happy, your comments will come across to others as important and necessary. Thus, you become important and necessary to them. Smile and look people in the eye when you talk to them. It shows confidence. No one likes a sourpuss.

3. ***Research and prepare.*** Know your client's likes and dislikes. What does the company/person stand for? Know and understand their needs inside and out. Realize corporate and personal situations can change on a daily basis and quite often do. What was once necessary can often be outdated within seconds—especially in a fast paced business environment. Always be prepared for change, accept it, and move forward.

4. ***Have follow-through.*** Do what you said you would do for people. If you do this on a consistent basis, they will trust you.

5. ***Display honesty, charm, and personality.*** These qualities can go a long way to make people comfortable. Don't be obsequious, but be yourself and allow others to be the same way. You will find that people respond to others who know who they are rather than to those who put on airs and falsehoods. In today's corporate environment, shuck and jive no longer work.

—Lance Walden
Northwest Regional Radio Promotions
Universal Republic Records

check out people and resources yourself without relying totally on the information given to you by others. This is an issue of personal responsibility and integrity. Reading and research can assist you in evaluating the information other people give you for truth, accuracy, and fairness. This is lifelong homework you need to do to stay on top of critical issues and decision-making choices. Whenever you are the decision maker, the consequences of communication choices sit on your shoulders alone. It is in your own best interest to recognize when you need to do personal research before you make a decision.

Communication is power. You use it with your family, friends, colleagues, and significant others in the workplace, job interviews, team environments, religious establishments, and clubs. You want to be liked by everyone, but that is not always possible. Communication is a personal challenge. Set your own standards for verbal and nonverbal message delivery. If you discover new techniques to improve your style, adopt them and use them effectively to build your own performance. Remain thorough and fair in every decision you make. It would be nice to think we can change other people or know what they really think, but we can't. We can only know and change ourselves.

When you learn to use language and behavior well, you are seen as an effective communicator. Mistakes in communication can happen. Analyze your error immediately and make sure not to repeat it. Everyone makes mistakes, but over the length of a career you will experience more successes than failures if you concentrate on the consequences of your messages.

You took a risk in communicating to the outside world when you went to school for the first time. You made it. Remember that. Every day gives you more insight into who you are and what you might become. It is important to accept the possibilities of success and move forward. Listen, observe, and analyze those around you. Absorb the good qualities they possess, if possible, and make them part of your communication strategy. You will be evaluated by the communication choices you make just as you evaluate the choices others make. Do not take words and behavior for granted. They are the keys to personal success. Success is within your reach, but you must constantly fine-tune your communication skills to meet ever-changing global needs and realities.

> Communication is something so simple and difficult that we can never put it in simple words.
>
> —T. S. Matthews

Writing the Final Report

(Adapted from *Group Discussion: A Practical Guide to Participation and Leadership 4/E* by Kathryn Sue Young, Julia T. Wood, Gerald M. Phillips, and Douglas J. Pedersen, 2007, pp. 154–158)

As you plan to write the final report, your strategy is important. Many groups try to divide the work and have everyone prepare a different part, but the same problems are inherent in group writing that are evident in group presentational speaking.

1. Group members have different writing skills. The differences result in some sections of the report being stronger and others weaker.

2. Group members have their own writing style. A reader knows immediately when the writing style shifts in the middle of a report.

3. Group members sometimes do not complete their work. If one person is in charge of an entire section and becomes MIA, the work will be incomplete.

If you choose to divide the work anyway, keep in mind you'll need time at the end for extensive editing to achieve a readable flow and to correct any errors. Since most groups are pressed for time as a deadline approaches, they often rush the written report—resulting in substandard results.

You can accomplish the writing in a number of ways. Many groups designate a writer or cowriters for their report. Usually this is someone who had a lighter load earlier in the project. If you use only one or two writers, it is imperative the other group members be available to offer ideas, suggestions, moral support, or snacks.

As one writer completes the rough draft, another person can begin the initial editing. Having two or three people involved in multiple revisions almost always guarantees a tighter, more professional report. When your group thinks the report is complete, have another person, who is not in the group, proofread the work for errors and clarity.

This may sound like a lot of work—it is. If you are used to turning in first drafts of your writing, break the habit. Too many groups put numerous hours of work into their projects but turn in a sloppy draft as their final report. Keep in mind that your credibility is enhanced or diminished by the written presentation of your work.

Here are some key guidelines for avoiding common writing errors.

- Make sure that you read all of your writing out loud. This will help you to find punctuation errors.
- Do not use contractions in formal writing. Don't should be "do not."
- Watch out for style shifts with group writing.
- Be sure to cite all articles properly.
- Know the difference between "definitely" and "defiantly." "Defiantly" is the first option that comes up in spell-check for Microsoft Word. "Defiantly" is definitely a different word than "definitely."
- "Nowadays" should never appear in your writing.
- A lot is two words (not alot).
- Be sure to number all pages.
- Be sure to use headings and subheadings in your writing.
- Be sure to use a preview and review if appropriate.
- Two complete sentences are joined by a conjunction, preceded by a comma.
  The dog ran, and the cat sat. The rat jumped, but he did not bite.
- Know which compound adjectives are hyphenated.
  My hard-hearted boss would not give me a raise.
- Create dashes by typing *two* hyphens with no space before or after the hyphens—see what I mean? (Software programs such as Microsoft Word can automatically convert two hyphens into the em dash [—].)
- Professional reports normally look better on heavier paper (25 percent cotton bond).
- Any time you use section dividers with plastic tabs, be sure they are typed. You can format them on a computer program.
- Above all, edit numerous times, proofread numerous times, and have someone else look over the writing.

Professional Perspective

As a supervisor in a human services agency, part of my responsibility was to review case notes documenting services provided to clientele. I was frequently amazed at the poor spelling, grammar errors, and unclear writing exhibited by caseworkers who were college grads, some with Master's degrees. The notes, used to develop client treatment plans, were often read by doctors, lawyers, judges, and juries and affected their decisions as well as their perceptions of our staff.

—Roberta J. Miller
Casework Supervisor, Retired

Bibliography

Adams, K. L., & Galanes, G. J. (2012). *Communicating in groups: Applications and skills* (8th ed.). New York: McGraw-Hill.

Andersen, P. A. (2008). *Nonverbal communication: Forms and functions.* Long Grove, IL: Waveland Press.

Associated Press (2007, February 28). "That's so gay" prompts a lawsuit. Retrieved from http://www.msnbc.msn.com/id/17388702/ns/us_news-life/t/thats-so-gay-prompts-lawsuit/

Basic resume formats. (n.d.). Retrieved from www.bazarorissa.com/jobs/resume/Resume%20Formats.htm

Battle of Breed's Hill/Bunker Hill. (n.d.). Retrieved from Worcester Polytechnic Institute, Department of Military Science website: www.wpi.edu/Academics/Depts/MilSci/BTSI/Hill/

BBC News. (2003, October 17). Short workers lose a small fortune. Retrieved from http://news.bbc.co.uk/go/pr/fr/-/1/hi/health/3200296.stm

Beebe, S. A., & Beebe, S. J. (2012). *Public speaking: An audience centered approach* (8th ed.). Boston: Allyn & Bacon.

Beebe, S. A, Beebe, S. J., & Ivy, D. K. (2010). *Communication: Principles for a lifetime* (4th ed.). Boston: Allyn & Bacon.

Beebe, S. A., & Masterson, J. T. (2012). *Communicating in small groups: Principles and practices* (10th ed.). Boston: Allyn & Bacon.

Bence, B. (2008 Dec). Top 10 secrets to mastering your personal brand. *American Salesman, 53*(12), 22–25.

Benjamin, J. (1997). *Principles, elements, and types of persuasion.* Belmont, CA: Wadsworth.

Boroditsky, L. (2001). Does language shape thought?: Mandarin and English speakers' conceptions of time. *Cognitive Psychology, 43,* 1–22.

Brickman, G. F., & Fuller, L. E. (1986). *Organizing for impact: A practical guide for the public speaker.* Dubuque: Kendall/Hunt.

Brotman, Barbara. (2007, June 14). Senn graduation truly a world party. *The Chicago Tribune,* pp. 1, 23.

Bruss, O. E. and Hill, J. M. (Spring 2010). Tell me more: Online versus face-to-face communication and self-disclosure. *Psi Chi Journal of Undergraduate Research, 15*(1), 3–7.

Bush, G. W. Rose Garden Press Conference. (June 14, 2006). Retrieved from http://www.whitehouse.gov/news/releases/2006/06/20060614.html.

Campbell, K. K., & Schultz Huxman, S. (2009). *The rhetorical act: Thinking, speaking, and writing critically* (4th ed.). Belmont, CA: Wadsworth.

Centers for Disease Control and Prevention (2011). Intimate partner violence: Fact sheet. Retrieved from http://www.cdc.gov/violenceprevention/pdf/IPV_factsheet-a.pdf

Clegg, B. (2001). *Instant interviewing.* Sterling, VA: Stylus.

Coombes, A. (2004, January 27). Bilingual job seekers rise above the crowd. *Chicago Tribune*, sec. 3, p. 4.

Daniels, A. C. (2000). *Bringing out the best in people*. New York: McGraw-Hill.

DeNoon, D. (2004). Child antidepressant use skyrockets: Use growing fastest in pre-school kids. Retrieved from http://www.webmd.com/content/article/85/98399.htm.

DeVito, J. A. (2011). *Essentials of human communication* (7th ed.). Boston: Allyn & Bacon.

DeVito, J. A. (2012). *Essential elements of public speaking* (4th ed.). Boston: Allyn & Bacon.

DeVito, J. A. (2012). *Human communication: The basic course* (12th ed.). Boston: Allyn & Bacon.

Dewey, J. (1910). *How we think*. New York: D. C. Heath.

Dewey, J. (1933). *How we think: A restatement of the relation of reflective thinking to the educative process* (2nd ed.). Boston: D. C. Heath.

Dunn, D. M., & Goodnight, L. J. (2011). *Communication: Embracing difference* (3rd ed.). Boston: Allyn & Bacon.

Dwyer, K. (2005). *Conquer your speech anxiety: Learn how to overcome your nervousness about public speaking* (2nd ed.). Belmont, CA: Wadsworth.

Ecoevaluator (n.d.). Filling our landfills. Retrieved from http://www.ecoevalua-tor.com/lifestyle/recycling/filling-our-landfills.html

Engleberg, I. N., & Wynn, D. R. (2010). *Working in groups: Communication principles and strategies* (5th ed.).Boston: Allyn & Bacon.

Fellingham, C. (2003, August). Extreme beauty. *O, The Oprah Magazine*, 158–160, 182–183.

The freedom trail—Road to American independence. (n.d.). Retrieved from www.bosto-nuk.com/history/and_trail.htm#header

Fogg, B. J. (2008). Mass interpersonal persuasion: An early view of a new phenome-non. Paper presented at the Third International Conference on Persuasion, Ber-lin. Retrieved from http://bjfogg.com/mip.pdf

Galanes, G. J., & Adams, K. (2010). *Effective group discussion: Theory and practice* (13th ed.). New York: McGraw-Hill.

Gall, D. (2010). Librarian like a rock star: Using your personal brand to promote your services and reach distant users. *Journal of Library Administration*, *50*(5/6), 628–637.

Gass, R. H., & Seiter, J. S. (2011). *Perspectives on persuasion, social influence, and compli-ance gaining* (4th ed.). Boston: Allyn & Bacon.

German, K. M., Gronbeck, B. E., Ehninger, D., Monroe, A. H. (2010). *Principles of pub-lic speaking* (17th ed.). Boston: Allyn & Bacon.

Golijan, R. (2011, February 8). Why are teenagers e-mailing less lately? MSNBC.com. Retrieved from http://technolog.msnbc.msn.com/_news/2011/02/08/6010428-why-are-teenagers-e-mailing-less-lately?gt1=43001

Golish, T. D., and Olson, L. N. (Summer 2000). Student's use of power in the class-room: An investigation of student power, teacher power, and teacher immediacy. *Communication Quarterly, 48* (3). 293–310.

Gormley, J. (1987). The idea for visually looking at organizational patterns was devel-oped by John Gormley and shared with KSY at The Pennsylvania State University.

Grice, G. L., & Skinner, J. F. (2010). *Mastering public speaking* (7th ed.). Boston: Allyn & Bacon.

Grow, B. (2011, January 27). In U.S. courts, Facebook posts become less private. MSNBC.com. Retrieved from http://www.msnbc.msn.com/id/41299930/ns/technology_and_science-tech_and-Gadgets/?

Half, R. (1993, November). How do you prepare for nonstandard interviews? *Management Accounting, 75*(5), 12.

Hall, E. T. (1966). *The hidden dimension.* New York: Doubleday.

Hall, E. T. (1968). Proxemics. *Current Anthropology, 9,* 83–109.

Hamilton, C. (2012). *Essentials of public speaking* (5th ed.). Belmont, CA: Wadsworth.

Hart, R. P., & Burks, D. (1972, June). Rhetorical sensitivity and social interaction. *Speech Monographs, 24,* 75–91.

HR World Editors (n.d.). 30 interview questions you can't ask and 30 sneaky, legal alternatives to get the same info. Retrieved from http://www.focus.com/fyi/hr/30-interview-questions-you-cant-ask-and-30-sneaky-legal-get/

Ivy, D. K., & Backlund, P. (2008). *GenderSpeak: Personal effectiveness in gender communication* (3th ed.). New York: McGraw-Hill.

Jaffe, C. (2010). *Public speaking—Concepts and skills for a diverse society* (6th ed.). Belmont, CA: Wadsworth.

Janis, I. L. (1972). *Victims of groupthink.* Boston: Houghton Mifflin.

Kilmann, R. H., & Thomas, K. W. (1977). Developing a forced-choice measure of conflict-handling behavior: The MODE instrument. *Educational and Psychological Measurements, 37,* 309–325.

Kito, M. (2005). Self-disclosure in romantic relationships and friendships among American and Japanese college students. *The Journal of Social Psychology, 14*(2), 127–140.

Knapp, M. L., & Hall, J. A. (2010). *Nonverbal communication in human interaction* (7th ed.). Belmont, CA: Wadsworth.

Knapp, M. L., & Vangelisti, A. (2009). *Interpersonal communication and human relationships* (6th ed.). Boston: Allyn & Bacon.

Koerner, B. I. (2003). What does a "thumbs up" mean in Iraq? Retrieved from http://www.slate.msn.com/id/2080812

Krugman, P. (2003, January 21). A touch of class. *New York Times.* Retrieved from http://select.nytimes.com/gst/abstract.html?res=F30C10F839540C728EDDA80894DB404482

Kursmark, L. The benefits of behavioral interviewing: How to get behind candidates' facades. Retrieved from http://content.monster.com/articles/3485/16602/1/home.aspx

Language guide. (n.d.). Retrieved from http://www.specialolympics.org/Special+Olympics+Public+Website/English/Press_Room/Language_guide/ default.htm

Larson, C. U. (2010). *Persuasion: Reception and responsibility* (12th ed.). Belmont, CA: Wadsworth.

Luft, J. (1969). *Of human interaction.* Palo Alto, CA: National Press Books.

Lumsden, G., Lumsden, D., & Wiethoff, C. (2010). *Communicating in groups and teams: Sharing leadership* (5th ed.). Belmont, CA: Wadsworth.

Martyna, W. (1978). What does "he" mean—Use of the generic masculine. *Journal of Communication, 28,* 131–138.

McKerrow, R. E., Gronbeck, B. E., Ehninger, D., & Monroe, A. H. (2007). *Principles and types of public speaking* (16th ed.). Boston: Allyn & Bacon.

Metcalfe, S. (2010). *Building a speech* (7th ed.). Belmont, CA: Wadsworth.

Moody, J., Stewart, B., & Bolt-Lee, C. (2002, March). Showcasing the skilled business graduate: Expanding the tool kit. *Business Communication Quarterly, 65*(1), 21.

National Institute of Mental Health. (n.d.). The numbers count: Mental disorders in America. Retrieved from www.nimh.nih.gov/publicat/numbers.cfm

O'Hair, D., Rubenstein, H., & Stewart, R. (2010). *A pocket guide to public speaking* (3rd ed.) New York: Bedford/St. Martin's Press.

O'Hair, D., Stewart, R., & Rubenstein, H. (2010). *A speaker's guidebook* (4th ed.). New York: Bedford/St. Martin's Press.

O'Keefe, D. J. (n.d.). Persuasion. Retrieved from http://www.dokeefe.net/pub/OKeefe08IEC-persuasion.pdf

Phillips, G. M. (1965). PERT as a logical adjunct to the discussion process. *Journal of Communication, 15*, 89–99.

Phillips, G. M. (1966). *Communication and the small group.* Indianapolis: Bobbs-Merrill.

Poniewozik, J. (2011, June 20). Birdbrained: Twitter is a danger zone—especially for its most adept users. *Time, 177* (25), 18.

Poundstone, W. (2003). *How would you move Mt. Fuji? Microsoft's cult of the puzzle—How the world's smartest company selects the most creative thinkers.* New York: Little, Brown.

Ramsey, L. (2011). First impressions: How seven seconds can make a deal. Retrieved from Sideroad.com/sales/first-impressions.html

Sapir-Whorf-hypothesis redux. (2002, Winter). *ETC.: A Review of General Semantics, 59*(4), 456.

Shockley-Zalabak, P. S. (2012). *Fundamentals of organizational communication: Knowledge, sensitivity, skills, values* (8th ed.). New York: Pearson and Allyn & Bacon.

Sprague, J., Stuart, D., & Bodary, D. (2010). *The speaker's handbook* (10th ed.). Belmont, CA: Wadsworth.

Starbuck, J. J. (2000, January). Ginger and peppermint. *Better Nutrition, 62*(1), 44.

Student Affairs (2011). Career Services. Virginia Tech. Retrieved from http://www.career.vt.edu/interviewing/Behavioral.html

Trenholm, S. (2011). *Thinking through communication: An introduction to the study of human communication* (6th ed.). Boston: Allyn & Bacon.

Tubbs, S. L. (2009). *A systems approach to small group interaction* (10th ed.). New York: McGraw-Hill.

Verderber, R. F., Verderber, K. S., & Sellnow, D. D. (2011). *Communicate!* (13th ed.). Belmont, CA: Wadsworth.

Verderber, R. F., Verderber, K. S., & Sellnow, D. D. (2012). *The challenge of effective speaking* (15th ed.). Belmont, CA: Wadsworth.

Von Bertelanffy, L. (1968). *General systems theory.* New York: Braziller.

Voorhees, R. (2002). *Old age is always 15 years older than I am.* Kansas City, MO: Andrews McMeel.

Weaver, M. (1999, April). Make your point with effective A/V. *Computers in Libraries, 19*(4), 62.

Wilmot, W. W., & Hocker, J. L. (2011). *Interpersonal conflict* (8th ed.). New York: McGraw-Hill.

Wood, J. T. (2004). *Communication theories in action* (3rd ed.). Belmont, CA: Wadsworth.

Wood, J. T. (2011). *Communication mosaics—An introduction to the field of communication* (6th ed.). Belmont, CA: Wadsworth.

Wood, J. T. (2011). *Gendered lives: Communication, gender, and culture* (9th ed.). Belmont, CA: Wadsworth.

Wood, J. T. (2012). *Communication in our lives* (6th ed.). Belmont, CA: Wadsworth.

Young, K. S., Wood, J. T., Phillips, G. M., & Pedersen, D. J. (2007). *Group discussion: A practical guide to participation and leadership* (4th ed.). Long Grove, IL: Waveland Press.

Zarefsky, D. (2011). *Public speaking: Strategies for success* (6th ed.). Boston: Allyn & Bacon.

Ziegler, H., & Lawler, J. (2003). *Feng shui your workspace for dummies.* Hoboken, NJ: John Wiley & Sons.

Index